Mohan Rakesh's
Halfway House
Critical Perspectives

Mohan Rakesh's
Halfway House
Critical Perspectives

edited by

SUBHASH CHANDRA

Asia
Book
Club

Published by
asia book club
New Delhi 110 058

ISBN: 81-7851-004-9

Printed at Chaman Offset Press, New Delhi 110 002

Contents

Part I

Mohan Rakesh's *Halfway House* A Critical Appraisal

by
Subhash Chandra

Part II

Critical Perspectives

for

my mother-in-law

Acknowledgments

I gratefully acknowledge my debt to the following scholars and publishers as I have profitably used their excellent works for writing this introduction:
Birendra Narayana and Bansal and Company for *Hindi Drama and Stage* (1981);
Carlo Cappola and Radhakrishan Prakashan, Delhi, for their *Anthology: Mohan Rakesh* (1974);
Om Shivpuri for "Nirdeshak Ka Vaktavay" and Radhakrishan Prakashan, Delhi, for the Hindi text of *Aadhe Adhure* (1969; reprinted 1995);
Pratibha Agrawal, Sanjay Kumar, Dilip K. Basu and Worldview, Delhi, for *"Halfway House": A Critical Commentary* (1999);
Seema Puri for her detailed notes on Mohan Rakesh.

Mohan Rakesh's *Halfway House* A Critical Appraisal

SUBHASH CHANDRA

Life and Works

Mohan Rakesh was born on 8 January 1925 in Amritsar and lived as a child in Jandiwala Lane. His father, Karam Chand Guglani, was a lawyer by profession but was more interested in literature.

Mohan Rakesh was initially named as Madan Mohan Guglani; later he was called Madan Mohan and finally he came to be known as Mohan Rakesh. His father was a prominent and respected citizen of Amritsar as he was an active social worker who held offices in various literary and cultural organisations. He took a keen interest in his children's upbringing and paid close attention to their academic activities. Mohan Rakesh inherited love for music and literature from his father. His father did not earn much from his legal practice and, therefore, the family was generally under debt. Rakesh racalls the names of the people whom his father owed money—Pundit Loknath and Nihal Singh (there were some other creditors, too)—and how once he was made to tell a lie that his father was not at home when Loknath called on them.

When his father died, he left heavy debts. Rakesh recalls the landlord's son's shouting for outstanding rent even as his father's dead body lay waiting for cremation the next morning. His mother's gold bangles had to be sold to pay the rent before the dead body could be removed from the house.

Rakesh, along with his elder sister, had to shoulder the burden of the family, when he was only sixteen years old. While his early schooling was done in Amritsar, he completed his M.A. in Sanskrit from Lahore. After the partition of India in 1947, he, together with his family, settled in Jallandhar where he continued his studies. He did his M.A. in Hindi and stood first in the university. His father's influence on him was great and perceptible, but he was also influenced by his grandmother, though in a negative manner. She was extremely superstitious, believer in the caste system besides being a disciplinarian. As a child Rakesh was forced to stay indoors in dark and damp rooms, because she restricted his movements. In fact, she made a fetish of discipline and order.

Rakesh remembers how he was not allowed to watch from the terrace of their house the dance of men and women, with baskets on their heads, in the courtyard of a house in the backlane. His grandmother's objection was that "They are Kanjars [low caste]." Rakesh could not understand what was wrong with being Kanjars because he enjoyed watching them dance and himself wanted to dance like them. He was also forbidden to play in the street. If he did, he would be contaminated by the magician Bhanshah and the leper Kuljug Prasad: "Even if we stay locked inside the house, their contamination takes hold by coming through the windows or skylight." (Cappola, 4)

This naturally fostered a deep dislike for discipline in Rakesh, who developed a rebellious streak in his personality. When he was confined because of the grandmother's commands, he relied on his imaginative resources and passed the time by creating imaginary worlds and moving in them.

The following lines draw a self-portrait of Rakesh which he wrote to project his mental state: "In the house, our energy is suppressed. When I am kept inside, I cry for a while and make myself sick. Besides, the world of the house and street, I have my own private world. Sometimes I travel with the rows of big black ants through holes in the dark. Sometimes I make tiny atoms fight with each other in the sun. I try to look for different faces from the broken plaster of the walls up to the running water of the tank. To change the plaster faces, I adjust the corner of my eye, I change the faces of the water by moving my hand. If the flow disrupts, the faces which I have made, I give them new forms." (Rakesh, 1974: 5) When as a child Rakesh had fever, he had to stay by himself but he had no problem spending time. He would contemplate the bars on the ceiling of the room, break and join them, "gather a whole world and build it in the courtyard, jump through the ventilator and walk all around the world, put together and destroy the history of the lines on every face, make up a story about everything you hear and then forget it." (Rakesh, 1974: 10)

Rakesh was given to day-dreaming "at home, in school, any place, at any time." While attending a class, he would begin to doodle on his slate. He would see the person in front as two individuals and would cease to listen to external voices. Even as the teacher lectured, he slipped into a trance. After completing his M.A. in Hindi, he got a job in Elphinstone college, Bombay, where he worked from 1947 to 1949. After losing this job, he remained unemployed for sometime and then got a teaching assignment for a short while in Jallandhar. He lost this job also because of his outspoken views on political issues and because of his mixing teaching with politics. For a brief period, he also taught in a Delhi college. For two years he worked as a teacher in a school in Shimla, but resigned on his own. After that he got back to Jallandhar and started teaching again and from 1957 onwards, he pursued his writing. For a short period, he also edited the well-known Hindi Journal *Sarika* (from 1962-63), but then quit the job, as he felt confined and hemmed in by the discipline of deadlines.

Rakesh was a versatile writer, who experimented with many genres, which included short stories, novels and plays. In addition to these, he also published collections of essays, biographies and travelogues. He breathed a new life in whatever he wrote, but it is as a dramatist that his work earned him accolades. In fact, his plays lent respectability to the Hindi theatre. His first play *Aashadh Ka Ek Din* received the Sangeet Natak Akademi Award for the best play in 1958. *Lehron Ke Rajhans* and *Aadhe Adhure* were two other full-length plays which he wrote. In

1968, the Sangeet Natak Akedemi again conferred an award on him for his eminence in the field of drama and his substantial and valuable contribution to its development. Together with Dharamvir Bharati's *Andha Yug*, Rakesh's plays bestowed a new dignity on the Hindi theatre. All of Rakesh's plays have been performed repeatedly by several leading theatrical groups.

Apart from the accolades he received as a sensitive playwright, he was also considered as an outstanding short story writer, as his stories poignantly projected the anguish of the common man, struggling to survive. As recognition of his concern for the language of theatre, he received Nehru Fellowship to carry out research on 'the dramatic word.' He was keenly interested in the power of the word in creating and conveying meaning on stage.

His married life became a saga of disasters. He was a very poor reader of people and, therefore, his choice of marital partners did not turn out to be right. Rakesh married thrice—the first two relationships ended in divorce; each time Rakesh took the initiative to separate from and convince his spouse to agree to the divorce. First time, it was an arranged marriage in 1950. He had met the girl briefly only a couple of times. There was hardly any compatibility between Rakesh and the girl who became his wife. She was egotistic, proud of the fact that she earned more than her husband did. Not that Rakesh did not make efforts to adjust. He did admit that "marriage means adjustments and compromises but it has to be made by both." But if both the partners want to live life on their terms, then the barriers become insurmountable and the problems unresolvable. The marriage lasted for a couple of years. Rakesh succeeded in convincing his wife for a divorce which eventually took place in 1957. His quest for marital happiness continued and he married a second time in 1960. This time, he got married to the sister of a friend. This girl also he had met only for a short while, after which he took the decision to marry her. This alliance also proved to be a disaster and lasted for a much shorter time than the first one. The second wife proved to be totally unpredictable in her behaviour and was a bit of a neurotic, reacting to situations too intensely.

Rakesh got fed up of his home and went to live at the office of *Sarika*, but had to abandon it because his wife reached there and created an ugly scene.

This marriage, therefore, too ended in divorce. Rakesh earned the label of home-breaker among those known to him. Some of his friends, with a bourgeois mindset, looked at his failed marriages in an uncharitable light. He was in the process of losing faith in the institution of marriage, when he found a true companion, Anita. She fortunately shared his convictions and lived with him till his death in 1972, displaying devotion and commitment. She did not get upset, even when Rakesh once told her that "you have the third place in my life; in the first place are my writings and in the second place are my friends." However, in spite of this stroke of good luck in Anita, Rakesh went on sliding downhill because of his excessive drinking, which perhaps was because of the several disillusionments and hurts he suffered in his dealings with the world and because of his authentic but extremely intense reactions to the inequities which are a part of reality, perhaps more so in the case of the Indian reality. He was strongly individualistic, extremely sensitive, suffering acutely at failed relationships, He did not like the mechanized urban existence which he thought caught people in Sisyphus-like hopeless situations.

He wondered why people did not throw away the superficial layers covering them while talking and why they shied away from self-knowledge and understanding; what force in circumstances compelled them to tell lies, show off, and hide the truth. He believed: "they should be themselves and live with confidence. What do they have to lose by living as they really are? Do they never realize, even for a moment, the extent of their hypocrisy? They do not suffer their own pangs of conscience?" (Cappola, 11) Rakesh was a genuine and intense individual. He felt that something was constantly burning inside him and he felt the veins in his head would burst any time. He felt disturbed to find many things clashing: "Yesterday's impressions with today's experiences, adolescent dreams with surrounding reality." (Cappola, 12) He was a restless soul, thinking deeply and intensely on sensual subjects. Sometimes while attending classes, his mind would go blank and the professor thought Rakesh was sick. One of Rakesh's aristocratic friends commented on his personality: "The trouble with you [is] . . . you can't create a balance among the impressions that you have. Your mind sways like a pendulum between this and that so that you can't ever relax and you are always tense." (Cappola, 12)

The research project on 'the dramatic word' for which he had received the Nehru fellowship remained incomplete, and Rakesh died, rather untimely, at the age of forty-seven, due to pernicious side-effects of excessive liquor intake, and his intense, extremist temperament.

Rakesh's friends included such well-known people as Kamleshwar, Rajendra Gupta, Rajinder Paul and Om Shivpuri and they felt his loss keenly. These friends vividly remember the emotional warmth which Rakesh brought to bear on his relationships. He enjoyed his friends' successes. When anyone of them went abroad, Rakesh enthusiastically accompanied him to the airport to give him a warm send off.

The Mystique of Rakesh

A mystique surrounds the personality of Mohan Rakesh who has been difficult to understand. Consequently, he has been dubbed simultaneously a messiah and a self-destructive individual. An evocative image used to describe Rakesh was that he was like 'a drop of mercury on the floor,' trembling and disintegrating into pieces in an attempt to attain stability. He was known to his friends as a person of restless temperament and immense impatience. In his own words, "This anxiety, this instability becomes a habit. A moment doesn't last in its desire to become the next one. Wherever you are, you get up and go somewhere else. Leave whatever you are doing and start something else. If you are sitting and reading, turn the page every two minutes to see where your chapter ends." (Cappola, 9)

It was this restlessness, perhaps, which made him hop from job to job; in fact he scoffed at people who stuck to one job for the sole reason of financial security. His credo was: "You need five hundred to live? Then borrow three thousand on interest and work for six months and earn six thousand." It was only after he resigned from several jobs, and remained unemployed for some periods which created for him acute financial crisis, that he took to full-time writing.

He was an intensely emotional person, with very strong likes and dislikes. He raged at phoniness, sham and hypocrisy. One recalls post-Second World War American novelist J.D. Salinger's Holden Caulfield in his classic *The Catcher in the Rye*. Holden castigated phoniness of all types and condemned hypocrisy so intensely that he became a symbol of authenticity of 'self' in the Sixties in America.

Rakesh gave way to angry outbursts during arguments (reminiscent of D.H. Lawrence, who shouted, trembled and blew his top off in an effort to convince his interlocutor about the rightness of the point he was making.) A large-hearted person, though never flush with money, Rakesh enjoyed spending money on his friends, with whom he spent time in coffee houses and restaurants in Connaught Place. Given to eccentric and obsessive behaviour, he was once looking for a suitable toy for his son in Karol Bagh and when he finally did find it, he went on a toys-buying spree, till he exausted all the money in his purse. But the same Rakesh haggled furiously with his publishers who he thought were paying him less for creative work than it deserved. He was no exception to the general belief that the publishers were a niggardly lot who thrived and enjoyed luxuries at the expense of the poor writer who slogged but got a measly sum for his labours. However, unlike many other writers, he fought hard for his rights. Being a stubborn individualist, acutely concerned about the authenticity of his self, completely conforming to the Sartrean model of an authentic being, Rakesh was dead against practising 'bad faith' which he thought was a sign of a weak personality and hypocrisy. He was shocked to observe how people wore layers of artificiality on their faces and every now and then he found the layer on someone's face broken away and the person revealed. Beneath the layers of love, sympathy, courage and enthusiasm, the real face would be very helpless, timid and unenthusiastic. (Cappola, 11) He regarded it his duty to wage a war against the publishers. His attitude was unprecedented in the Hindi publishing world. He was a sentimental person, always ready to help his friends, and an idealistic individual, who thought that the tribe of creative writers, of all people in the society, needed to cherish and practise certain values for creating a better society.

Unpredictable as he was, at times, he would suddenly runaway to isolated places like Dalhousie or Srinagar and live in Dak Bungalows in remote, isolated areas. This invited the charge of irresponsibility and indiscipline from his friends and detractors who could not understand his need for isolation for doing his creative work. He believed that he could come out with his creative best only in such peaceful, undisturbed and isolated places and, therefore, it was imperative for him to get away from the bustling life of the metropolis of Delhi. Kamleshwar, one of his close friends and admirers, agreed that Rakesh did lead a disorganized life, but clarified that deep down, he observed a fantastic discipline, the discipline of the mind and the creative spirit.

His disorderly living notwithstanding, the process of his writing was always well organized and ordered. Behind the chain-smoking, at times even shabbily dressed, Bohemian, there was a Rakesh who had an enviable clarity of artistic purpose.

His artistic creed consisted in commitment not to any particular philosophy or ideology, but to his self and his times. It was his firm belief that if the artist is truly committed to the authenticity of his self then like a blind man groping alone in the dark with a stick, he could hit out at the powers of terror and darkness with his entire self. The line of the famous song of Rabindranath Tagore: "Jodi tor daak shune keu, naa ashe, Tobe ekla chol re," (If no one responds to your call, then walk on your chosen path alone), could be aptly applied to Rakesh. He did not mind treading alone the path of creative integrity, even though it created problems for him at times.

Rakesh began by writing short stories, and went onto write novels and plays, "From 1948 he had also been keeping a diary intermittently, and portions of this diary, written between 1948 and 1968 were published under the title *Mohan Rakesh ki Diary* in 1985." (Agrawal: 1999: 93) Rakesh was an important part of the new writing that emerged after Independence and which was mainly the work of the city-based, city-oriented, middle-class writers. These writings mainly focussed on the problems which were the creation of the urban life and which concerned the middle-class. During the 35-40 years after Independence, the writers of the "new writing" diverted their attention from the larger social or cosmic problems to the middle-class individual and his struggle to find happiness. Their concern has been the "personal happiness and sorrow, the forging of one's identity as well as personality, the establishment of new values, the new parameters of the man-woman relationship, the desire for personal freedom which, when too powerful, takes the shape of licence, the apprehension of loneliness." (Agrawal, 93) Prem Chand's era which was marked for social awareness and projection of social problems was succeeded by an age in which the individual became central. Not much was written about education, unemployment, the generation gap, the fast changing social scene and the go-by given to values in the mad race of competitiveness, and the younger generation going astray in the absence of concrete moral values. The period from 1950 to 1972, on the contrary, explored the psychic complications of the modern middle-class man, caused by his angst and frustration from breaking human relationships. Rakesh was an active part of this creative milieu and his writings constitute an in-depth study into the psyche of the city-bred, city-harassed, middle-class man.

As mentioned earlier, Rakesh started his creative career as a writer of short stories. Between 1944 and 1972 he wrote a total of 66 stories of which 12 were published during his lifetime. The form of the story (*Nai Kahani*—New Story), created by Rakesh and his contemporaries like Rajendra Yadav and Kamleshwar was different from that of the stories that had been written earlier. Stylistically, these stories used a language which was natural and simple. In fact, the language of everyday use was adopted as the vehicle of creative expression. Thematically, a large body of writing took up man-woman relationship (Rakesh dealt predominantly with this theme), in addition to personal failures, frustrations, despair and collapse of traditional values, leading to extreme individualism. There was a certain amount of openness in the portrayal of sexual relations which was in sharp contrast to the earlier writings. In the case of Rakesh, his stories were mostly extensively based on the experiences and impressions he had noted in his diary. Talking of his stories, Rakesh said:

> Most of my stories are about people living through the torture of relationships in their loneliness, where I have tried to depict through the individual, his environment. This loneliness is not the loneliness of the socially isolated individual but the loneliness that comes from living within society and it leads not to any kind of cynicism but to the need to live through it. The attempt is not to see the individual and society as mutually opposed and mutually exclusive, distinct from and separated from each other but rather to see them as related in such a fashion that the individual reflects the dilemmas of society and society reflects the torture of the individual (From the flap of *Sampoorna Kahaniyan*).

One reason why most of Rakesh's stories took up the subject of man-woman relationship was the changing identity of woman during the Sixties and the Seventies. The women got a measure of economic independence by entering the job market. Because of their increased level of education, women acquired a greater self-awareness and by virtue of their jobs got greater opportunities to inter-act with men outside home. This necessitated a crucial change in the mindset of men and required a different equation between husbands and wives. In fact, the institution of marriage itself came to be interrogated and the traditional idea that marriage had to be rescued at any cost was not found sacrosanct. In Mohan Rakesh's stories, novels and plays, one rarely finds man-woman relationships leading to love, happiness, wholeness and surrender; on the contrary these relationships, whether in or outside marriage, are fraught with tension, dislike, suffocation and alienation, in spite of his protagonists' desire and attempts to find happiness and joy. The very titles of some of his short stories are suggestive of this mental condition. "Doraha," "Dhundhlaa Deep," "Aparichit," "Aadami aur Deevar," "Marusthal," "Lakshyaheen," "Insaan ke Khandahar." These stories and novels are largely based on his personal experiences and for that reason they contain an intensity of emotion which is difficult to match but, because of this factor, at times they seem to lack the breadth of canvas that comes from creating diverse characters, circumstances and emotions. Nonetheless, their artistic merit remains undisputed.

Mohan Rakesh wrote three novels (again the titles of the novels are noteworthy for their sadness and despair) *Andhere Band Kamre* (1961), *Na Aanewala Kal* (1968) and *Antaraal* (1972).

While in the field of short story, there were three prominent writers at that time viz., Rajendra Yadav, Kamleshwar, and Mohan Rakesh, there was none who could match the competence of Rakesh in the genre of drama. Rakesh wrote three full-length plays: *Aashadh Ka Ek Din* (1958), *Lehro Ke Rajhans* (1963) and *Aadhe Adhure* (1969). Rakesh virtually dominated the field of drama. With his very first play, he established himself as an unrivalled dramatist.

In 1959, he was awarded the first prize by the Sangeet Natak Akademi for his first play. He also penned some one-act plays, *Dhwaninatya* (audio plays), *Beejnatya* (seed plays and radio plays) which were published under the title *Ande Ke Chhilke, Anya Ekanki Tatha Beej Natak* and *Raat Beetne Tak Tatha Anya Dhwani Natak*. He left one play, *Pair Tale Ki Zameen* unfinished, which Kamleshwar, his close friend, completed later, on the basis of the notings left by Rakesh.

Aashadh Ka Ek Din (1958), like his other plays, takes up the man-woman relationship, but in addition to that it also reflects Rakesh's concern for the issue of royal patronage and creativity. There is a conflict between the two—it was his belief that the creative powers of an artist get atrophied, if he kowtows to the powers that be. This is what happens to the protagonist of *Aashadh Ka Ek Din*. Rakesh noted, to his chagrin, how some of the creative writers, to garner small and big gains, indulged in sycophancy and in this play, he highlights the dangers of sycophancy. Act II of the play explores the psychology of the royal officials who have arrived from the capital of Rangini-Sangini and draws a parallel with the modern officials and students of art who tend to get involved in futile discussions and arguments, getting lost in issues of secondary importance and at times indulging in arrogant behaviour. Act III also underscores the conflicts between creativity and the reality of life which often entangles a writer in the struggle for survival. Even though the play is located in the past, the issues it raises and the concerns it depicts are undoubtedly modern and relevant even today.

Lehron Ke Rajhans (1963) focuses on man-woman relationship in a more intense manner. The vitiating factors are identified as clash of egos, split personalities, and breakdown of communication. Why does breakdown in communication occur? Graham Greene provides an answer in his novel *The Quiet American*: "Wouldn't we all do better not trying to understand, accepting the fact that no human being will ever understand another, not a wife a husband, a lover a mistress, nor a parent a child." (60) This breakdown of communication inevitably leads to sadness, loneliness and the anguish of not being able to communicate. This play is unambiguously modern in its concerns, since despair, loneliness, and the sense of futility are modern phenomena. *Halfway House* published in 1969 also takes up the clash of egos of man and woman, and depicts the disintegration of not only the individuals but the institution of family (I will revert to an exhaustive discussion of *Halfway House* later), and a complete breakdown of communication among the family members.

A Comparative Study of the Three Plays

As noted earlier, *Aashadh Ka Ek Din* deals with man-woman relationship, and dramatizes the separation of Kalidas from Mallika whom he loves deeply. Mallika also emotionally responds to his love and talks about "choosing feeling with feeling." She sends him to the capital, because she wants him to gain recognition and fame and is ready to embrace him when he gets back—it is another matter that his return is not shown. Kalidas does leave, but feels pained at doing so. For him going away from Mallika is wrenching away an important part of his own self. In *Lehron Ke Rajhans*, the man-woman relationship unlike *Aashadh Ka Ek Din*, is not tender and loving; on the contrary it is soured by the self-centeredness and ego of Nand and Sundari, who progressively become lonely because of their bickerings, and their inability to mould themselves according to the desire of each other. They are aware of each other's shortcomings, but still they refuse to or are unable to understand each other sympathetically. Constant tension and bitterness between them turns them into islands unto themselves. The relationship becomes full of hostility towards each other. Act III shows their perverse delight in hurling accusations at each other. Nand finds it difficult to stay with Sundari; and she in turn cannot stop him from leaving. Like the earlier play, there is a parting in this one also, but this parting is marked by hard feelings, dissatisfaction and defeat. They seem to have been cursed never to achieve happiness and contentment through each other. *Halfway House* is the culmination of the theme of disintegration of man-woman relationship. In this play, the man and the woman are not only married, they also have a family, consisting of two daughters and a son. This family seems to be a gas-chamber in which the members are getting choked; they are unable to breathe normally, as it were, and feel suffocated because of the oppressive, rancorous atmosphere that lies like a pall on the family. Each one of them seems doomed to suffer, whether it is the head of the family, Mahendranath, or his wife, Savitri (the only earning member who is supporting the family) or the boy Ashok or the youngest adolescent, Kinni. One difference between *Aashadh Ka Ek Din* and *Lehron Ke Rajhans* on the one hand and *Halfway House* on the other is that while one does not know whether Kalidas and Nand ever returned to Mallika and Sundari, but Mahendranath does return every time he threateningly leaves home, as if he were tied to the stake from which he cannot get away. But then others also are unable to escape the hell that they are in—Ashok has no job and, therefore, has no alternative, Binni, though married, keeps returning to her parental home (she is there for the most part of the action in the play), Kinni is of course too small. Savitri, who keenly longs to get away from the place she has come to abhor, makes a desperate attempt to go away, but has to come back, as if fated to live with the family and suffer. She is in an extremely tricky situation (perhaps each one of them is): cannot live there, but cannot escape either.

In all the three plays, the women play a crucial role. Their thinking, their attitudes and their decisions become catalysts in giving direction to the events in the plays. That they act, and then suffer for their actions is another matter. However, they are fully conscious women, who are aware of the complexity of their circumstances, and respond sensitively to the varying crises they are placed in. While Kalidas (*Aashadh Ka Ek Din*), Nand (*Lehron Ke Rajhans*) and Mahendranath (*Halfway House*) are weak, divided and insecure personalities, Mallika (*Ashadh Ka Ek Din*), Sundari (*Lehron Ke Rajhans*) and Savitri are stronger and decisive in their thinking. All these women are emblematic of different emotional states; the three plays can be truly categorized as woman-centered.

Even though Rakesh declares in the beginning of the play: "if the woman of the family were replaced by another, she would put up with me in a different way . . . or she would assume my role and I assuming hers, would have to put up with her," the focus is undeniably on the woman. and it is clear that the woman is more important in the scheme of the play.

Rakesh was fully conscious of the demands of the theatre and, therefore, kept the unities of time and place in mind while composing the plays. *Aashadh Ka Ek Din* spans a long period of time, no doubt, but *Lehron Ke Rajhans*, and *Halfway House* encompass the action in not more than thirty hours. One could of course, point out one or two instances which are not in keeping with the stageability of the plays: for example showing a fawn on the stage creates problems and generates some bit of confusion; similarly the presence of the monk Anand in the bedchamber of Sundari appears unrealistic. However, *Halfway House* does not suffer from any such incongurities.

As far as the language of the plays is concerned, one finds similarities in terms of the sharpness and pointedness of dialogues. The language is polished and chiselled, primarily because, as mentioned earlier, Rakesh had a special fascination for the "word." In order to suit the historical background of *Aashadh Ka Ek Din* and *Lehron Ke Rajhans*, the language used is Sanskritized which succeeded in creating the appropriate atmosphere, but the language is not obscurantist and inaccessible to the audience/reader. Even the few difficult words can be understood with the help of the context. The use of the words is not excessive, just the required number of words to explain the situation or express an emotion. Economy and appropriateness are the hallmarks of the language and it is difficult to find a single superfluous word which can be done away with. Consequently, there is a tautness in the plays, which contributes to the effective expression of stressful situations. It is difficult to find such judicious, restrained, and discreet use of the language in any other play of his contemporaries.

All the three plays generally end with long dialogues, at times monologues, which tend to slow down the pace. Mallika's long monologue in *Aashadh Ka Ek Din* and Nand's long monologue in *Lehron Ke Rajhans* impressively articulate the problems that are exercising their minds. In *Aashadh Ka Ek Din* even though Kalidas's dialogues, before Vyom arrives on the scene, are in the form of an exchange, actually they could be considered monologues, because while talking to Mallika he seems completely lost within himself. However, in *Halfway House* the long speeches of Juneja and Savitri are not strictly monologues, because Juneja and Savitri are not reflecting or exploring themselves (a characteristic of a monologue); rather these speeches refer to others, and are made with the purpose of communicating with others. For this reason, we find that the pace of the play does not slow down, unlike the earlier two plays.

The Plot of *Halfway House*

Even though The Man in the Black Suit, who could be taken as the Chorus of the play, tells us that "this play is as undefined as I am," the play does have a recognizable plot. One has to remember that the plot of *Halfway House* is not of the traditional type, which contains statement, complication and resolution. It does not conform to the Aristotlean norms of beginning, middle and ending. The only sense in which the play remains undefined perhaps is that it is, as the Chorus says, difficult to pinpoint the determining agency. Is it the Chorus (or any of the men, who are the same as the Chorus) or the woman, or the circumstances, or the questions that are the result of the inter-relations of the characters? In this sense., the plot is difficult to define. But, just because the play has a different type of plot does not make the play plotless.

The plot encompasses the life, experiences, frustrations, bitterness and despair of the members of a family who seem to be caught in a desperate situation. The plot conveys a higher level of meaning about human existence, but of that later. For the time being, it is important to remember that Mahendranath (husband), Savitri (wife), Ashok (son), Binni (the elder daughter married to Manoj) and Kinni (the younger school-going daughter) are members of a doomed family whom nobody can help. Not that there are people eager to help: Singhania, the stupid and lecherous boss of Savitri, is interested only in showing off his power and status, vis-a-vis the family, and a hint is made in the play about his sexual attraction for Savitri, Manoj, once Savitri's lover, has married Binni and remains off-stage, but complicates Binni's and her parents' lives by continuously taunting her about the 'infection' she has brought from her parents' family, which does not let them live in peace, Jagmohan, whom Savitri wants to use as a support to get out of her marriage and family, confines his interest to having an affair with her, and that too, on his own terms, not the least concerned about what plagues her family. We have one person, Juneja, Mahendranath's friend, who is sincerely anxious to solve the tangle that has knotted the lives of the members of this family, but he ends up a failure in his efforts. But why does Juneja fail in spite of his sincerity? Who is responsible for the impasse that has been created in the family out of which there does not seem to be a way out for anyone? These questions I would address in due course, but for now, as part of the plot, we find Savitri is frustrated, angry and upset at her having to sustain the family, because Mahendranath has turned into an idler, lacking in self-confidence and the desire to engage himself productively, though he does not desist from passing snide remarks at Savitri for her extra-marital relationships. This further exacerbates matters. Savitri becomes bitter at her lot in having once loved and married a nincompoop, like Mahendranath, an utter failure in life not only economically, but also as a husband and as a father, not giving support to his wife, and neglecting the children all of whom seem to have gone astray.

In spite of her frustrations, Savitri is keen to bring order into the household, and feels responsible for the children. In the very first scene, she is shown picking up Mahendranath's pyjamas lying on the back of a chair and folding them to keep them in place. She also picks up the tray lying in the room: "Everything is left for me to do." (7) Her concern for Binni's unhappy marriage gets revealed in her attempts to find out what is wrong with Binni's marriage. It is noteworthy that when Binni tells her mother that Manoj is neither unfaithful nor ill-tempered, nor unwell, Mahendranath does not hesitate to make a satirical comment: "No, no problem at all." It is Savitri again who questions Kinni as to where she had gone, when she returns in after her long absence from home. The older girl (Binni) is right when she says, "You're the only one who feels responsible here. If you too . . ." Savitri had got Ashok a job with Air Freeze, which he left. He also quits college without completing his studies. Savitri fails in her efforts to get Ashok a job through Singhania. The reasons remain unclear—these could be Singhania's shrewdness under his stupid exterior (he cannot be stupid, after all he has a job worth Rs. 5000 per month) or Ashok's indifferent, and even mischievous response to Singhania. But Savitri's failure further adds to her frustration and she begins to find her stay in the family increasingly difficult.

What gives fillip to her ambitions is the return of Jagmohan to the city. He is an old flame, but things could not work out with him earlier. She is keen to pick up the thread and revive her relationship with him, with the hope that he would provide her with an escape route from the hell-hole which her home has turned into. In the meantime, Mahendranath has left home and has begun to stay with Juneja.

In Act two a suggestion is made through the stage direction that Savitri, too, had decided to clear out. When she gets back home, unlike earlier times, she "glances at the disorderly room but doesn't try to tidy it." Binni is informed by her that Jagmohan is coming to pick her up and she decisively announces to Binni: "When you come next time I may not be here"—she is so sure of Jagmohan's love for her. Of course, she is mistaken, and is in for a rude shock. An indication of how Jagmohan is going to treat her is again provided in a stage direction. She puts her hand on his but he "takes her hand away." The play operates in a subtle way through innuendoes and suggestions. Savitri is keen to get away from home, but despite everything, there is something which binds her to the place: while leaving with Jagmohan, she asks him as to when he thinks she will be back because "I ought to leave a message," Why leave a message, if everything is over between her and the family? Why worry about saving her family the anxiety? There is that connection, that bond which makes the desire complex. Wanting to escape and yet not wanting to.

However, the acrimony that characterizes Savitri's and Mahendranath's present relationship is reason enough for the two to divorce and get away from each other. The intensity of the hostility between the two is described by the Older Girl (Binni) to Juneja who has come to have a talk with Savitri for a possible reconciliation. "When I lived here it was like being . . . you can't even imagine what it was like. . . . Daddy's rages when he tore Mama's clothes to shreds . . . when he gagged her and beat her up behind closed doors . . . dragging her by the hair to the WC . . . (shudders) I can't even recount the fearful scenes I've witnessed in this house.' If any outsider had seen all this, he would have wondered why they hadn't." (63-64) The irony of the situation is that even Juneja, in spite of his desire to sort things out between Savitri and Mahendranath despairs of the situation ever improving. "You really think that nothing can be done?" asks Binni sadly and his reply is "Perhaps something can be done for a day. Or even for a week. But forever? Nothing!" The obvious choice then for the two of them is to go in for a divorce and that is what Binni has on mind. But it is not an easy proposition. Savitri, after having been rejected by Jagmohan, has nowhere to go. And Mahendranath, in spite of Savitri's numerous affairs with other men, still loves her and cannot live without her. And, therefore, a marriage of 22 years standing, with three children, one of them married, is in a piquant situation; it cannot break, and it does not work. The net result: suffering for all. Anguish for all. Never ending. Even as Juneja is having a discussion with Savitri, who is venting her pent up feelings of injury and hurt, and Juneja is saying that Mahendranath will never come back, Mahendranath comes home, unasked, unwell, unhappy.

The Issues Involved: Human Relationships
Man-Woman Relationships

Like many other works of literature, the play deals with human relationships, which as E.M. Forster tells us, are never constant. The axes explored along these relationships are: man-woman, husband-wife, parents-children, employer-employee (especially with the gender aspect taken up), brother-sister, sister-sister, and even neighbour-neighbour. The title of the play suggestively hints at the incomplete human beings which populate the world of the play and, therefore, posits a scenario, in which human relationships are bound to be complex, unfulfilling, tangled and tortuous. But it is noteworthy, that in the whole play there is not one relationship, which could be called happy and symbiotic, with the sole exception of Mahendranath-Juneja relationship. It is a dark, grim world which Rakesh creates, devoid of affirmation, redemption, or a ray of hope. Savitri-Mahendranath relationship, of course, forms the epicentre of the play around which it revolves, and it appears it is this relationship that sets the tone for all others, too. While exploring this relationship, the gender issue becomes important, since the question of representation of woman by a male writer assumes significance. In the intensely soured relationship between the husband and the wife (and its attendant consequences in the form of disintegration of the family), apportioning of responsibility by the author for what goes wrong between Mahendranath and Savitri needs to be examined. Rakesh insisted that *Halfway House* is not anti-woman and for this purpose he made the Prologue speak thus, right in the beginning: "If the woman of the family was replaced by another, she would put up with me in a different way . . . or, she would assume my role and I, assuming hers, would have to put up with her. The play would remain equally undefined and it would be just as difficult to decide who has the determining role . . . I, the woman, the circumstances that surround us or the questions that arise out of our interaction with each other." (5) The implication is clear that neither the man, nor the woman is to blame for the blighted situation that has developed in the family. But a close reading of the play reveals that Rakesh arraigns the woman for the tragedy which overtakes all the members. Rajinder Nath, a celebrated director, underscores this point in his respsonse to the reading of the play, given by Rakesh himself to a select gathering of close friends: "portrayal of Savitri was not very sympathetic. It seemed as if she were being held responsible for this 'hell'/no exit' situation." (Basu: Intro, xiii) Rakesh was shocked. He tried to reassure them that that was not his intention. That he had read an earlier version of the play to the well-known actress, Dina Pathak, and she had pointed out that, if she were to perform the role of Savitri she would feel that not enough lines had been given to her to adequately express her feelings. After listening to her views, Rakesh had revised the play, and incorporated the long speech for Savitri towards the end of the play to redress the imbalance. But the imbalance still remains. Savitri's presentation has a negative dimension to it. Perhaps, it is in spite of the playwright. 'The pen does not lie' or as D.H. Lawrence says, 'trust the tale.' "In spite of the author's conscious intention, the play tells a different truth. This imbalance against Savitri can be recitified, only to a limited extent, by combined efforts of the director and the actor, but in reading the play it does remain.

Family and Home

Family as an institution creates a small social unit which is cohesive, mutually supportive and a site for balanced and integrated growth of children, who develop into responsible, sensitive individuals, contributing to the well-being of the society, as also to each other's happiness. In its early stages, family began only as a reproductive or biological association, it acquired the highest importance as a social unit for several significant reasons. Sociologists MacIver and Page observe: "Of all the organisations, large or small which the society unfolds none transcends the family in the intensity of its sociological significance. It influences the whole society in innumerable ways, and changes reverberate through the whole social structure." (Prabhu: 1958: 203) Like any other social institution the family emerged to fulfill certain very basic biological, psychological and social needs of humans. The following three functions could be termed as primary: (i) the more stable satisfaction of the sex need of man and woman (ii) procreation, care and nurture of the young and (iii) the sharing of a home and all that it involves. MacIver and Page go on to aver that only in a *successful* family are these three functions so balanced that each of them reinforces and enriches the satisfaction of the others. In a family, sex does not remain an isolated phenomenon, which is the case in extramarital relations and in prostitution. It forms a part of a larger experience of living and sharing and caring. It has been established that the nurture of children, to make them bodily and mentally healthy, can take place within the favourable environment of the family than that of the state nursery or other public or private agencies. Even though in a country like the erstwhile U.S.S.R., the institution of family registered a radical change in its form, after the great 1917 revolution, a central point of continuity between the old and the new form, according to Burgess and Locks, is "an intangible but a very real thing, viz., deep family feeling and the affection and solicitude of parents for children, which survived the Revolution and now again is being expressed freely and openly." (204)

Males like fox, martin, wild cat, eagle, sparrow, hawk, pigeon, stork, black-bird, swallow etc. whose young are difficult to provide for, select one from among several females at the first period of oestrum. They remain attached to each other even when the time of propagation has passed. They journey together, remain side by side in flocks, "provide for themselves, and at each succeeding period of oestrum, again yield to love, and do not "seek a new mate till the former is dead." (Walker: 1987: 75) Homo sapiens belong to this category, and therefore, promiscuity in sex is as unnatural to them as it is to such animals and birds. The behaviour of anthropoid apes, man's nearest kins, further confirms the instinct for family and absence of promiscuity. They "always live in pairs and are not promiscuous," (Sur: 3) and do not part company until separated by death. Among men even the savage races of the world are known to "live under a well-regulated marriage system." Havelock Ellis says, "Marriage in the biological sense is a sexual relationship entered into with the intention of making it permanent, even apart from whether or not it has received sanction of law or the Church." (Sur: 2) Family, the smallest sociological unit, implied marriage, implicit or explicit, which in turn lent this unit stability, togetherness and mutual care. Commenting upon the benefits that result from family, Alexander Walker observes: "The advantages resulting from the state of marriage are that the two sexes may reciprocally satisfy the natural desires which are felt equally by each . . . that they equally submit the exercise of the reproductive organs to a healthful regularity; that they may equally perpetuate their common species; that they may equally by respective duties, provide for the children proceeding from their mutual union, that they may equally assist each other throughout life by reciprocal affection and cares; that they may in old age receive the cares of their common progeny: and that they may, in health and well being, reach that age which all these circumstances generally enable married pairs to attain." (1987:78) Walker goes on to assert that "History proves that marriage is essential to the well-being of human society." (80) This conforms to the Vedantic view of marriage according to which "marriage partners are to serve each other. Elevate, help, teach, strengthen each other, but above all, *serve*."

Let us now consider the marriage between Mahendranath and Savitri and the state of the family they have created between themselves. After the initial erotic attraction between them, they get married and procreate three children to raise a family. They remain together, of course, but not through choice. It is the failure of Savitri's attempts to walk out of her marriage, and settle with somebody else that force her to continue with Mahendranath. Mahendranath, in turn, comes back home because, as Juneja says, he loves Savitri and cannot live without her. But the way he treats her—physical bashings of Savitri included—does not exactly make the family environment conducive for anyone. Savitri's continuous accusations that Mahendranath is a good-for-nothing person, a complete failure in life, who is not capable of anything—neither earning to support the family, nor willing to take up responsibility of any kind—is one factor which vitiates the family atmosphere. Her constant frustration at not being rich and her chasing the mirage of riches by running after different people sets an unhealthy example for the growing children. Mahendranath's frequent satirical barbs attacking Savitri on the issue of her extra-marital liaisons do not contribute to alleviating the worsening situation. Nor does he provide a role model for the children to emulate. Consequently, Ashok grows into an idler who has given up his studies mid-way through college, and whiles away his time reading trashy (pornographic) magazines and cutting pictures from them. Savitri's treatment of Mahendranath and her flirtations with other men have filled Ashok with rage against his mother. (Here it would be pertinent to point out that while the older girl, Binni, sympathises with the mother,

Ashok's sympathy lies with the father). Binni was unhappy before she got married and went away, and is unhappy in her marriage, too (she has married the erstwhile lover of her mother, Manoj). As her husband points out, she has brought an infection from her parental home which spoils their marriage. Kinni is growing into a troublesome brat—reading pornographic magazines on the sly, talking sex with her friend, Surekha, in the neighbourhood and misbehaving with almost everyone in the family. But she is not to blame for what she is becoming and the manner in which she behaves. Nobody is there to look after her school needs, and to pay attention to her problems. She becomes an object of Savitri's frustrations who beats her up for the child's not so unreasonable demands. This is the family that is presented in the play—a complete reversal of the ideal projected by the sociologists, a total travesty of the Vedantic concept of the family mentioned earlier.

Home is a space one wants to come to after the day's struggle and tensions. At home one relaxes, and eases out the stress that has been accumulated throughout the day. And one very potent factor which helps one to relax is the love one gets from the family members. The family members reciprocate each other's affection and care and, thus, home becomes a site where one feels replenished emotionally and gets the nervous energy to face the next day. No doubt, occasional disagreements and quarrels between members of a family are a natural phenomenon, but they do not affect the empathy that exists for each other, and the basic understanding of each other. Perhaps, it is this emotional support one gets from the family, that protects one's sanity and prevents one from becoming a nervous wreck. But the home in *Halfway House* does not provide emotional succour, or support. This home is the site of perpetual discord and acrimony. Here there is no pleasure, joy or happiness. This home is a place which repulses its inhabitants: escape from it is uppermost in the minds of the persons who inhabit this space, (It is another matter that there is no exit for them from this torture-cell that this home has become). They try, but do not succeed in getting away. Binni married Manoj, because she wanted to run away from the trouble-spot called 'home.' But by some perverse quirk of circumstance, she still remains tied to the place, even after her marriage. It appears her fate is sealed, along with the other members of the family. She has to remain rooted to this distorted version of 'home.' And this home is like a long tunnel, at the end of which there is no light. It is a *cul-de-sac*, into which are huddled, Savitri, Mahendranath, Ashok, Binni and Kinni, who (unlike a traditional family in which members sustain each other during crises) keep tearing at each other, injuring each other and stoking the fires of anger, frustration and bitterness. This home has become a place where the members inhale the miasmic air of rancour and lead cantankerous lives.

So, marriage, between Savitri and Mahendranath went haywire in the first two years of the ceremony, the family began to disintegrate ever since because the essential bond of love vanished from their lives, and the home turned into a ground splattered with poison which insidiously kept seeping into their systems and destroying them. The fairy-tale like ending "and they lived happily ever after" is inverted into 'they lived unhappily ever after,' because Savitri comes back from her tryst with Jagmohan rejected and disappointed, Mahendranath gets back home from Juneja's where he had gone to stay, in a fit of anger and the children, of course, have nowhere to go.

Other Relationships

There is no love lost between Ashok on the one hand and Binni and Kinni on the other. He is brutally frank with Binni in telling her that she escaped into marriage, because she was disgusted with home. Binni chides him for being an idler, not interested in his career, wasting precious years of life. One does not see any warmth of affection between the two. There are no tender feelings (except towards the end when an ill Mahendranath comes back home and both Ashok and Binni share concern for their father.) This is the only moment when they act like loving brother and sister, joined by their concern for their father. Otherwise, one witnesses, either a cold, indifference characterizing their relationship, or angry exchanges between the two. Ashok-Kinni relationship does not provide any different pattern either. Ashok is forever trying to chastise Kinni for her fascination for pornographic magazines (which ironically Ashok himself brings home to read. This is an instance of the gender bias, though Ashok cloaks it under the argument that she is too young to read all that stuff). And Kinni's grouse against Ashok is that he has been giving away her things to Varna, his girl friend, and is rough with her. And what kind of relationship do the children have with the parents? They have grown into distorted personalities which could be traced to their resentment against their parents, who have failed to provide them with worthy role-models and a congenial atmosphere in which to live, like other children, and grow into adults with healthy psyches. If anything, they provide negative role models to their children, the direct effect of which can be seen on Binni whose marriage with Manoj is more of a running away and is as troubled as her mother's, and on Ashok who seems to be becoming the exact replica of his father—an idler, a parasite, but not short on taunts and satirical remarks. And Kinni's excessively keen interest in sex is partly attributable to Ashok's procuring the magazines, but largely it is because of her desire to understand what goes on between Savitri and her male friends. The relationship between the children and the parents, therefore, is not a happy one.

Why is it that Rakesh chooses to divest this play of any redeeming relationship in the family? Ashok's concern for his father, and Binni's sympathetic feeling for the mother hint at the possibility of mutual tenderness, but this possibility does not develop into anything more substantial partly because Ashok's and Binni's feelings are mixed with an undercurrent of resentment and partly because Rakesh's perception of an urban middle-class family is based on his experience and he does not want to be unrealistic.

Language and Dialogues

Mohan Rakesh's interest in and fastidiousness about language is well known. He wanted to work intensively in the area of language in relation to the stage—how language could intensify or dull the dramatic impact of dialogues, how appropriateness of the 'word' could articulate the nuances of feelings being experienced by a character; above all, he lay stress on the accessibility and comprehensibility) of language to the audiences. Even though he used Sanskritized language in *Aashadh Ka Ek Din*, the language remained dramatic and easily communicable. In *Halfway House*, the language is simple and colloquial but no less dramatic. The apparent simplicity of the language of *Halfway House* could be rather misleading, inducing belief that it might have been easy to write. But that would be grossly incorrect. As R.K. Narayan (whose language is also simple and easy to understand) asserted that one had to work more assiduously and harder to bring the effect of simplicity to the language. It is not surprising, therefore, that Rakesh's subject for the Nehru Fellowship Project was: "The Dramatic Word."

Two distinguishing features characterize the dialogues in *Halfway House*: (1) Most of the statements, or even questions, are followed not by comments on the statements or answers to the questions asked. Let us see some of the examples: the scene: the younger girl, Kinni, in her school uniform runs into the house through the street door and finding Papa and Binni at home expresses surprise at their presence at home to which Savitri says:

The Woman:	What did you say?
The Younger Girl:	You tell me, does one know what's going on? When I came from school no one was at home. And now you're all here . . . even Binni-Di is here.—Why are you so quiet?
The Woman:	You tell me about yourself . . . where did you go?
The Younger Girl:	Somewhere . . . what does it matter? Was anyone at home that I should stay here? Is the milk hot? (20)

The second instance: the scene in which Ashok and Binni are talking; Ashok speaking about the vitiated home atmosphere.

The Boy:	There is something in this house that . . .
The Older Girl:	(shattered) You think so too . . . ?
The Boy:	Don't you know?
The Older Girl:	(averting her eyes) How should I know? (46)

The second feature of the dialogues is the pauses or the silences into which the sentences spoken by characters trail. We observe, almost every sentence either has a pause/pauses and/or ends in silence. There are two implications of these characteristics of the dialogues.

The first is related to the central theme of the play: the play throws up questions, but there are no answers. There is no resolution to the main problem. Neither Savitri, nor Mahendranath, nor the children can find their way out of the impasse in which they are caught. The play ends where it began. Everybody is unhappy to be living in that family, yet everybody is forced to live there. The second implication is the problem of communication. The characters find it difficult to express themselves. The dots at the end of the sentences could also indicate the impatience of the other character who cuts the speaker short, which, in a way, reflects the predicament of communication.

Taken together, both these implications point to the fragmentation of the family. Each individual tends to become an island unto himself/herself, without much contact or rapport with the others.

Universality of the Play

Some critics tend to run down the play as being too limited in canvas, as it deals with only one family. However, this criticism is not valid. The woman-question in the context of changing socio-economic environment in India in the Fifties/Sixties as also in other countries of the world, gives the play a much larger scope, which these critics ignore. Women entering the employment market, their new-found economic independence, and consequent confidence in themselves, infused a new awareness and need for self-fulfilment in women which became a point of clash with the 'family' which remained in the grooves of patriarchal attitudes. We know that as a result of Women's Liberation Movement, the institution of family, gender roles of motherhood, reproduction and rearing of children came to be examined and questioned by women. Man-woman (husband-wife) relationship was sought to be redefined with a view to giving a fair deal to the woman. Societies are in a flux even now because of women's efforts all over the world to get a niche in the social space. Besides, there are other issues—parent-child relations, employer-employee relations which transcend the context of the particular family in the play. Also, as mentioned earlier, the play has an absurdist dimension which refers to the human condition.

Rakesh's Views on Diverse Subjects

According to Mohan Rakesh, the most important problem for a creative writer is to maintain the authenticity of his self. Lack of economic independence, forces the writer to make compromises, which militate against his self. One such compulsion is the necessity to write 1,500 to 2,000 pages a year to sustain himself economically. This inevitably tells upon the quality of the writing.

Rakesh holds both the readers and the publishers responsible, to a large extent, for forcing writers into compromising situations. The readers do not buy enough books; they tend to borrow books from the libraries, and the publishers of Hindi books, being small-time businessmen are, on the one hand, unable to organize campaigns to promote the sales of books and on the other, pay paltry sums to writers for their creative labours.

According to Rakesh, creative writing is a full-time job, which demands commitment. Like the other arts, writing also demands total dedication and commitment. Creative writing is like a *sadhana*, requiring sincere, hard work. The two essentials for a creative writer are talent and exposure to life.

While it is necessary that a writer should have a definite viewpoint about life and issues, and situations, he should not isolate himself from the broader struggle of life. It is desirable for a creative writer that he should evaluate each event and circumstance objectively and independently and place his perceptions before others courageously. Creative writing is not a political strategy to acquire power and prizes, as some pseudo-writers tend to think. It is a process leading to evaluation of the things happening in society. A true artist wants to possess the independence to disagree with the dominant political ideology, to be able to caution the politicians and point out to them their errors. The writer's views may tally with a political party's position or its ideology, but it is essential that he should remain free from the political regimentation of the party. This is his true independence, and this is what gives to his writing the strength and the power to move.

Rakesh raises an important question: should a writer accept State's financial patronage? According to him, there is no harm in doing so, provided the writer can maintain independence of his views in spite of the facilities he receives from the State. But the experience shows, he says, that the writer tends to feel beholden to the State, and this enfeebles his writing. Therefore, he thinks, it is more important for a writer to preserve his individuality than getting financial support from the State.

Talking of other countries, Rakesh informs us that Writers's Groups and Writers's Forums have played a crucial role in protecting the creative independence. But unfortunately, the scenario is different in India. A few groups were formed, but they broke up, without playing any meaningful role. Absence of such forums left the writers to fend for themselves. But for this state of affairs, believes Rakesh, writers themselves are to blame.

Rakesh finds a schism between the common man and literature of his times. Reason: rapid change in social milieu and disintegration of traditional cultural values. The scale of scientific and technological progress is unprecedented. Politics without values and without any philosophical bases, the shattering of traditional framework of human relationships regarded as the axis of human progress is unparallelled. Therefore, the crisis of creativity, facing the writer today, cannot be compared with any earlier crisis. The writer feels impotent and helpless in the face of such a situation. He has to assimilate the emerging values. Talking continuously about the past values is living in the past. The new values demand new forms of expression, new craft, new patterns of arrangement. If a creative artist cannot grasp this new tone of life, then, in spite of all his claims to modernity, he is not modern. Relating to the present has only one meaning and that is the effort to cross the threshold of today while gazing into the future. This is the only way to recognize and understand the potentialities of the present.

Mohan Rakesh is of the view that the process of writing a play and the process of dramatizing a play are two different processes and each has its own problems. During the course of dramatization, the director conceives the form of the stage, in order to express fully what the script according to him seeks to communicate to the audiences. This often necessitates a seemingly arbitrary surgery which begins to be performed on the writer's script—dialogues are changed, situations are modified, and even characters are interfered with. The playwright's position becomes that of an outsider who, if he complains, is seen to be creating problems for the director, without any knowledge of the theatre. Mohan Rakesh does not agree that the playwright should remain a respectable spectator or an outsider in the whole process of dramatization. The experimentation with writing and the experimentation with the creative stage need to interact symbiotically for an effective dramatization. It is essential for the writer to become an integral part of the process of theatre in order to bring together the two processes.

Words play a significant role in the theatre. Unlike Cinema, which is basically a visual medium, theatre is mainly an audio medium, where whatever is seen is the transmutation of what is heard. There is nothing more important than the word, apart from the actor and the director. The director coordinates the actor and the word. But this situation enhances the responsibility of the word, which in other words means the responsibility of the playwright. In Rakesh's view, the playwright today is not discharging that responsibility adequately.

The Contemporary Hindi Theatre

The regional character of the language, depth of emotions and literary achievement of Prasad's plays was so great that it undermined the importance of stage. With the rise of amateur theatre, the stage again began to play a significant role. Because of the increasing demand for the amateur theatre during the Seventies and Eighties, some social, historical plays, especially one-act plays, were written, keeping in view the requirements of the theatre. But our amateur theatre is also modelled on the lines of the Western theatre. Therefore, its own individuality has not been carved out. Western plays have generally been written keeping the set of a drawing room in mind. Our own social plays focus on the middle-class family's house, where things like table, chairs, bookshelf and table lamp become essential. If a bit more of Indianness is needed, a picture of Mahavir is hung in the background. The conception of this type of stage limits the play mostly to the urban elite. It also limits for the playwright the scope of presentation of themes. It seems contradictory to keep in mind the Western stagecraft and talk about the development of our native theatre. The development of the Hindi theatre does not mean that theatres equipped with ultra-modern devices should be constructed where Hindi plays could be staged. The emphasis should not be on improved technological stage facilities, but on the cultural vision. The real Hindi stage will develop not through state-sponsored programmes, but through capable playwrights, actors and directors. If the plays portray the conflicts of human existence, then the stage will also have to mould itself accordingly. The Hindi theatre will have to become representative of the cultural fulfillment and aspirations of the Hindi-speaking region. Our stage has to be much more open and broader in order to express the rhythm of our life. Our native colour sense should guide us to create the relevant backdrop by using yellow (haldi), pale yellow (chandan) and dark brown (Geru) instead of green or grey; the former colours will be appropriate for presenting all kinds of scenes on the stage and will be pleasant to look at. A canvas in the mould of modern Western theatre, sets made of cardboard and wood, background music and light and sound effects could be considered later. If we begin with a specialised theatre, we would not be able to make it conform to the needs and tastes of the common man. Jagdish Chandra Mathur has conceived of theatre in three forms: realistic, commercial and rural. Commercial theatre can of course be developed by people other than us, but we are better equipped to conceive of and implement a problem-oriented realistic theatre and rural theatre. If we pay proper attention to colours and sounds, then a play dramatized on a very simple stage can also be effective.

The Hindi Drama

The genesis of the Hindi drama lies in the Sanskrit drama, which itself is shrouded in obscurity. However, there are references to the plays in the Vedas, and evidence is extant about the dramatic performances in the period of the *Ramayana* and the *Mahabharata*. The most decisive indication of the presence of the plays in the early Indian period is the expert treatise on dramatic art, *Natyasastra* by Bharata. Then there was a decline in the Sanskrit drama. Even though the reasons for this are not very well-known, but the founding and expansion of the Mughal empire in a large area of the country played a major part in this. Bharatendu provides a convenient starting point of reference for the beginning of the Hindi drama. He is the first author who took part in the presentation of the plays. Bharatendu was also the first writer who imaginatively and consciously combined the living folk forms with the tradition of Sanskrit plays. In his hands language got radically transformed to become an effective medium of greater communicability.

The religious fanaticism of the conquerors who attacked India and the destruction wreaked in the wake of these frequent invasions disadvantaged not only the genre of drama, but all forms of fine arts in India. However, the creativity of the vast majority of people could not be killed altogether. The elite, who were interested in arts, took recourse to indigenous forms of plays like *Kirtaniya* and *Ankiya* and *Nata* respectively. The indifference of the literary historians to the value of these plays notwithstanding (as these plays are considered different from Hindi), the significance of these plays in inspiring similar attempts in the neighbouring regions cannot be overestimated.

In the seventeenth and eighteenth centuries, the plays which were based on religious themes remind us of *Kirtaniyas* or *Ankiyas* or *Natas*. Simultaneously, the folk theatre, which portrayed the characters of Rama and Krishna at once demonstrated vitality and avoided persecution on the basis of religion. In fact, there was almost an upsurge in religious plays in the areas of North Bihar, Bengal and parts of South India. This religious fervour gave rise to *Rasa Lila* and *Rama Lila*. *Gambhira* was probably created on the same lines by the Saivaites of Bengal. The year 1657 A.D. constitutes an important landmark when the King of Calicut, Mahadeva, started a new form, known as *Krsna Natakam* based on the famous treatise *Gita Govinda* by Jayadeva. Taking a cue from King Mahadeva, King Kerala Verma followed suit and started *Rama Natam*. In the North, religious sentiments gave rise to *Rasa Lila* and *Rama Lila* based on the lives of Krishna and Rama respectively. Like folk plays, *Rama Lila* is put up on an open stage. Full-throated singing and circular dance movements are the distinguishing features of this form.

The Sanskrit plays prominently dramatized the story of Rama. Bhavabhuti's *Uttararamacharitam* perhaps constitutes the beginning of the plays about Rama, which continued upto the seventeenth century in different parts of the country—both in the North and the South.

The saint poet, Tulsidas is regarded as the origin of *Rama Lila* in the cities of Ayodhya and Varanasi. The text for *Rama Lila* is excerpted from Tulsidas's *Ramacharitamanasa* in which the spoken word is divided into that of the narrator, his associate and the cast. An important feature of these performances was that the stress was not on dramatics, but rather on pageantry. In fact, pageantry, mime and songs were made use of in the performance of *Rama Lila*.

There were a few other folk forms in the Hindi-speaking areas, viz. *Nautanki, Maca Sapera, Bahurupia* etc., in addition to *Rama Lila* and *Rasa Lila*. These were also open air performances. In these genres the dialogues were rhythmic, very strongly underlined by percussion, and the acting was highly stylized.

An important contribution to this genre was made by Wajid Ali Shah who experimented with the then form of Thumri and the stage presentation was called *Rahasa*. He made use of the methodology of changing the location as was done in *Rama Lila* and *Rasa Lila*. However, he did not follow the religious framework of *Rama Lila* and *Rasa Lila*. The form he developed acquired a definite shape when Amanat Ali (1816-1858) wrote *Indra Sabha*, which was enacted in Wajid Ali Shah's court. After some time, the practice of shifting from place to place in a *Rahasa* performance was given up. His court became the permanent venue and he himself performed the lead role.

The Hindi Drama in the Modern Times

A crucial change came about in the field of Hindi drama, after India became independent. The Forties saw the founding of three Akademis by the Government of India—Sahitya Akademi, Lalit Kala Akademi and Sangeet Natak Akademi—to promote literature, fine arts, and performing arts respectively. The Song and Drama Division was also established by the Government to utilize the performing arts for projection of government's official policies and ideals.

The very well-known theatre group IPTA was born as a result of the desire of political parties to make use of the performing arts for the propagation of their ideologies and programmes. The members of IPTA, succeeded in impacting the middle-class population with their ideology, which they projected as people-oriented.

Hindi authors got bigger opportunities to write plays, as several universities introduced plays for students of Hindi literature in B.A. and M.A. Against this background, the Hindi drama entered the modern phase.

Ramabrksa Benipuri came out of jail with a full-length historical play, *Ambapali*, which portrayed the life of the great dancer of Vaishali, who eventually embraced Buddhism. This play is perhaps in the tradition of Prasada.

A notable development in the post-Independence drama scene was the establishment of Prithvi Theatres by the famous film actor, Prithviraj Kapur. The theatre toured the country and staged plays like *Pathan, Diwar, Gaddar, Ahuti, Kisan, Paisa,* etc. Coming in the wake of great communal massacre, his plays mostly took the basic theme of Hindu-Muslim unity, and provided the much-needed healing touch. These plays were realistic presentations. The Hindi theatre world accorded them an overwhelming response and Hindi authors got familiarized with the plays produced in a realistic manner with their possible limitations and potential.

Even though some of the problems taken up for presentation in these plays are still relevant to the social life of the country, before long the plays went out of demand. Prithvi Theatres died a premature death. No doubt the performances drew packed houses, and Prithviraj obtained donations after each show. But the theatre could not survive. It died even before the death of its founder.

Nonetheless, the credit goes to the Prithvi theatres that the Hindi world could see plays produced in a realistic manner. Also the performances held a great attraction for budding authors and actors. Prithviraj had a unique inflection and a huskiness in his voice which many young actors attempted to copy. His style of acting was a mixture of stylisation of Parsi company days and demands of the modern theatre. The imitations of his style continued till the Sixties in amateur theatres.

IPTA, as mentioned earlier, was an organisation with the leftist ideological base and it came up with some impressive productions. Shambhu Mitra from Calcutta and Balraj Sahni from Bombay made a substantial contribution to the IPTA movement. However, in spite of good performances put up in towns and cities by the group, the movement did not last long, primarily because it was not broadbased enough to create any political impact. The 1952 elections decisively proved that there was no chance for the leftists to capture power. It was realized that the use of performing arts as a means of political propaganda and capturing power could not succeed. Hence, within a very short span the IPTA movement petered out. One major reason for the early demise of the IPTA movement was the patronage provided by the government through its various institutions which acted as a damper to the growth of IPTA. Getting recognition and facilities through the governmental agencies was comparatively easier. IPTA tried to depend on the mass support for its sustenance which turned out to be an uncertain and risky affair. However, it goes to the credit of the movement that it helped several talented actors and directors to come to the fore in the field of performing arts.

This was the socio-political backdrop against which the modern Hindi drama developed.

Upendra Nath Ashk, as already mentioned, had published his first full-length play *Jaya Parajay* in 1937 which had an historical theme, inasmuch as it dealt with the feudal age. But taking advantage of long prefaces, introduced by Lakshmi Narayan Mishra, Ashk explained why he shifted from historical to social themes: "Instead of glorifying the past, it is essential for us to think about the future and about eradication of the evils of the society to make it healthy and march towards prosperity. . . . And we should attempt such creations that touch different aspects of the society." (Narayan, 1981: 100) In his very next play, *Swarga Ki Jhalak*, Ashk dealt with the problem of marriage of the educated youth. Then came *Chhata Beta*, a fine and delicate play, in which the sixth son is the symbol of the ideal, as conceptualized by the father: the ideal so much desired but never achieved. In *Quida Aur Udan*, an experimental play, two facets of woman—inactive, passive, imprisoned and active, rebellious, and questing for her identity—were depicted. *Bhanwara* portrayed the life of a very highly educated woman who hops from man to man, but remains dissatisfied in life. *Anjo Didi* (1955) presented Anjali, the protagonist, as living in a world of her grandfather. She insisted on enforcing strict discipline, bringing about the ruin of the family through her fanaticism. The excessive idealism coupled with unremitting discipline filled the world of the play with morbidity.

Jagdish Chandra Mathur, a senior Government official, wrote *Konark* or *Bhagna Ragini* which was also an interesting experiment in that it had no female cast and yet projected a fullness of life. Also perhaps for the first time, a setting was visualized which did not stress any of the known methods hitherto followed in Hindi drama.

The Fifties saw a significant contribution from the Song and Drama Division of the Ministry of Information and Broadcasting which presented a play *Hamara Gaon* by Ramesh Mehta. Undoubtedly, it was a propaganda play which may have been derided by the elite theatre but it was the first play in Hindi which used realism in the true sense of the term. Its humour and wit were immensely enjoyed by the common people whom it targetted.

Alongside the realistic plays, experimentation continued in the Fifties. Two significant performances need to be mentioned in this context. *Ambapali*, a Hindi play by Benipuri and *Raktakarabi* (Bengali) by Tagore were staged, even though they were regarded as literary plays (not stageworthy) by a group of young critics, who were under the influence of Western literary criticism. Staging of *Raktakarabi* by Sambhu Mitra is now considered a landmark in the development of Indian Theatre, as the Hindi world got a chance to see a play produced in a non-realistic style which achieved the twin objectives of (i) heightening its impact and (ii) maintaining the lyrical values of the whole concept. There is hardly any external action and yet the movement, because of its pace and tempo, is not adversely affected by the presentation.

Jagdish Chandra Mathur picked up the trail and came up with a puppet play *Kunwara Ki Tek* in which Kunwar Singh actively participated in the mutiny of 1857 despite old age. It is an attempt to utilize the traditional skill of the puppeteers of Rajasthan and provide them with a completely new story. He followed it up with another puppet play, *Gagan Sawari*, which is a fantasy. A weaver, fed up with his present life, tours the country in his dream meeting beautiful girls in different places, but is rejected by all because he is a shirker who dislikes work.

He also wrote two collections of one-act plays *Saradiya* and *Pahala Raja*—the latter was published in 1969. In *Saradiya*, he makes use of the Maratha history, using Sarje Rao and Narasimha Rao, to give the central idea a suitable medieval background.

Translations had suffered a setback earlier, but with the increased opportunities for production, adaptations and translations were done more frequently; while some were acknowledged as translations, others posed as originals. Ramesh Mehta wrote some entertaining adaptations/originals and his plays remained extremely popular for quite some time, though they continued to be regarded rather superficial. Bachchan, the Hindi poet, translated Shakespeare's *Macbeth* as faithfully as possible and made it stageworthy in Hindi. It was produced on the Radio and presented on the stage in New Delhi in December 1958 with B. Narayan as the director.

Andha Yug by Dharam Vir Bharati constitutes an important landmark in the development of Hindi drama. It comments on the ravages of war and has chosen the last days of the battle of the *Mahabharata*, with its variety of characters and dramatic situations to interpret characters and incidents in the light of the psychological make-up to relate them to the contemporary times. It was ably produced by Ebrahim Alkazi. In terms of technique, its format was designed as having a prologue, an epilogue, an intermission and five acts. Two sentries are used to comment on the incidents, situations and characters. Chorus of a sort is used to indicate the happenings in the background, describe the set and to underline the symbolism.

Some of the subsequent attempts at playwriting resulted in *Ek Kanth Vispayi* by Dushyant Kumar, *Samasya Ki Ek Rat* by Naresh Mehta, *Sukh Sarovar* by Lakshmi Narayan Lal, *Uttar Priyadarshi* by Ajneya, *Agni-lik* by Bharat Bhushan Agrawal, *Katha-Mahal* by Prabhat Kumar Bhattacharya etc.

Mohan Rakesh's *Aashadh Ka Ek Din* shifted the emphasis from the famous and great men to the commoners. Although the play delineates the life of the famous Sanskrit poet Kalidas, the attempt is to probe his inner self and reveal the essential man.

Rakesh's other plays *Lehron Ke Rajhans* and *Halfway House* have been discussed separately in the introduction for their thematic and technical dimensions in the context of contemporary drama scene.

Works Cited

Agrawal, Pratibha. "Mohan Rakesh" in Dilip K. Basu, pp. 93-106.

Burgess and Locke, qtd. Pandharinath H. Prabhu, *Hindu Social Organization: A Study in Socio-Psychological and Ideological Foundations* (1958).

Camus, Albert. *The Myth of Sisyphus* (Harmondsworth: Penguin, 1975).

Cappola, Carlo. "Mohan Rakesh: A Self Portrait" in *Anthology: Mohan Rakesh* (Delhi: Radha Prakashan, 1974), pp. 4-14.

Havelock, Ellis in A.K. Sur.

Greene, Graham. *The Quiet American* (Middlesex: Penguin: 1962).

Kumar, Sanjay. "*Halfway House*: A Critical Commentary," in Dilip K. Basu (Delhi: Worldview, 1998), pp. 132-44.

MacIver and Page, qtd. Pandharinath H. Prabhu.

Narayana, Birendra. *Hindi Drama and Stage* (Delhi: Bansal, 1981).

Nath, Rajinder. "Introduction" in Dilip K. Basu, IX-XIV.

Rakesh, Mohan. "A Self Portrait" in Carlo Cappola.

Sur, A.K. *Sex and Marriage in India: An Ethno-Historical Survey* (Bombay: Allied, 1973).

Walker, Alexander. *Woman: Physiologically Considered as to Mind, Morals, Marriage, Matrimonial Slavery, Infidelity and Divorce* (Delhi: Mittal, 1987).

The Director's Viewpoint: Om Shivpuri

Translated from Hindi by
NILIMA CHANDRA

This was written on the occasion of the first presentation of the play by Dishantar in Delhi in 1969 which was directed by Om Shivpuri himself.

Editor

From the point of view of a director, *Aadhe Adhure* seems to be the first meaningful Hindi play about contemporary life. It portrays some of the subtle ironies of modern life. Its characters, situations and mental states are realistic and convincing. Its structure is compact and stage-worthy. The entry and exit of characters are well organised from the point of view of dramatization. Behind the entire conception of the play, there is an innate stage consciousness. *Aadhe Adhure* is a portrayal of the life today, making effective use of the living Hindi idiom. At the very first reading. I had found the language quite gripping. Needless to say that the most remarkable feature of this play is its language. It has successfully captured the tensions of contemporary life. The choice of words, their order and placement are such that they effectively convey the intended meaning. It is because of this power of the written and the spoken 'word' that the play continues to retain its magical effect, whether performed on an open-air stage or in an auditorium.

As far as the explication of the play is concerned, the play is meaningful to me in several ways. At one level, the narrative is a statement about the strong mutual attraction and the subsequent tension between man and woman. Mahendranath loves

Savitri intensely. Savitri also must have been in love with him at one time, but after marriage, she has begun to feel disillusioned with Mahendranath because while she has high expectations from life, he is without work and, therefore, has no source of income. Savitri has turned bitter because, on the one hand, she bears the burden of running the household, on the other, she suffers the sharp pang of not being able to achieve anything in life. Her children do not provide any solace to her either—fed up with their rude behaviour, she longs to spend the rest of her life with a "complete" and successful man. But this aspiration of hers is not fulfilled, perhaps because the quest for perfection is a Utopian exercise. Living on the earnings of Savitri, Mahendranath has become a pathetic figure.

His status is no more than that of a servant in the house where he was once the master. Now, he has no say in the family. He is aware of Savitri's relations with other men and once in a while gives vent to his anger and frustration by abusing them. Every weekend, he goes away from home hoping to preserve his shattered self-esteem, but returns after a few hours—exhausted and defeated . . . because this is his destiny.

At another level, this play is about the disintegration of a family. Each member of this cursed family is isolated from the others. They have turned against each other, vitiating the atmosphere of the house. The 'Older Girl' escapes the moment she finds the opportunity of running away with a sympathetic Manoj. The boy, whiling away his time in cutting out coloured pictures of film actresses from magazines, waits for his chance to get away. He is empathetic towards the father, but is full of rage against the mother. He does not believe that his elder sister fell in love with Manoj: he regards that love as a means of escape.

The 'Younger Girl' does not feel attached either to the parents or to her brother and sister. She is very bitter as her small needs remain unattended to. She feels neglected. Consequently, she begins to talk insolently and starts taking interest in sex-related matters, which does not become her tender age. She becomes increasingly irritable because she has to put up with the snide remarks of the neighbours concerning her father's unemployed state, mother's male friends and sister's elopement.

It is only from Binni that Savitri, who slogs both at the office and at home, gets a little sympathy, though even Binni seeks an answer from her to the question as to what it is in this house which, even after getting away from here, keeps lurking like a dark shadow between her and Manoj.

Ashok is against Savitri making friends with influential people and bringing them home, because he begins to feel smaller than he actually is when such people come over. All in all, the interpersonal relationships between the members of the family are multilayered and complex.

At another level, the play shows that human beings can never be fully satisfied especially those who desire too much from life. Mahendranath, Singhania, Jagmohan and Juneja are four men with different qualities. While making her choice, Savitri chose Mahendranath and married him, but she did not feel satisfied with him. However, if she had selected Jagmohan as her marital partner, things would not have been any different, because she would not have found the qualities of Juneja in Jagmohan and her situation would have remained unchanged.

At yet another level this play for me is a projection of the universality of human experience, diversity of people notwithstanding. For this purpose, the playwright has adopted the device of using one actor for five different roles. It does not make a crucial difference in the situation if Mahendranath is substituted by Jagmohan or Jagmohan is replaced by Juneja, because 'man' behaves the same way in a given set of circumstances. In order to stress this particular point, some of the dramatizations of the play focus on a mask at the start of the play.

The locale of *Aadhe Adhure* is a sitting room which has a sofa, chairs, a table, a cupboard and a few files etc. Years of financial difficulties faced by the family have turned this once fresh and cheerful looking room into an old and shabby one. The crockery is chipped. The walls are dirty. Members of the family are cut off from each other. They live in an atmosphere which is bitter and stifling.

I found a box-type set appropriate for the dramatization of

this tension. And many early stagings of the play adopted this set.

Some of the early performances of the play were presented in closed auditoriums. When the play was sought to be staged at the *Triveni* open-air theatre, some of my friends expressed their doubts about the suitability of the open-air stage for the play, as the openness of the stage was likely to diffuse the tension and the intensity of the play. But I was convinced that newer strategies would have to be evolved to attract audiences for the serious theatre. If a play is capable of imparting a deep, artistic experience, and if it focusses on the vicissitudes of life, then perhaps a small disturbance from the road or the honking of a car should not adversely affect its artistic quality. I am glad that my belief has been vindicated. The openness or closedness of the stage made no difference to the impact of the play. In either case, the rapport established with the audience was equally intense. During those days I realized that the box-type set created many practical problems. On the one hand, it was expensive and time-consuming and on the other, it increased dependence on the stage props. Therefore, I mustered courage and gave up the use of the box-set; and even this did not, in any way, reduce the impact of the play.

I like simplicity of presentation. Therefore, instead of using elaborate lighting effects, I chose a simple lighting arrangement appropriate for the play. At the beginning a spotlight was used to highlight certain objects in the room. These objects later became a part of the general lighting. Similarly, at the beginning of the second act, two lights were focussed on the 'Boy' and the 'Older Girl' but gradually they also got assimilated in the total lighting. I preferred the same simplicity regarding the costumes. The main actor had to perform five roles. For this purpose, he changed only the upper garment—first of all he wore a black suit (The Man in a Black Suit), then took off the coat and wore only a shirt (Mahendranath), then a coat with closed neck and a cap (Singhania) and then a high-neck shirt (Jagmohan) and finally a long coat (Juneja). There was no change in the costumes of Binni, Kinni and Ashok. Only Savitri changed her sari for the second act, because that was the need of the situation.

Another remarkable feature of the presentation was the total absence of make-up. The heroine wore only such make-up as women like her put on in real life. Apart from this no other actor/actress used face-powder or any other make-up.

A significant thing about this presentation was the close co-operation between the playwright and the director. Rakeshji was always present with us right from the first rehearsal till the first performance of the play. We consulted each other over every small detail. Quite often, there were disagreements and discussions. But both of us were immensely satisfied with the final product.

Portrait of a Perverse Marriage: A Comparative Study of Mohan Rakesh's *Halfway House* and John Osborne's *Look Back in Anger*

DEEPSHIKHA KOTWAL

In a comparative study of Mohan Rakesh's Halfway House *and John Osborne's* Look Back in Anger, *the writer contends that unable to overcome an adversarial social order, both Savitri and Jimmy direct their rage against their respective spouses. Kotwal raises questions about the validity of the institution of marriage and concludes that pending answer to these questions, both Savitri and Jimmy are compelled to remain in "Hell" and "Zoo"—which their families have become.*

Editor

> Once again, the same thing all over. I am amorphous. And this play is as undefined as I am.
>
> *Halfway House*

> It's always so depressing, always the same.
> We never seem to get any further, do we?
> Always the same ritual.
>
> *Look Back in Anger*

Mohan Rakesh and John Osborne have a lot in common as both of them explore the issues of alienation, identity-crisis and the desire for personal freedom that plague the middle class. As trend-setters in their own spheres, they make a few statements which induce people to reflect on them. John Osborne represents the post-Second World War generation that felt betrayed and sold out by the older generation. He claimed that he did not like the kind of society in which he found himself and *Look Back in Anger*, published in 1956, synergises the prevailing mood of anger and protest in England at that time. His authentic portrayal of the frustrated young misfit Jimmy Porter, began the Angry Young Man Movement in British drama. Mohan Rakesh subscribed to the credo, "the real commitment of a writer is not to any particular philosophy but to himself, his times and the life of his times."[1] Leftist politics dominated the theatre in the late sixties leading to disenchantment with contemporary society. Rakesh represents the post-Independence urban middle class bogged down by the weight of personal dilemmas. In *Aadhe Adhure* or *Halfway House*, published in 1971, Savitri, the frustrated protagonist wages a lonely struggle as a middle-class woman juggling with her roles as wife, mother and breadwinner. Osborne and Rakesh give voice to the middle-class angst and ennui at a personal and individual level through their protagonists Jimmy Porter and Savitri, while reflecting through them the larger malaise that afflicts society. Porter and Savitri, thus, function as a microcosm of the larger macrocosm of contemporary society. It was this immediacy of the subject matter in both the plays that was responsible for their resounding appeal. In the words of Mohan Rakesh:

> Most of my stories are about people living through the torture of relationships in their loneliness. This loneliness is not the loneliness of the socially isolated individual but the loneliness that comes from living within society and it leads not to any kind of cynicism but to the need to live through it. The attempt is not to see the individual and society as mutually opposed and mutually exclusive, distinct from and separated from each other but rather to see them as related in such a fashion that the individual reflects the dilemmas of society and society reflects the tortures of the individual. (95)

Despite the critical flak which has been directed at Osborne's old-fashioned structure and at Rakesh's dreary prologue and theatrical gimmickry involving one actor playing multiple roles, we cannot deny that the two dramatists have genuinely succeeded in matching the form to the truth which they seek to convey. Both plays use a very simple colloquial but intensely dramatic style to focus on the immediacy of the theme. *Look Back in Anger* and *Halfway House* are highly thought-provoking and disturbing plays in which there is a splendid amalgam of the subject with the style.

In their respective plays, Osborne and Rakesh have made an accurate dissection of a perverse marriage. The marital wrangling between Savitri and Mahendranath in *Halfway House* and Jimmy Porter and Alison in *Look Back in Anger* brings to mind the marital discord in Strindberg's *Dance of Death* and Edward Albee's *Who's Afraid of Virginia Woolf.* Osborne and Rakesh have explored the dissensions which have wrecked the institution of marriage at a time when society is rapidly deconstructing traditional norms of family and home. Both the plays present an absurdist scenario of a family which is torn asunder, a house which is not a home, a couple which is poles apart. In addition to the basic theme which is common to *Look Back in Anger* and *Halfway House*, the two plays share several commonalities. Jimmy and Savitri as protagonists dominate the action as they are set against weak and spineless spouses, Alison and Mahendranath. Extra-marital relationships are a part of both the failed marriages, and Cliff and Juneja serve as confidants and guides to the warring partners. The two plays portray the dilemma of the couples conclusively but fail to offer any radical solutions, hence the ending of both the plays remains tame and inconclusive.

The setting of the two plays is identical and in keeping with the parody of a real family and the home as a sanctuary of peace. Jimmy Porter shares a pokey little bed-sitter in the attic of a large Victorian house with his wife, Alison and friend Cliff. An old oak table, a large double bed, two arm chairs, book shelves, a gas stove and an ironing board make the room seem even smaller than it is. Jimmy and Cliff spend most of their time sprawled in the armchairs, surrounded by a "jungle of newspapers and weeklies," while Alison wearily irons clothes and keeps making a dreary thudding noise with the iron. Jimmy endlessly puffs obnoxious smelling cigars or loudly blows his trumpet creating an ear-shattering cacophony. The smoke-filled room with three people constantly stumbling against each other in its overcrowded confines, brings to mind the image of three animals who have been caged together for too long. In fact Alison describes her house as a "Zoo."

The setting of *Halfway House* showcases an average middle class house which is functional rather than aesthetic. The dilapidated living room has a door in each side wall, the one on the right opens into the street, while the one on the left leads to an inner room. The way to the kitchen is through a small courtyard. The living room is overcrowded with old and broken furniture, teapoys, cane poufs, a writing desk, piles of old books and some magazines are scattered all around adding to the general air of confusion and disorder that prevails in the house. The inhabitants come in through one door and exit from the other frequently after verbal altercations with each other. Savitri struggles to bring some order by picking up books and papers, punching cushions into shape but it seems an exercise in futility because the house, like the people living in it, seems at sixes and sevens always. The disorderly exterior of the house becomes an image of the deeper malaise that is rending the family apart. As Binni, the elder daughter, says:

> And I come here to look for the cause of my trouble! Can you tell me, Mama, what is it and where it is? Is it in the doors and windows of this house. In the walls, the ceiling, the floors? Why can't I see it? Can you see it, Mama? Can Daddy? Can Kinni? Can Ashok? (19-20)

Jimmy Porter belongs to a generation that has no roots in the past and no hope for the future. His wife Alison represents the upper middle-class which was responsible for England's past glory and present despair. Jimmy hates this class for his present misfortune (a university graduate forced to run a sweets stall) but also envies it for its stable past. His relationship with Alison represents this paradoxicality, because he loves and hates her at the same time. Jimmy's working class background was anathema to Alison's family and they were dead against the relationship. To spite them, Jimmy marries Alison. In order to possess Alison, Jimmy had to submit to the conventionality that he hates. Her virginity angers him, because by being a virgin, she is pulling him into the vortex of social convention: "And afterwards, he actually taunted me with my virginity. He was quite angry about it, as if I had deceived him in some strange way. He seemed to think an untouched woman would defile him."[2] His outbursts flow from his overriding need to possess Alison's complete unquestioning love and yet he contradicts this by saying, "She has the passion of a python. She just devours me whole every time, as if I were some over-large rabbit." (37)

Their relationship of four years has now settled into a predictable pattern. She stands, for what seem whole days, at the ironing board, ironing clothes, dressed in an old shirt of Jimmy. He carries on an endless tirade against her, her family and her friends. She refuses to be goaded into speech and this infuriates Jimmy even more. He calls her a "Monument to non-attachment," "Lady Pusillanimous" and says she's a "great one for getting used to anything." Jimmy is angry because, "Nothing I could do would provoke her. Not even if I were to drop dead." (19) Jimmy feels she has betrayed him by coming over to him in marriage while remaining physically and spiritually in the world of her parents. She was attracted to him because of his rebellious and unconventional behaviour which was in stark contrast to the polite and staid manners of the men in her circle, "Jimmy went into battle with his axe swinging round his head—frail, and so full of fire. I had never seen anything like it. The old story of the knight in shining armour." (45) Alison is the proverbial doormat who is battered, brow-beaten and trampled upon but continues to endure silently. The only time the couple seem to relate to each other is when they revert to the world of make-believe, where Jimmy becomes a growling, cuddly bear and Alison the tiny and tamed squirrel. This game becomes a trivial evasion of the completeness found in any marriage:

> It was the one way of escaping from everything—a sort of unholy priesthole of being animals to one another. We could become little furry creatures with little furry brains. Full of dumb, uncomplicated affection for each other. Playful careless creatures in their own cosy zoo for two. A silly symphony of people who couldn't bear the pain of being human beings any longer. (47)

What Jimmy needed was a strong woman who would stand up to him as well as inspire him to look up to her. Unfortunately, Alison liked to "sit on the fence because it's comfortable and more peaceful." (66)

Just as Alison accepts her role as the dominated partner in marriage, so does Mahendranath in *Halfway House*. Savitri scathingly refers to her husband as "a puppet" and a "pawn," "half a man." The couple have been married for twenty-two years, their elder daughter Binni has escaped the family hell by marrying her mother's friend, Manoj. But she seems to have created a private hell of her own. She does the exact opposite of what her husband likes, cuts her hair short, because he prefers long hair and goes to work when he wants her to stay at home. "I cut myself off from him for days on end. But then, slowly we start treading the same weary path. Everything happens in the same way . . . until we reach the same abyss once again." (19) The son Ashok is feckless and irresponsible and Savitri is desperate to see him settle down to a permanent job. The youngest child Kinni is a spoilt and insolent brat who reflects the consequences of growing up in a fractured family. A confused Binni, a frustrated Ashok, an indisciplined Kinni, the spineless Mahendranath and the officious, dominating Savitri, are the perfect ingredients to create a halfway house. Savitri is the breadwinner of the family and it explains her dominance over the other characters. Mahendranath, after losing his money in business and wasteful expenditure, has been jobless for years, "I'm responsible for ruining my life, your life, all our lives? And I still stick to this house because I'm a parasite, because I like living off my wife." (11) Savitri constantly compares her husband to the other men she meets! Singhania, Jagmohan and even Juneja who symbolize power, wealth, confidence, status—all the things she craves for but her husband is unable to give. She is a woman straddling two worlds, the one of personal fulfilment and the other of family responsibility: the traditional Indian woman who wants her husband to provide for her and her children and the New (Indian) Woman who is suffocated in her marriage and seeks greener pastures. It is this dichotomy in her personality which makes her options so limited. After tolerating a hell for twenty-two long years, she decides to create a heaven with her former lover Jagmohan. She is forever compromising her integrity as a woman by using some man or the other as a crutch. I tend to disagree with R.L. Nigam who says that the name Savitri is used ironically, "The Savitri of yore found her life meaningless without her husband; our Savitri finds her life meaningless (to say the least) with her husband."[3] It seems that the contemporary Savitri cannot conceive of life without a man, like the Savitri of legend. She constantly seeks male support in different ways: from her lecherous boss Singhania, from her caddish lover Jagmohan and even from the sermonizing Juneja. She says, "From now I'll only bother about myself . . . you look after your own lives. I don't have many years to live now. But however few they may be, I'll no longer spend them like this." (43) Her grand rebellion fizzles out into a damp squib. She is forced to return to her halfway house and her half a man, as Jagmohan refuses to play ball.

Mahendranath on his part is forever sobbing on Juneja's shoulders and seeking his assistance in steadying his rocking marital boat. Like Ashok, he resents Savitri's liaisons with other men but is unable to put his foot down because he is solely dependent on his wife. That is why his occasional rages, when he gags and beats up his wife, only serve to play up his ineffectiveness in his house and provide an outlet for his pent-up frustration. Osborne and Rakesh have shown how against the backdrop of generalized social experience, the only enemy in sight is the spouse. The rage which fills Jimmy and Savitri against a frustrating social order is directed at their spouses. Why do the spouses not react to the humiliation they face daily? Alison is egged on by her friend Helena "to get out of this mad-house." Juneja is determined to make Mahendranath stand up for himself, "He's not as helpless either, as he thinks. If he'd look around he would see a whole world is before him. I'll try to open his eyes to it." (77) Alison returns home after a miscarriage and finds that her friend Helena has taken her place. Helena mouths some platitudes about how selfish she has been and leaves the field clear for Alison. We see Alison grovelling and crawling before Jimmy begging for forgiveness:

> Don't you understand? It's gone!. . . . That—that helpless human being inside my body. . . . All I wanted was to die. . . . I was in pain, and all I could think of was you, and what I'd lost . . . if only he could see me now, so stupid, and ugly and ridiculous. This is what he's been longing for me to feel. . . . This is what he wanted from me! (95)

Jimmy takes her in his arms and they revert to their fantasy world of being a bear and a squirrel. He can relate to Alison better now because like him she has experienced pain and anguish. The play ends on an ambiguous note. Will the warm animal love they share as a refuge from the harsh reality lead to happiness or is it only a temporary escape into whimsy? Both possibilities are left open.

The conclusion of *Halfway House* is equally controversial. A hegemonic male-centred discourse is created to shift the entire blame for unhappiness in marriage on Savitri. Juneja seeks to reclaim the "pawn" Mahendranath and demolish the image of Savitri as the superior partner. "But every other year you've tried to free yourself by looking around for another man. In the beginning I was one of these men." (73) Savitri has been at pains to convince her children that her social contacts were necessitated by economic considerations and were for the betterment of her family. On the other hand, Juneja, by listing her male friends starting with himself, Shivjeet, Jagmohan, Manoj and Singhania, tries to prove that her promiscuous behaviour is responsible for her husband's shame and her son's rebelliousness. This duality hints at the opposing pulls in Savitri's personality as well as the manner in which Juneja as a man and Savitri as a woman interpret the same situation. While Savitri claims she does not want her husband back, "I've absolutely no need of the pawn as you saw, this man neither moves ahead himself nor permits anyone else to do so." (77) Juneja claims he will not allow him to come back, Mahendranath returns home despite his "blood pressure," because he loves his wife or because she is a habit he is too timid to break.

The element of repetitiveness in the two marriages is heightened by the similarity in the characters of Jimmy Porter and Savitri. They are both highly individualized and they search for completeness in the "other." Alison says Jimmy's problem is, "He wants something quite different from us. What it is exactly I don't know—a kind of cross between a mother and a Greek courtesan, a hench woman, a mixture of Cleopatra and Boswell." (91) Savitri had got married to, "fulfil a need . . . an inner . . . void . . . to be self-sufficient . . . complete." Instead, she found her husband to be a puppet in the hands of his friends, especially Juneja, whom she tells,

> Ever since I've known him, I've always found him leaning on someone or the other. Particularly on you. He's never been able to do anything without asking you. If we want to buy something he must ask you. If we want to go somewhere, he must ask you. When he wanted to marry me, he had to ask you. He can't even breathe without asking you. (68)

Juneja thinks Savitri is an overambitious woman who could never be happy with any one man, because she wants to enjoy as many different things as she can at the same time.

The marriages of Jimmy Porter and Alison and Savitri and

Mahendranath seem to bear out the truth of the statement that familiarity breeds contempt. Are we deconstructing the linear image of marriage as the bedrock of a stable society and the family as a sanctuary? Is it time to explore a more pluralistic arrangement of personal fulfilment and interpersonal responsibilities? In the meantime, there seems no apparent way out of the impasse. The "zoo" and the "hell" remain inviolate.

NOTES

1. Mohan Rakesh, *Halfway House*, ed. Dilip K. Basu (Delhi: Worldview, 1999), p. 97.
2. John Osborne, *Look Back in Anger* (London: Faber and Faber, 1957), p. 30.
3. R.L. Nigam, "*Aadhe Adhure*: A Comment," in *Halfway House*, p. 91.

Halfway House: A Powerful Dramatization of Modern Sensibility

O.P. SHARMA 'PRAKASH'

In his comprehensive article, Sharma argues that Halfway House *is a play which deals with problems peculiar to the modern sensibility. According to him, Rakesh not only marks a break with the earlier plays dealing with myths or history, with this realistic play, but he also evolves a new stage consciousness subsuming a simple but effective stage-setting, capable of reinforcing the meaning/ message sought to be conveyed.*

Editor

Mohan Rakesh wrote only three plays and left a fourth unfinished. With this meagre but worthy capital, he has very deservingly become a celebrity in the Hindi world. Along with Jagdish Chandra Mathur (with *Konark*) and Dharamvir Bharti (with *Andha Yug*), Rakesh succeeded in giving Hindi drama a new shape and status. Right from *Aashad Ka Ek Din* to *Halfway House*, he presented plays that were commercially a big success. In the context of *Halfway House*, it was perhaps for the first time that the tickets of any Hindi play were sold in black. Rakesh freed the Hindi drama from the run-of-the-mill type that revolved mainly around mythological, historical or pseudo-social themes. Instead, he made his plays representative of the real life and the complexities of the modern-day-living. He brought radical changes at the level of technique, so that it could cope with the new sensibility. In a broader sense, we can say that Mohan Rakesh basically deals with only one subject in all his three plays and it is man-woman relationship. This inclination starts right from the short stories and culminates in *Halfway House*. Though very limited and nearly a personal subject, in *Halfway House* it transcends the inner circle to encompass the universal world of human relationships. The plays of Mohan Rakesh are known for bringing in a freshness and newness in the Hindi plays after Jaishankar Prasad. It was because of him that the Hindi plays graduated from text to stagery. With Rakesh the Hindi play comes of age and turns modern. His very first play *Aashadh Ka Ek Din* was adjudged the best by Sangeet Natak Akademi in 1959. After 10 years i.e. in 1969 he added to his laurels by writing *Halfway House* that became the talk of the theatre during those days. It has been performed by different directors in different styles in many languages.[1] The plays of Mohan Rakesh, including *Halfway House*, are convincing and credible because they have been created out of a genuine experience. With whatever he lived, sweet or sour, and as a very sensitive person having extraordinary command over the language, he produced impressive short stories, novels and plays. But more than a fiction-writer, his reputation and recognition rests with his plays. In the first two plays namely *Aashadh Ka Ek Din* and *Lahron ke Rajhans*, Rakesh deals with the perplexity of the modern man through historical characters of Kalidas and Nand. But in *Halfway House*, he dares confront the realities directly. The story of a couple with strained relations that survived despite twenty-two years of fighting each other becomes the medium. Also included in the family are the son, the elder daughter and the younger daughter. It is a family almost on the brink of disintegration. It is a family of modern times whose feelings and attitudes are determined by their surroundings, inside as well as outside the home. It would be more appropriate to call this home merely a house, a half-way house. The members are living in utter disharmony. Day in and day out, the fighting between the husband and the wife does take its toll. The children become unmanageable.

The boy is a drop-out having no employment and simply cutting pictures of beautiful actresses from the magazines. The elder daughter elopes with the paramour of her mother. She carries the 'unhealthy' air of her parental house as a result of which the wretchedness creeps into her new married life. At the same time, she fails to understand where the fault lies.

All the members are sick of one another; most of the time, they are quarrelling, accusing each other. Whether parents or children, they find no charm in their lives. There is a feeling of hollowness in their very existence. They seem to be frustrated. Everybody feels that nobody would ever be of any help to him or her. There is an air of helplessness throughout and no effort to make a breakthrough succeeds. The parents feel that the children are disobeying them; that they are rude and going astray. Kinni is going beyond her age of thirteen years. She is keen to know the reality of sexual relationship. In fact, it is the psychology of adolescent stage. Nobody cares to treat her sympathetically or understand her that way. Nobody has the time to explain things to her or guide her. She wants her part of the recognition. This is the psychological need of the children. Since Ashok is not employed and has left studies incomplete, he too is condemned which he resists forcefully. Ashok, Kinni and Binni represent the youth suffering because of the generation gap. The defiance of authority, be it parental, social or moral, is a common feature of our times.

The failure of the institution of marriage is depicted through the unsuccessful family life of Mahendranath and Savitri but in *Halfway House* it does not die out altogether. Mahendranath returns ultimately; so does Savitri. They may venture out again. There is every possibility; but they go away only to return. There is no way out. There is no escape from the hell. Knowing well that the atmosphere of the house will tell upon them, still they return because there is no option but to linger on. This is the helplessness of the modern man. This phenomenon generates a sense of tragedy, the tragedy of the persons living in our own age. Savitri tries out the options. She feels over-burdened since no other member comes to her rescue. On the contrary, they all add to her difficulties. Kinni demands time to talk to the lady in the neighbourhood, to boil milk for her, to attend to her requirements for school. Savitri is also striving to arrange a job for

Ashok through her boss, Singhania, whom she wants to welcome in a befitting manner to achieve the purpose. Mahendranath is simply useless, not even helping in household chores. Neither Kinni nor Ashok nor Mahendranath appreciates Savitri's tiring efforts to improve the position of the house. On the contrary, they smell motives in her efforts. Tired and fed up, she wants to step out for good with her old associate Jagmohan who at the eleventh hour fails to match her expectations. Dejected and broken, she returns home cursing the total male community. "All of you . . . everyone of you . . . alike! Exactly the same. Different masks, but the face. . . ? The same wretched face . . . every single one of you."[2] The return of the broken hero, defeated and crest-fallen is vital for the continuation of tragedy; both Mahendranath and Savitri exemplify man's destiny of 'no-exit.'

The character of Savitri has another significance. It is through Savitri that the playwright illustrates the principal question of completeness. In search of an ideal husband who would be complete in all respects, she travels from person to person. She is in search of a person who would be rich like Juneja, learned like Shivjeet, high-positioned like Singhania, sweet-tongued and tiptop like Jagmohan and handsome and liberal like Manoj. The million-dollar question is, how can one person alone possess all these qualities? If one has one quality, he lacks the second; if the second person is blessed with the latter, he would lack the former. She fails in her pursuit of having a complete man because she fails to understand that neither all blessings nor all banes are never concentrated in one man alone. Savitri was going against the laws of Nature. Therefore she was bound to fail. To quote Juneja's words, "If any of these men had been a part of your life instead of Mahendra, you would still have felt that you had married the wrong man. You would still have encountered a Mahendra, a Juneja, a Shivjeet or a Jagmohan and thought and reacted in the same way because the meaning of life to you is how many different things you can have and enjoy at the same time. One man alone could never have given them to you. So no matter whom you married you would have always felt as empty and as restless as you do today." Whichever way we may classify these words, the writer succeeds in underlining a hard truth of real life which gives us strength to live with limitations.

The plight and pain of a working lady are also highlighted through the character of Savitri. She presents the image of new woman rising to struggle for her legitimate position.

The play shows the collapse of the traditional values—social, moral and familial. With the erosion of values and judgement-parameters without appropriate replacement, a situation of vacuum has developed in our lives. We have become like rudderless boats moving without direction. All characters of *Halfway House* are suffering because they are directionless. They are, therefore, disinterested in almost all sorts of activities. They are simply killing time. Therefore, they are frustrated and, consequently, irritated. They flare up on every small bit. They all are boiling inside for want of proper channelisation.

Halfway House is a story of a family in the process of disintegration. An eminent critic has described the play as the crisis of the family. I would amend it to say that in fact it is the crisis of identity of the individual. Modern man demands individual dignity, recognition as also the honour of his choice. Mahendranath, Savitri, Ashok, Binni, Kinni—all are trying hard to interpret their existence. They desperately try to find the meaning of the life they are leading. Whether they succeed or not is for the future to answer. But the beauty lies in their constant efforts and search.

Hollowness of relationships is depicted in *Halfway House*. All relationships particularly in the family need to be re-defined. This is the strain of the time. In a team of husband and wife, who will husband whom, who is the boss and who is the subordinate, who is the planner and who the mere executive, who will lead and who will be led—these are some pertinent questions that need to be addressed and the same have been incorporated in the plot. It would be relevant to point towards the ego-clash of husband and wife that forms a common scene of our contemporary life. The play basically presents a picture of bloated ego and false prestige which cause disturbance and disintegration.

The play does not present a cut and dried solution to the problem. There are several questions in *Halfway House* with almost no answers. It can safely be said that compromise and complementary roles can revive the lost harmony and peace. False faces not only generate distrust but also are injurious to mutual relationship. Mahendranath does not trust Savitri and Savitri has a condemnatory attitude towards him. The family moves on the path of ruination.

Halfway House expresses tragedy, helplessness, vacuum, egoism, rise of individualism, feeling of futility, search for meaning in one's existence, defiance of authority, loss of traditional values, a feeling of loneliness and alienation in contemporary life. Rakesh himself led a life full of ironies, contradictions and controversies. Therefore, he could give such a genuine, forceful account of these traits. *Halfway House* presents the modern sensibility in all its intensity, forms and dimensions.

The plot of *Halfway House* is made of an average middle-class family-life. Ostentations, taboos, worthless traditional customs, cowardice to break them for fear of social stigma, financial stringency, to live beyond one's means—all these characteristics of the class appear vividly in the play. The members of Mahendranath's family suffer from these ills and pay for it.

Very special is the nature and treatment of the subject-matter. There is no story in the traditional sense. Instead, there are only tense situations, that go into the making of the play. The other fibre interwoven is the mental attitudes of the characters. Everybody is in a soup. Everybody is uneasy. There are family quarrels typical of a middle-class, hurling allegations and counter-allegations at each other. There are no big events, only small bits. The plot is compact because it is not too detailed. The situations are hard and complicated making the play tense as a whole. Tension causes confrontation that gives movement to the plot. Again, the attitudes of Savitri, Mahendranath, Ashok, the younger girl, even of outside friends like Juneja are sharp and rigid. Generally, the attitudes are mutually hostile although no big headlong collisions take place. There are, instead, dissensions, disagreements, opposition and a tendency to have a showdown, lending impetus to the movement.

It may be noted that Mohan Rakesh has departed from the traditional style of plot-building and its development. The play ends from where it starts. There is but slow progress, if at all we can call it so. The movement is subtle. Apparently, there is insignificant furtherance, yet the play grips the audience. The movement of the play is not horizontal or linear; it is circular. It deepens as it moves. Therefore, it becomes more and more intense and thereby more and more absorbing. Rakesh deserves the credit for writing a convincing play without any outside happenings that usually formed the basis for plot in Hindi drama during those days. He breaks new ground and develops his own craft.

The plot is limited and, therefore, compact. It is also compact because the sensibility is so strong and so complete. The theme is focussed with no unnecessary material being dragged in. Mohan Rakesh had a keen eye to distinguish affordable episodes from the unaffordable ones. Quite a few incidents have been communicated through information instead of being actually shown on the stage. Binni's elopement, the preceding parts of lives of Mahendranath and Savitri are only mentioned. Such a device was called 'suchaya' i.e. through information in Sanskrit drama.

The characters have already been partially discussed. Though weak and unsuccessful, the characters of *Halfway House* are quite attractive, as they appear to have come from life itself. The playwright handles them with great skill. He moves them perfectly in tune with the theme. They are alive, real and representative of contemporary life. They represent different aspects and stages of life being led.

The characters confirm that home surroundings do condition the psyche of a person, particularly during the formative years. They are victims of the mismanagement in the family and the maladjustments of the parents. The younger daughter is obstinate and rude because she feels ignored and unwanted. The elder daughter too runs away, perhaps to get rid of the tense atmosphere at home. Ashok is bitter because there is absolutely no guidance and nothing worthwhile to be done. He does not approve of Savitri bringing the boss home, inviting persons who cast amorous glances at his sister, make them feel inferior. The children consequently turn rebels. More often than not, they confront and defy their parents. They strive to break open. However, the characters of *Halfway House* are psychologically appropriate and sound.

All the characters are unsuccessfully fighting against the circumstantial odds and are consequently tense and restless. They are perturbed most of the time. They want to avoid difficult situations. They appear to be almost exhausted. Indecisive as they are, their fate is always trembling in balance. They are small, ordinary but wonderful creatures.

Mohan Rakesh's major contribution to Hindi play-writing is the new technique—a technique that is in harmony with the new experience. The subject matter of *Halfway House* is very plain, generally familiar to most of us. He could carve out an interesting play, out of uneventful material, because of his superb craft. He was a playwright with stage-consciousness. This consciousness has also influenced his technique. The play has limited duration. It shows the life of a family during twenty-six hours when Savitri returns from office till the next late evening when Mahendranath too returns. The action is also short and continuous. An exhausted Savitri criticizes the unhelpful attitude of the other members; feeling sick, she leaves the house and comes back being unsuccessful in convincing her one-time lover, Jagmohan. Soon after, a tired, indisposed Mahendranath also comes back. In between are the incidents of elder daughter's visit, Kinni's complaints and undesired guests.

All action takes place in Mahendranath's house; in his drawing-room, to be exact. The unity of action, time and place has lent the play a unique cohesion. Continuity of action adds to the pace. The characters are real, recognizable and natural.

The tendency for experimentation has made Rakesh introduce many new strategies like that of one person playing four roles. Nemi Chandra Jain has not appreciated this new device[3] but it does reinforce the theme that all men are basically alike; only their outer appearances differ.

The Prologue is a totally new idea in the technique of playwriting. It is equally controversial as critics are both for and against it. The code of playwriting does not permit the writer to address the audience directly. The Man in Black Suit is actually the writer himself. Part of the speech of the Man in Black Suit is not sustained by the later development of the play; so it becomes contradictory in itself. Yet it has its own purpose. It prepares the audience mentally to receive the play. It also partially hints at the type and purpose of the play the audience is going to witness. The Prologue appears to be a modern version of the 'sutradhar' (the introducer-narrator) of Sanskrit drama.

Mohan Rakesh does away with the inherited essentialities of the earlier playwriting—the 'Mangla-charan,' the hero, ideal characters, multi-acts and scenes, the curtain etc.

The stage properties are limited and simple. A room alone would suffice. A sofa-set, a cupboard, teapoy, dinner table and chairs, tea set, a cheese tin, an opener and a pair of scissors etc. are the commonest household goods. Their availability and setting pose no problem. The same scene continues throughout. The fade-in and fade-out lights serve the purpose of the curtains.

The language of *Halfway House* is marvellous from the point of view of the stage. The success of the performance of the play owes much to the kind of the language used. It is significant that Mohan Rakesh did research on the use of the "word" in the theatre. He advocated that in a play, the audio part is far more important than the visual.[4] The zenith of the visual has already been reached in the genre of cinema and the stage, in no way, can excel it. Therefore, relying more and more on the sound and its rhythm can improve the communication on the stage.[5]

The language of *Halfway House* is plain and simple, quite appropriate for the members of a middle-class family, but at the same time it is powerful enough to convey the tension, the mental disturbance and irritation of the characters. Simple words have been imbued with deeper meanings and implications of the context. In the language of a play, the implied meaning is more important. The language of *Halfway House* meets this requirement. This language has scope for innovation when used purposefully by the expert actors.[6] Repetition and omission of words reflect the hidden restlessness and pain of the characters. The unspoken conveys more than the spoken.

The Older Girl:	What is the matter, Daddy?
The First Man:	Matter? Nothing.
The Older Girl:	There is something
The First Man:	It is nothing, your mother was saying . . .
The Older Girl:	What was she saying?
The First Man:	Nothing . . . actually. . . . I was just say ing. . . . *Halfway House* (14-15)

Hesitation or unwillingness on the part of the speaker:

The Woman:	Sit down. Tell me the truth. Is there any thing. . . ?
The Older Girl:	No. Nothing and yet . . . everything.
The Woman:	For instance . . .
The Older Girl:	For instance . . . everything. (16)

The language has different colours and shades depending on the user. It is cool at the hands of Mahendranath, sharp when used by Savitri and Juneja, light and funny when Singhania speaks, pointed and witty in the case of Ashok, obstinate and rude in the case of Kinni and confused when Binni wants to articulate her problem. Like the craft, the language of Mohan Rakesh is mature in *Halfway House*. He believes in economy of words. He uses fewer but appropriate words. At the end of the play, Mahendranath returns home. "Carefully Mahendranath carefully," says the Fourth Man [Juneja]. (111) Only two-three words but the advice, concern and note of precaution, and Mahendranath's weak physical condition are effectively conveyed. In contrast to his earlier plays, the language of *Halfway House* is neither lyrical nor literary. It is the language of the common man, man in the street, in accordance with the requirements of the play.

The symbolic use of words, situations, properties and even light and music are peculiar to Rakesh's craft. In the opening scene, the stage-properties are described thus—"a disorderly living room in what was once a fairly well-to-do middle-class home, several pieces of broken furniture—sofa set, dining table, cup-board, dressing-table etc. having lost their proper function appear to have acquired uses dictated by the limitations of space. Teapoys, a couple of cane-poufs, a shelf of dilapidated, old books and the writing desk and the chair add to the overcrowding effect of the room." (8) This language obviously provides an instant insight into the state of affairs and the position of the characters, totally worn out but lingering on somehow.

Lets's take the example of the use of light and music. The occasion is when Mahendranath returns home towards the close of the play—"the lights dim . . . the woman gazing stonily at the street door, lowers herself into a chair. The Older Girl looks at the Woman and then towards the street-door. A soft, mournful melody strikes up. Then almost in darkness the First Man enters on the Boys arm." (111) Light but melancholy dying music explains the position and future of Mahendranath and dimming of lights on the woman and the elder daughter convey weakening of their once strong position.

By drawing a cartoon, Ashok makes a mockery of the unwanted guest. Again, his jumping and pretending that there is an insect in his trousers is nothing but showing his hatred for Mama's boss. Similarly, saying that a sharper instrument is needed to open the cheese-tin carries undercurrents of deeper meaning that only some revolutionary steps could change the situation prevailing in the house.

Halfway House contains more of action and less of speech. The gestures of characters are far more important than the words they utter. There is not a single page without parenthetical directions for the characters.

With *Halfway House* Mohan Rakesh has given a new idiom much needed for the Hindi drama. He has initiated writing of realistic plays of contemporary life. His simple but effective craft has not only enriched the stage-worthiness of Hindi plays but also made them popular. Rakesh has been instrumental in creating a decent and cultured audience for the Indian theatre. All his plays have been commercially successful not only in India but in other countries also.

NOTES

1. See Jai Dev Taneja, *Mohan Rakesh: Rang Shilp Aur Pradarshan* (New Delhi: Radhakrishan, 1996), pp. 287-315.
2. *Halfway House* by Mohan Rakesh, ed. Dilip K. Basu (Delhi: Worldview, 1999).
3. *Natrang*, Oct-Nov. 1972, p. 39.
4. *Sangeet-Natak*, Oct.-Dec. 1971, p, 21.
5. *Natrang-21*, pp. 10-12.
6. Siddh Nath Kumar, *Halfway House: Samvednaa Aur Shilp* (Ranchi: Saroj Prakashan, 1987).

Stage-Setting and Stage Directions in *Halfway House*

SUBHASH CHANDRA

Chandra foregrounds the significance of the stage-setting and stage directions in Halfway House, *as they effectively contribute to communicating the meaning of the play. In fact, the rare economy of language is made possible through appropriate stage setting/directions.*

Editor

A general tendency in drama-criticism is to respond to them as one would do to fiction, taking up for discussion and scrutiny elements like imagery, plot, characterization, and moral vision. The obvious reason for this type of criticism, to a large extent, lies in the dual function of the plays: their being staged and also being read as texts. So, much of Shakespeare criticism, all over the world, is the response to his plays as written texts. There is nothing wrong in this, of course. But what I wish to suggest is that little attention is paid to the stage-craft in the plays when they are read, even though the meaning of the play is communicated on the stage largely by the combination of words, gestures of the actors, and the stage-setting (which includes lighting, sounds and arrangement of things on the stage and even costumes,) I propose to focus on the stage-setting and stage directions in Mohan Rakesh's *Halfway House*, with a view to demonstrating how the seemingly small and insignificant details on the stage, not only substantially contribute to the meaning of the play that is sought to be conveyed by the playwright but also, equally importantly or perhaps more importantly, mentally prepare the readers/viewers of the direction the action in the play would take—action in this play is not to be understood as the traditional Aristotelian concept of action, but rather as the mental atmosphere of the characters, and the state of their interrelationships, which are an important area of exploration in the modern Hindi drama, dealing with the urban middle-class and their predicaments.

Rakesh was not a votary of an elaborate setting or sophisticated mechanical devices to manipulate the stage. He advocated, on the contrary, a simple stage, of course appropriate to the demands of the play to be mounted, but without a large number of highly technical props. This is, however, not to say that he did not pay attention to the details of the stage-setting. Quite the contrary. As he was finickily concerned with the suitability of the "word" as a playwright, (it was not for nothing that he was awarded the Nehru Fellowship for conducting in-depth research into the subject of the "word"), so was he attentive to the details of the stage-setting and stage directions.

The very first scene outlines a stage-setting which is amply suggestive of the kind of world (in this case the family) we are about to encounter. We know, the situation of the family, in which both human relationships, and the human beings themselves are falling apart under the strain of socio-psychological forces, which potently operate in an urban environment, especially in relation to the changing family structure, in which women have acquired education and economic independence. Savitri (wife) and Mahendranath (husband) have been straining at the leash that is family, the children, Ashok (the boy), Kinni (the younger daughter) and Binni the elder daughter (married, but still a part of the suffering family), have grouses against the parents (the parents keep scolding them for their erratic and irresponsible behaviour), and keep quarreling between themselves. It is a family only in name; otherwise it is a crumbling structure and each member feels frustrated, sad and lonely.

Now let us have a look at the stage-setting: "A disorderly living-room in what was once a fairly well-to-do middle-class home." (4) In a "disorderly room," one could not expect a family, living harmoniously, and the members acting responsibly. The disorder in the room is clearly symbolic of the disorder in the lives of the family members. Further on, we are shown "Several pieces of broken furniture—sofa-set, dining-table, cupboard, dressing-table" etc. (4) The brokenness of furniture, speaks about the poor financial state of the family. Metaphorically, 'furniture' suggests 'rest' and 'grace,' and therefore, its brokenness, conveys restlessness and impatience that characterizes the family, as also the lack of decorum we witness in the interactions between the members. In the same scene, there is "a shelf of dilapidated, old books,"—we know that none in the family evinces interest in studies or learning.

At the start of Act One, we again see a stage which is evocative of attitudes, situations and behavioural patterns. The younger girl, as we know later in the play, rages against the callousness of the adults in the family: her school requirements remain unfulfilled, the adults do not discharge their responsibility of looking after her and preventing her from going astray, nor do they protect her from the crises she faces, as a result of her waywardness.

All this is compressedly foretold by the scene: "A high-school satchel lies open on a teapoy with half the books spilt out." The open satchel and the spilt-out books not only underscore Kinni's irresponsibility and her lack of interest in studies, but also her anger. The satchel has been thrown down with the force of anger, resulting in some of the books spilling out.

In the same scene, another significant object is a pair of pyjamas, hanging from the back of a chair. Importantly, this pair of pyjamas belongs to Mahendranath who has been reduced, because of his failures in business, to the status of a non-entity. Savitri's telling him that he is not a "man," his own confession that he is a "parasite," and Ashok talking back to him, are all pointers to his very low position in the family. Mahendranath has lost the feeling of self-worth and self-esteem. How to represent a defeated, self-deprecating, parasitical man on the stage: Nothing could be better and more powerful symbol than a pair of pyjamas, dangling at the back of a chair. Mahendranath is nothing more than this evocative object which the dramatist has chosen to represent him through.

A short stage direction, when Savitri enters this room, goes to the crux of the relationship between Savitri and Mahendranath. "Savitri picks up the pyjama *with distaste* (italics mine), and is about to throw them into a corner, but then starts folding them." (7) The only feeling now left in Savitri for Mahendranath is "distaste" (though once she loved him), because of Mahendra's lack of dynamism, loss of initiative to make another start, and his irresponsibility towards the family. She was about to discard Mahendra, when she decided in favour of Jagmohan, after his return to the city, like she thought of throwing the pyjamas into a corner. But she came back home, as things did not work out with Jagmohan. After this stage direction, it is important to note the comment she makes: "Idle all day, but he can't look after his clothes . . . or even clean the table." (7) So, we find the words and the stage direction coalesce to enforce each other: in fact, this kind of stage-setting, and stage directions, enable the writer to practise economy of words. This economy builds pace and introduces raciness and force in the words.

Thus, the action of picking up the pyjamas with "distaste" exhibits her dislike for the man, for the pyjamas metaphorize the owner, intending to throw them into a corner, stands for her action of leaving Mahendranath (and the family) for Jagmohan, and her eventually folding the pyjamas even though irritatedly and keeping them in the cupboard hints, in a subtle way, at her eventually not discarding Mahendra. As we know, a whole lot of words are needed to dramatize what has been condensedly presented on the stage through the device of the stage-setting and stage directions. If we look at the gestures vis-a-vis the pyjamas, the whole spectrum of her feelings towards Mahendranath gets communicated. Having folded them and kept them, she "picks up the pyjamas again and keeps them in the cupboard, though angrily. The duality in her thinking—her desire to leave Mahendra and the family and her loyalty to the family seem to be evenly balanced—and equally potent.

Another stage direction: She picks up the scissors, magazine cuttings and journals and puts them into the drawer of the writing-desk; puts the books into the satchel and places the satchel upright on one side. It could be argued that she does all this because her boss Singhania would be visiting her and she does not want him to see them in the room. But this argument is only partly true. If this were the only reason, she need not have folded the pyjamas; instead of picking the magazine cuttings and journals and putting them into the drawer and putting the books into the satchel and placing the satchel upright on one side, she could have just flung them somewhere to put them out of sight. But she does not do that. Why?

As a contrast, let us see what the other adults, Ashok and Mahendra, do for the house. We have already seen that Ashok whiles away his time cutting out pictures from magazines, and then leaving them wherever, and Mahendra needs Savitri to give his empty tea cup to, then at best he can only 'pretend to be busy,' (14) and quite importantly at another time, "starts rolling up his newspaper *and tearing* little pieces from it absent-mindedly." (italics mine, 2) While Savitri, besides being a working woman, indulges in purposive, responsible actions, the two male adults only contribute to the disorder.

And how does Mahendra keep the files back: "starts stuffing files back, helter-skelter." (24) Interestingly, he is the one who is supposedly tied down to Savitri, through his undying intense love for her (it is for this reason that he comes back home at the end of the play), and through her to the family and house-hold. And yet, it is Savitri who puts things back in the proper manner, even though she makes an abortive attempt to get away. Furthermore, keeping the files helter skelter is revelatory of Mahendra's character—the playwright wishes to tell us that he is a sloppy man, with no desire to do things right. Will it be an exaggeration to say that this one gesture of his provides us a clue as to why he failed twice in business endeavours?

Before I end the paper, I would like to comment on the stage direction/setting at the end of the play. These directions replace a lot of words which would have been required to indicate to us the future of the family as a unit or the fate of individual members in it. "The lights dim, leaving only the Older Girl and The Woman illuminated." The playwright wants the reaction of the mother and daughter to be noticed clearly. And what is their reaction? The words preceding these stage directions are spoken by the Fourth Man: "Carefully, Mahendranath, carefully," (79) which tells us that Mahendranath is ill. But his illness does not evoke a sympathetic emotion either in the daughter or the mother. As far as the Older Girl is concerned, she only looks at the mother and then towards the street door from which Mahendranath would enter. No feeling, no gesture indicative of possible help to Mahendra from the daughter. But Savitri's reaction foreshadows her continued antipathy towards her husband. Then "A soft mournful melody strikes up. They are almost in darkness. The First Man enters on The Boy's arm." The very last stage direction is: "As they come forward, the music becomes louder and the light fades out slowly." (79) The melody is mournful, appropriately sad for the present state of Mahendranath and also for his bleak future which is underscored by the "almost darkness" into which Mahendranath steps.

Juneja's concern is reflected in "Carefully, Mahendranath, carefully." While Ashok's words "Look out Daddy, look out" are indicative of his sympathy for his father. The two women's silence and motionlessness joins them into a pair—while Binni feels sorry for the mother, there is hardly any word or gesture for the father who gets back home in a sick condition.

The stage directions and stage setting are not elaborate and yet they effectively contribute to communicating the nuances of situations and characters. The overall economy in language which makes the language racy and incisive is made possible through the supplementarity of stage directions. It may be stretching the point too far, but the experiment is worth conducting: read only the stage directions and most probably you can get the central thrust of the play.

A Thematic Interpretation of One Actor and Five Roles in *Halfway House*

ARTI MATHUR

Arti Mathur takes up for examination the dramatic device of one actor for five roles, used by Mohan Rakesh, and concludes that it is not a meaningless gimmick employed by the playwright. Actually, through this device, Rakesh underscores the lack of choice for Savitri who finds herself in a cul-de-sac because in patriarchal order all men are the same.

Editor

The forceful representation of ideological entrapment in a middle class urban family sets the modern play *Halfway House* apart from the kind of drama that prevailed in different regions of India. The modern Indian playwright has attempted to liberate drama from heavy symbolism, use of masks and other conventional theatrical gimmickry practised in depiction of grand themes. Consequently, "city artists are no longer conscience-stricken enough to wear rural costumes, paint their faces and replicate folk and tribal forms. The city-play has come of age and theatre in the century to come is likely to deal in a more unabashed manner with grimy, urban reality, the drama of everyday existence."[1] The struggles of the common man have become a recurrent theme for playwrights such as Mohan Rakesh. In *Halfway House*, the playwright moves towards the poignancy of inner conflict, using imagery and symbols from everyday life. The most striking feature of the play is Rakesh's use of the same actor for the five male characters. The interplay of similarity and dissimilarity between the five men in the play is contextualized within the rubric of everyday experience. The device of one actor playing five different roles is to highlight the idea of an individual woman's lack of options in the existing set of circumstances. This paper will focus on demonstrating the validity of this dramatic device that has raked a major controversy amongst various critics.

There is a contention amongst critics whether the device succeeds in fulfilling its objective. Critical opinion on the same actor playing five different roles varies from endorsement of the technique to complete debunking of it. Productions such as those of Nemi Chandra Jain, Jagdish Sharma and Virendra Narayan attempted to prove that it is meaningless for one person to appear in five different roles. But in Rajinder Nath's opinion it is a "powerful theatrical device which is fully integrated with its thematic concerns" to show how "conveniently and according to one's convenience the same man can put on different masks according to the situation in which he is placed."[2] A detailed examination of each of these characters bears out the truth of Rajinder Nath's idea of each man being different only at a superficial level.

The first male character, who is not really a participant in the action of the play but performs a peculiar introduction to the main concerns of the play, is the speaker of the Prologue. The Prologue attempts to set up contraries by highlighting the concept of definite versus indefinite. Paradoxically, while the speaker associates himself with unlimitedness, the play is primarily about limitations, social entrapments and the futile attempts the characters make to free themselves of these bonds. The persona facing the audience is a Man in Black Suit with a cigar. He directly addresses the audience in a rather confrontational manner. With a direct gaze at the audience his words, "Once again . . . the same thing all over again" (4) bring into sharp focus the repetitive monotony of life. The dilapidated environs of the setting combined with the somberness of the speaker suggest disappointment with the ceaseless cycle of events in life. In other words, the normative circumstances of life appear stifling and static to him. In order to free himself of this stasis, he takes refuge in an indefinite or amorphous state of things. He even introduces an element of suspense regarding his exact role in the play. In fact, he declares that he has no definite role to play. He claims rather ambiguously, to be "amorphous" and "everything concerned with me, including this play, is as undefined as I am." (4) The implications of 'amorphousness' are akin to nondescript, indescribable and indefinite in meaning, qualities that are actually a contrast to the solid figure in black upon the stage. Nevertheless, the term matches well with the diffused gray dusty pallor that pervades the entire setting of the play. The speaker's perception that he is "undefined" suggests that he does not want a single conventional identity. Hence, he has given up trying to figure out "who am I." However, he continues to aspire towards an evolving identity that is capable of overflowing boundaries. This directly reflects the only option left for Savitri at the end of the play to get out of the 'hell' she is living in by developing an evolving identity. The acknowledgement by the first speaker of "what I am on this stage, I am not outside" (5) could perhaps be one of the ways to resist being fixed with a single identity. However, there is meaninglessness in this multiplicity because of mutual unconcern or concern with oneself borne out by the statement "but why should you care what I am outside only, . . . You stare at me for a moment but you're not in the least concerned with me or with my life." (5) In the context of the play, we perceive multiplicity to be a kind of repetition of the first, in the form of the five men who come into Savitri's life. A selfish sameness about them renders their individuality worthless. In the light of this remark we can well believe the Man in Black Suit's capability to exchange places with any other male character. But that he can take Savitri's place too, as suggested in the Prologue, in the given scheme of things is a problematic claim. It negates Savitri's gender specific struggle against social constraints. The nature of her struggle is peculiar to her circumstances as well as symptomatic of the predicament of middle class women caught in a web of transition and tradition.

Savitri's enforced role as the chief provider of her family without any help from her husband delineates her situation at the beginning of the play. This remains a major factor of disagreement between Savitri and her husband Mahendranath. It is the primary cause of all the acrimoniousness in their attitude towards one another. The fact that Savitri refers to him as "the curse" of her life is characteristic of their relationship. Even before he actually enters upon stage, his 'pyjama' represents Mahendranath. The impact of his 'pyjama' constantly thrown around with contempt is enough sign of ridicule with which his family treats him. This piece of clothing, ironically 'amorphous,' without any shape or body, stands out in the general mess of the room awaiting its rightful place. This empty discarded object highlights Mahendranath's uselessness. Through Savitri's accusations and Mahendranath's own admission, we realize that he is a good-for-nothing fellow. Significantly, one of his earliest responses to his wife is that "I was doing nothing." (7) We are informed that he has not been the earning member of the house for quite sometime. Savitri's accusations reveal that he is unwilling to replace this lack in one capacity as bread earner with taking over or even sharing the responsibility of the household in any other way.

Mahendranath's rocking chair is symbolic of his fluctuating attitude. For instance, the manner in which he expresses disapproval of the wife bringing her boss home is characteristically spineless since he is not able to sustain it with any authority. Instead, in ostrich-like fashion, he leaves the house on some pretext or the other each time the boss comes home. The reason perhaps is that he prefers to avoid direct confrontation and comparison with a more successful man. He hints at Savitri's possible liaisons with her boss and with other men in the past, but his weakness makes him more or less accept this and his protests remain feeble. Nevertheless, Mahendranath is not all meekness but has a terrible temper, too. The older girl in the play exposes him as full of rages and the cause of fearful scenes of domestic violence. Savitri's frustration with Mahendranath is apparent when she declares: "1 don't want you for anything." But there is an element of illusion in her statement because she thinks that merely by raising her hands to a Jagmohan or any other, she can attain all that has been denied to her by Mahendranath. At the same time it is clear that Mahendranath is definitely not the kind of man Savitri could continue to love or respect.

Unlike the tense, humourless and near tragic portrayal of Mahendranath, the boss enters the play introducing an element of humour. Singhania is associated with comic mannerisms including crude public behaviour. His Nehru jacket and trousers are in themselves not so radical, but when combined with his characteristic pompous manner, the overall impact outwardly is of a completely different personality from Mahendranath's. Singhania is supercilious, arrogant and full of egotistic assumptions about all the people he meets. His conversation proceeds with abruptness, superficial logic and is falsely comprehensive. A typical example of his conversation when the woman inquires about a job for her son proceeds like this:

Second Man:	Yes, yes . . . you did mention something. For a cousin of yours . . . no, that was Mrs. Malhotra. Who was it you mentioned?

And later,

Second Man:	Yes, yes . . . oh yes . . . you told me. He was with Air India for a while . . .
Woman:	With Air Freeze.
Second Man:	Yes, Air Freeze. Hmm . . . hmm . . . (turns to the boy who smiles in the same way once more) Won't you come nearer?
Boy:	(points to his nose) I have a slight . . .
Second Man:	Oh I see, I see . . . the climate of this country is such, what can one do? Now take the climate of Italy for instance. I did a lot of travelling last year . . . one has to in my position. . . . I went all over Europe but . . . no other country can compete with Italy! Do you know what is so special about. . . . It's delicious! Where did you get it? it's already five past seven. I think . . .

His bumbling way of communication creates more confusion than throw light upon any subject. He has an anecdote to relate on every subject, which of course is never narrated to its conclusion in his hurry to show off as a man of the world. Though he talks of vastly different subjects, each subject brings him back to himself. He sports a fashionable 'forgetfulness' that he thinks compliments his high status in society. Thus, his affected manner of forgetting people's names is a deliberate strategy to make them feel insignificant. For the self-opinionated Singhania, the world comprises two categories of people: those who seek favours and those who dole out favours. He tries to include most people in the former category. For instance, he persistently believes that the older girl appeared for an interview obviously implying that her placement is due to his goodwill. The older girl had of course not appeared in any such interview. However, we cannot deny the fact that though the boss's world-view may be highly reductive, it has some basis in reality. It is a mere chance that Savitri is not seeking favour for her daughter but for her son. Singhania is the successful man in whose image Savitri would like to mould her son. Despite the element of exaggeration in the portrayal of Singhania for dramatic purposes, he remains unappealing, banal and exploitative. The boss represents the class of exploitative employers who prey upon weaknesses of people in subordinate positions to their advantage. What he offers to Savitri is opportunity for her son and the role of 'Aunty' to Savitri vis-a-vis daughter and whatever else the latter job entails. Thus, as an alternative option for Savitri, he represents only another face of tyranny and so is entirely unsuitable for the woman. Nevertheless, she continues to entertain him in the hope of gaining even a little from his higher status.

Like Singhania, Jagmohan is a successful and worldly man, but unlike him he is not just tolerated but truly admired by Savitri. His greatest appeal for her is apparently the strong stand he adopts in pertinent as well as impertinent matters. In comparison to Mahendranath, Jagmohan is definitely not an "idler whom one can summon and dismiss just as one pleases." Jagmohan possesses all the outward signs of leading a stylized life. He wears trendy clothes, drives a New India car and gets involved in sporadic affairs necessary to complete his rakish picture. He arrives at Savitri's house in the absence of her husband in sporty clothes, making it obvious that this is a social visit. His bold stance is a contrast to the clandestine ways of the boss, who uses innuendoes and crude gestures. The term of endearment 'cuckoo' that Jagmohan uses for the woman is suggestive of past intimacy. Savitri does allude to the fact that Jagmohan had once been interested in her. At that time, we are told that his circumstances were not so affluent and Savitri was more ambitious, hence the relationship had stalled. However, there are enough indications that since then the man has progressed and moved up in the world. The "great difference between yesterday and today" (56) exists even more poignantly for Jagmohan than Savitri. She is only one of the women he picks up and then drops when the affair gets too demanding. Savitri is still under the illusion that he loves her and is still waiting for her acquiescence all these years. Accordingly, she treats him as the key that would unlock the hell she lives in. It is for this reason that she even accepts his snide remarks without showing any ill-will. She pretends to ignore his indifference to her 'momentous' confession that she was finally ready to break free of her husband and insists that "I never misinterpret what you say." (55) But the scene of Savitri's return to her home clearly shows his rejection. In the new role reversal brought about by his economic well-being, he is interested in Savitri as far as she is ready to play the game on his terms. The escape route offered to her, if at all, is clearly only another twist to the kaleidoscope of exploitation and hence, not a viable option. She rejects the terms, apparent from the angry manner in which she snatches her hand away from Jagmohan while getting out of his car.

At this point in the play, Savitri's arrival back into her house coincides with Juneja's presence there. He speaks with great confidence when he analyses the cause of Savitri and Mahendranath's misery. In fact his authoritative manner is indicative of his representing the playwright's point of view. This is partly borne out by Juneja's description of what really might have occurred between Jagmohan and Savitri that left her angry and defeated. The accuracy of Juneja's description is confirmed by Savitri's amazement when he recounts the whole incident between her and Jagmohan as if he had been a witness to it. The purpose of Juneja's revelations is to make Savitri recognize her responsibility in souring her marriage. Juneja accuses Savitri of rendering her husband incapable of acting on his own due to her dissatisfaction, cribbing and domination over him in the last twenty years. He says with conviction that "today Mahendranath thinks he is helpless. You have made him believe that despite the circumstances he has no other way of life open to him, no other solution, except to remain with you. And haven't you done everything to ensure that, if nothing else, you should at least be able to hold this wretched pawn in your hand?" (77) On these grounds, he makes the strange request to Savitri to "free" Mahendranath from her "trap." According to him, Savitri was discontented even twenty years ago in her marriage when she confessed to Juneja that "he [Mahendranath] was sloppy, had no backbone. . . . But the names of the people who had made him so were different then. You put the blame on the parents then." In effect, Juneja thinks it is not Mahendranath's unemployment which is the cause of Savitri's discontent. He points out that Savitri had in fact started complaining about her husband even before he stopped earning for the family. At that time she had other justifications for her dissatisfaction.

He reveals the chain of men whom Savitri cultivated in her attempts to free herself from her husband including Juneja himself. He further contends that "the point is that if any of these men had been a part of your life instead of Mahendra, you'd still have felt that you'd married the wrong man. . . . Because the meaning of life to you is how many different things you can have and enjoy at the same time. One man alone could never have given them to you, so no matter who you married, you would always have felt as empty and as restless as you are today." (74) The logic of Juneja's argument is that Mahendra's uselessness is merely an excuse for Savitri who craves for fulfillment from multiple sources. This man-eater image of Savitri drawn by Juneja does tend to leave the reader disturbed regarding Savitri's moral uprightness. However, strangely enough, Juneja's high voltage disquisition elicits only a bitter laugh from Savitri. The truth that confronted Savitri might have rendered her dumbfounded with shame. Instead, there is a challenging tone in her laughter, which is rather disconcerting for the audience who have been taking Juneja most seriously. The attitude of the characters may appear less problematic if we consider Juneja's word also questionable. In fact, there are hints in the course of the play that warn us against identifying Juneja with the playwright or treat his discourse entirely as truth.

Significantly, the play reveals that Juneja defrauded Mahendranath of his rightful share in their joint business venture. Savitri, of course, has never forgiven him for this act. But Mahendranath has remained indebted to Juneja because of the sums he owes to him. The couple later borrowed money from him to support an ambitious lifestyle for which Mahendranath continues to feel gratitude towards Juneja. In the play Juneja enters the house through the back door, symbolic of his place vis-a-vis Mahendranath's family. At one level, this implies easy familiarity with them, at another level his act is suggestive of sneaky behaviour. Savitri detests him for being Mahendranath's spy. She feels that his visits are a pretext to carry back reports about her male visitors to Mahendranath. She bitterly regrets that her husband is completely dependent on Juneja for everything. Both Savitri and Juneja counter-accuse each other of being responsible for Mahendranath's weakness. It is not easy to find out who is to blame more, but at the same time that Juneja does contribute to the degeneration of Mahendranath's family is irrefutable. Juneja's discourse definitely has its limitations. He suffers from a static mind that constantly qualifies his outlook. This is obliquely symbolized by his visits abroad where, by his own admission, each time he did not visit any new place. The incident that casts a major shadow on Juneja's veracity and grasp of the other's situation is his failure of judgement regarding Mahendranath's return to Savitri. Juneja is convinced that this time the husband has finally decided not to return to the woman, but of course, like always Mahendranath does return. Juneja is convinced that it is Mahendranath's love for Savitri despite all the wrongs she had committed which prompts him to come back to her each time. But we cannot accept this reason since the circumstances of the play clearly delineate the fact that Mahendranath too, like Savitri, has no option to go anywhere else. Hence, he returns just as she does. Accordingly, Juneja misinterprets Savitri's dilemma too.

Savitri is responsible enough to think that if her husband cannot provide for the house, she can. She is not helpless in her situation but has enough confidence and ambition to forge ahead under any circumstances. At the same time, she has not integrated into the modern situation completely and is still in the clutches of the past. Hence, she continues her futile search for the perfect man, but these men with no notion of gender parity cannot possibly fulfill her. Her belief that she could find a better life for herself is genuine, until her final confrontation with Juneja. She finally discovers, not her guilt, but that her search for a real man is illusory. Her moment of recognition is when she realizes the essentially exploitative nature of men and their refusal to change. It dawns on her that the four different men in her life are essentially the same, each wearing a different mask.

Contradicting his own belief, Rajinder Nath's performance staged for Sangeet Kala Mandir in 1974 had five different actors to play the five roles. The outcome was that it defocused the central concern of the playwright and hence was not repeated. Without the dramatic interplay between their similarities and differences, the men appear too diverse and the idea of each concealing behind a mask becomes diffuse. The device of the same actor playing the role of the five men ruthlessly snatches away their supposed individuality to reveal the underlying similarity and lends meaning to Savitri's painful recognition that "everyone of you . . . all alike! Exactly the same. Different masks, but the face. . . . The same wretched face." (76) Though Juneja's tirade against Savitri attempts to establish Mahendranath's victimhood, Rakesh through the use of the same actor for the role of the five men skilfully tilts the balance of sympathy towards Savitri, demonstrating her helplessness, and despair in a situation which becomes a cul-de-sac for her primarily because all men are alike.

NOTES

1. Nirupama Dutt, "The City at Play," *The Express Magazine* (August 15, 1999), p. 4.
2. Rajinder Nath, "Introduction." *Halfway House*, trans. Bindu Batra (Delhi: Worldview, 1999), p. xi.
4. R.L. Nigam. "*Halfway House*: A Comment," *Ibid.*, p. 90.
5. Dilip K. Basu. "*Halfway House*: Some Stray Comments Only," *Ibid.*, p. 129.
6. Uma Shankar Jha and Premlata Pujari, *Indian Women Today: Tradition, Modernity and Challenge*, Vol. 3 (New Delhi: Kanishka, 1996).

Savitri: A Schizophrenic Woman

SUBHASH CHANDRA

Chandra argues that Halfway House *is not anti-woman as is believed by several critics. Savitri is not to be held responsible for the near disintegration of the family. She is a woman divided against herself, a schizophrenic, who represents the larger dimension of cultural schizophrenia of the urban middle-class. This dimension, Chandra contends, lends universality to the play.*

Editor

A majority of critics, while discussing diverse aspects of the play, don't forget to touch upon the woman-question and accuse Rakesh of being mysogenistic, inasmuch as he has been unjust in representing Savitri in an unsympathetic light, especially towards the end of the play, using the agency of the Fourth Man, Juneja. If one goes by the thrust of Prologue's peroration, he claims that he is everyman, undefined. Savitri asserts during her climactic exchange with Juneja, that all men are alike, with different masks, meaning thereby that all men are the true descendants of Manu, for woman is the slave of her husband and by extension of the family. If anything goes wrong with the family, she is held responsible and is castigated. On being told by Rajinder Nath and others, when Rakesh read *Halfway House* to them in his Rajinder Nagar barsati, that Savitri had been portrayed negatively, Rakesh was surprised, He maintained that he had tried to be fair to Savitri. Dina Pathak, who played Savitri in one of the productions, told Rakesh that she had much more to say than what Rakesh had apportioned for her. Rakesh wrote a long speech for Savitri, to be spoken towards the end of the play, in her encounter with Juneja and this he thought had redressed the imbalance against her and to a certain extent it does. But the charge that the play is anti-woman is not withdrawn, because Juneja forcefully demonstrates that Savitri, because of her unlimited ambition, unrealistic aspirations in life, and a string of extra-marital relations, is responsible for ruining the family. Juneja's speech is valorized because it has logic on its side.

The contention of my paper is that it is neither Savitri, nor Mahendranath nor even the social system, as suggested by Nigam which is responsible for the near-disintegration of the family. Besides sustaining the family economically by becoming its breadwinner, after Mahendranath's losses in business, Savitri's efforts to restore order in the family (she is the one who notices the disorder in the room when she enters and tries to put things at their right places—by this small action, the dramatist is making a significant point about Savitri's devotion to the family and its wellbeing) her concern for Binni's unhappy and floundering marriage (her own unhappiness in the family notwithstanding), her desire to put things right for her elder daughter, and above all, to arrange a job for the idler son, Ashok (whose only preoccupation is to cut out pictures of heroines from magazines and to read smut) are all pointers that negate the thesis that it is Savitri because of whom the family goes under. Is Mahendranath then responsible for what happens. It may appear to be so because of his apparent lack of interest in sharing responsibility of the family and his having turned into a defeatist failure who goes on trying to justify himself, by repeatedly mentioning what he has done for his wife and children in the past (one sure sign of failed men, who have compulsive, psychological need to refurbish the present with the gloss of the past). His lack of dynamism to make a fresh beginning to succeed and establish himself as a productive man, and re-earn his status in the family and respect of his children and wife, hardly get him any sympathy of readers/audiences. If Savitri does not exactly behave like an ideal mother, nor does Mahendranath provide an inspiring role model to the growing children. But it is equally true that he is unable to leave the family for good, and more importantly, he continues to love Savitri (albeit he has bullied and beaten her in the past twenty years). Juneja confirms and communicates as much to Savitri. And by his returning home, unasked (having left never to come back), demonstrates Mahendranath's commitment to the family. How could a man for whom there is no other refuge than his family could want to destroy that space. The third possible destroyer, the social system, we need to remember, remains an abstraction till human beings interact with it and find it inimical to their interests. If one attempts to transgress social taboos, and social boundaries, then there is a problem, and a certain cost has to be paid. In this case, the cost is paid by Savitri, for attempting to exercise the choice of being the New Woman who seeks to prioritize self-fulfilment.

But Savitri is a split personality. There are two Savitris in this woman. For all the bravado and loud talk of leaving Mahenranath and the children to fend for themselves, she has a strong lurking desire to protect and sustain the family. I would like to adduce textual evidence, in addition to what I mentioned earlier in the essay, that Savitri remains concerned about home, family and children. The climactic moment is when Savitri tells Binni: "When you come next time, I may not be here."[1] A conscious decision has been taken. Savitri sounds firm and decisive, which shocks Binni. But it appears the decision has not been taken, after all. Matters have not been fully sorted out in her mind, as far as Mahendranath and the children are concerned. Otherwise, why become absent-minded at this stage? When there should be calm, in the aftermath of the decision, there is disturbance, agitation and even anger. In this disturbed, absent-minded condition, her necklace breaks, which cannot bear the physical pressure of the upheaval Savitri is undergoing mentally. The stage directions are instructive here: (in fact the stage-setting and stage directions provide an important clue to the central thrust of the play, and support the verbal, gestural movements by the characters, intended to convey to the readers/audiences the meaning of the play. Another essay is included in this anthology on the role of stage-setting, and stage directions. "She goes to the cupboard, puts the necklace away and takes out her jewellery box to select another" but there is no indication that she does choose another. She is in the midst of her soliloquy: she "puts the jewellery box back, tries to close the cupboard but, when the door does not close properly, she opens it again and bangs it shut." At this time she is waiting for her supposed "saviour" Jagmohan. So, she should be focussed on him, alive to any sound or movement associating it with his arrival. But no, she is so oblivious of her surroundings that she does not notice when Jagmohan comes: ("The Woman does not notice him.") It is only after stumbling against the sofa, absent-mindedly, that she sees Jagmohan, who has already entered the room. She admits her obliviousness when she tells him: "Oh I didn't hear you come in," (53) And when she says that "I was waiting for you," (53) she is being true and untrue at the same time. She had been ostensibly waiting for him and did leave with him. But she was also thinking of the home, the family and the people at home. The most important point on which I would hinge the burden of my argument is her question to Jagmohan: "When do you think I'll be back . . . ? *I ought to leave a message.*" (italics mine) Why bother about leaving a message? Juneja is coming to talk things over, but why bother about Juneja, whom she holds responsible for the ruin of Mahendranath? Of course, later on, she goes, without leaving a message, going out of the house, when nobody is around. But that is the whole point. Her desire for leaving the message is as significant as her finally leaving without bothering to do so. Here we have two Savitris. One the traditional, home-bound, family-bound woman (with the ring of the mythological Savitri, after whom she is named, and there is no irony involved here) and the New Woman, who is conscious of what she has been doing for the family, who has seen the glitter of the material world, with opportunities and better life and who has come to believe that her self-fulfilment lies in walking out of the family and fulfilling her desires. This is the new Savitri (with an ironical ring to the name).

Therefore, Savitri is as helpless as Mahendranath, when it comes to leaving the family. I do not agree with Nigam that the social system does not let her walk out on Mahendranath and start a new life, with or without another man. In the Sixties and Seventies, divorces were not unheard of. In fact, Ashok's hint that things should change confirms that even he was aware of husband-wife separations, and divorces. She cannot leave the family, because there is a tradition-bound 'self' which will not let her do so howsoever she may fret, fume or beat her head in frustration. And since this split in her personality is a 'given,' the situation cannot and will not change.

It is, therefore, not right to regard the play as anti-woman. Perhaps, Rakesh's shock was justified when his listeners, including Rajinder Nath, told him that it was an anti-woman play, and that Savitri's character had not been portrayed with sympathy. Because he did not intend to represent Savitri in negative light, he was quick to make amends, when Dina Pathak told him that as Savitri she had more to say than the dramatist had allowed her. Rakesh promptly gave a long speech to Savitri to rectify the imbalance. But perhaps the problem lay elsewhere and that problem was unrectifiable. Savitri's schizophrenia could not be changed—the two opposite pulls in her character could not be reconciled. Probably, there was larger purpose behind it.

Savitri metaphorizes the cultural schizophrenia of the urban middle-class, which for ever attempts to juggle standing on two stools—they remain rooted in notions of morality (the axiomatic middle-class morality!) and traditional values, on the one hand, and, on the other, aspire to join the ranks of the rich and the wealthy and in the process lose out on their peace of mind and happiness because what they want is impossible: the conciliation of the two realms of traditional moral values and the almost amoral sometimes immoral mores of the ultra rich is impossible. Through Savitri's character, *Halfway House* remains not only limited family drama, depicting personal anguish and frustrations of members of this family, but also transforms into the saga of the modern, urban middle class, their inhibitions, their ambitions, their conflicts, and consequent angst.

A question that needs to be answered is why Rakesh chose Savitri to stand for the urban middle-class's predicament. Why not Mahendranath, or Juneja, or any other man in the play? The reason for that is that in the post-Independent India, like elsewhere in the world, the issue of women's liberation had gained attention. Important social changes were taking place in society: increased opportunities for education and employment for women, their economic independence and their consequent demand for a larger space for themselves beyond the threshold. However, these women, mostly from the middle-class, were simultaneously housewives, too, looking after the family, shouldering the responsibilities of the mother and the wife as efficiently, as they were required to be at their workplace. The schizophrenia of the middle-class, urban middle-class, therefore, could be effectively focussed on through a woman character who, at her personal level, was situated in similar fashion.

The play, thus, effectively articulates, a larger dimension than merely the family tragedy: the play acquires universality—cultural schizophrenia of the urban middle-class cuts across regional and even national boundaries. It is not surprising, therefore, that the play won several awards and became one of the most frequently staged plays, always drawing large appreciative audiences.

NOTE

1. Dilip K. Basu, ed., *Halfway House* (Delhi: Worldview, 1999).

Lust for Life: A Study of Savitri in *Halfway House*

NARESH K. JAIN

In a sympathetic study of Savitri, Jain sees the genesis of complexities in man-woman relationship in Halfway House *as arising out of emergence of a new economically independent woman and the changed equation of power between the sexes within marriage. According to him, Savitri's loyalty to the family is unquestionable. She is beset by problems because she is also driven by desire for personal fulfilment by her enormous appetite for life which does not accord well with the postulates of a patriarchal society. She is a woman more sinned against than sinning.*

Editor

Like his other plays *Aashadh Ka Ek Din* (1958) and *Lehron Ke Rajhans* (1963), Mohan Rakesh's *Halfway House* is centrally concerned with man-woman relationship. The dramatist's exploration of the theme takes place in different form in each play. In *Aashadh Ka Ek Din*, though Kalidas and Mallika love each other, theirs is an asymmetrical relationship. While for Kalidas, love is only a part of his life and he is intent on realising his ambition of becoming a great poet, it is Mallika's whole existence and means total self-surrender. She loves the poet in him and wants to see him realize his greatness, and she does so too but only "at the unbelievable cost of all that is valuable in her total existence." In the second play *Lehron Ke Rajhans* the playwright takes up a young married couple who drift apart because of incomplete understanding of one another.

In *Halfway House* Mohan Rakesh deals with a middle-aged

couple, Savitri and Mahendranath, the dissonance in whose lives is reflected in the fragmented lives of the children. The contemporary setting of the play makes it possible for the playwright to probe the complexities of man-woman relationship arising out of the emergence of a new economically independent woman and the altered equation of power between the sexes within marriage. In spite of some ambiguity in the text, the play could be said to look at the relationship from the viewpoint of the woman.

The contours of the relationship are determined by the conflicting ideas of marriage held by Mahendranath and Savitri—traditional male-dominated marriage versus marriage as a companionship and as a means for self-fulfilment.

Mahendranath is the older patriarchal ideal of marriage in which man is the head of the family and the dominating partner whereas the woman has a subservient position. This accounts partly at least for the marital quarrels between them and the savage beating Savitri receives from her husband in the early years of marriage. Binni tells Juneja of the brutality inflicted on Savitri: "you can't imagine what it was like . . . Daddy's rages when he tore Mama's clothes to shreds . . . when he gagged her and beat her up behind closed doors . . . dragging her by the hair to the WC . . . (*Shudders*) I can't even recount the fearful scenes I've witnessed in the home. (64)

But fuller evidence is provided by Savitri's long speech to Juneja specifying how Mahendranath expected her to conduct herself:

> How can you refuse to go there? . . . You think you're an educated woman . . . you don't even know how to behave! He wants to change the way I walk, the way I talk, the way I. . . . That same Mahendra who smiles meekly among his friends, becomes a fiend when he comes home. One never knows when he may snatch one's eyes out or drink one's life-blood! (70-71)

Mahendranath's behaviour stemmed from a settled conviction that the husband was the lord and master and also the final arbiter of taste and decorum and propriety and that the best a woman could do was to fall in line with the wishes of her husband. That being Mahendranath's conviction, it was inevitable that he should resent any part of her conduct that went against what he held to be proper in a wife. Hence his use of physical force. In more prosperous times, he tried to please her by purchasing all kinds of substandard articles but that only showed his lack of understanding of his wife as it suggests that like a typical male he thought of his wife as a mere consumer. Even the fact that she was educated was ironically used against her. Mahendranath was always worried about his position among his friends: "Why do you always compromise my position among my friends?"—a complaint that reminds one of Torvald Helmer's charge against Nora in *The Doll's House.*

Savitri's expectations from marriage, on the other hand, suggest a belief in marriage as a loving companionship. She begins by articulating her expectations by first asking Juneja his definition of a man: "What is it that makes a man really a man?" (68) When Juneja shrinks from giving an answer and asks her to say what she wants to, she asks a rhetorical question: "doesn't being a man involve something more? Personality? Strength of character?" (68) She then goes on to say that we all marry because each one of us has a need, an inner void that we need to fill in. But significantly she adds: "For that he has to be complete in and for himself."[2]

This implies an ideal of marriage as a companionship, a relationship between equals, between two separate selves, each of whom has a minimum of autonomy and each will provide what the other lacks. But as she tells Juneja, Savitri discovered very early in marriage that Mahendranath was not even half a man.

It was inevitable that a relationship based on such conflicting ideas should lead to acrimony and bitterness and loneliness.

When the play opens, the marriage is twenty-two-years old, marked by a reversal of roles, which has, however, not been accompanied by a change in male thinking. Though Mahendranath now leads a parasitical existence and has further marginalized himself by abdicating all domestic responsibility, he still deeply resents the loss of his accustomed authority. In a revealing outburst which combines both rebellion and lament, he compares himself first to a rubber stamp and then to a mere piece of rubber. (38)

The wife, on the other hand, has long been the sole breadwinner of the family but she still hasn't yet acquired the authority that comes with being the economic provider. To borrow a metaphor from Yeats, the centre has not been able to hold itself and so has not been able to hold the family together. This void has led to the fragmentation of the family best illustrated by the feeling of abandonment experienced by the younger daughter, Kinni. Her accusations of her parents and her siblings as mere clods of earth gives us an idea of how a family divided against itself appears to a young child.

The two leading drives that motivate Savitri are her loyalty and devotion to the family and her need for personal fulfilment. But her integrity is questioned on both these counts. While the first is questioned by both the males in the family, by the son more than by the father, the second is grossly misinterpreted.

Her exertions on behalf of the family are questioned and her motives are suspected. Her invitation to her boss in the hope of seeking his help to find a job for her son and later the visit itself bring to a boil the deep accumulated resentment of both the father and the son.

Traditionally an unwritten code of wifely conduct requires that the woman of the house should not have any truck with any male outside the approved family circle, for such contacts are viewed with suspicion both within and outside the family. The violation of this stipulated code of conduct is partly responsible for the suspicious hostility with which the visits of Singhania and later of her former admirer Jagmohan are viewed by Mahendranath, his son Ashok and his mentor Juneja. While Mahendranath takes refuge in irony and a mocking tone and a ready excuse to stay away during the boss's visit, Ashok is more forthright.

The scene of confrontation between the mother and son is a key scene because the son here represents the point of view of his absent father. At first he is reluctant to say anything—though his reluctance to speak is more vocal than speech—but when pressed he openly suggests to her to decide things one way or the other. Sensing his mood, when his mother says that time has come for her to decide for herself, he at once says: "you really should, you know." (42)

His disgust with Singhania expressed through his cartoon-drawing and his play-acting about having caught and crushed a worm is justified. But what is not justified is his and Mahendranath's suspicion that Savitri has illicit sexual relation with Singhania or Jagmohan. I don't think we can fault Savitri for the ill manners of her boss. Singhania's crude behaviour is, in fact, just another instance of the threat of sexual exploitation under which female employees often have to work in offices. Being the sole breadwinner of the family, she finds, she cannot avoid inviting the boss to her place for he may be able to help her son get a job, or so she hopes. Savitri is merely being polite when he makes his visit. There is no evidence, direct or indirect for the suspicion of any sexual liaison between them. But in his suspicion, Ashok shares his father's patriarchal attitude—whom to invite and whom not to. The resentment/anger of the father-son duo proceeds partly at least from the fact that her act of inviting outsiders constitutes an act of transgression, a crossing of the *lakshman rekha*.

Ashok's beating of his thirteen-year-old sister Kinni for reading Casanova and talking sex with her friend Surekha could also be traced to a similar attitude that empowered the males in the family to legislate what a young growing girl should read and talk about and what she should not. The son's beating of his sister could also be seen as a replication of his father's thrashing of his wife, both resulting from an incapacity to understand the woman or the young girl as a person.

While her devotion to the family's interests ties her closely to the family, Savitri's need for personal fulfilment impels her to look beyond it. But this is problematic because of the ambiguity surrounding its presentation. Up to almost the middle of Act II Savitri comes through as a woman who is more sinned against than sinning but who remains undeterred, and demands more from life than life gives her. We get a hint of this appetite for life in her final words to her son as she decides to live life for herself at the end of Act I: "Very well, then. From now on I'll only bother about myself . . . you look after your own lives. (*Silence*) *I don't have many years to live now. But however, few they be, I'll no longer spend them like this.*" (43, italics added)

But Juneja in his defence of Mahendranath hurts her very avidity for life as an accusation in her face. His main argument is that no matter whom she had married she would have remained dissatisfied:

> The point is that if any of these men [whom Savitri fancied in an attempt to escape] had been a part of your life instead of Mahendra, you would still have felt that you had married the wrong man. You would still have encountered a Mahendra, a Juneja, a Shivjeet or a Jagmohan and thought and reacted in the same way. *Because the meaning of life to you is how many different things you can have and enjoy at the same time.* One man alone could never have given them to you, no matter whom you married, you would always have felt as empty and as restless as you do today. (74, my italics)

This accusation is largely a speculation on the part of a character who is acting as both the prosecutor and the judge. Juneja is not an unbiased observer either and like a clever lawyer chooses to ignore inconvenient facts. One glaring example of this is his reaction to the eyewitness evidence which Binni furnishes to him regarding her father's brutality. All that he says in response is: "What you're saying is not new to me." (64) Moreover he makes claims for his friend for which there is little evidence in the text. Immediately after making the aforesaid remark, he adds: "Still I say that he loves her." (64) Mahendranath's coming back at the end, more helpless than ever, merely marks the end of a little rebellion presumably like several others before. But it cannot be construed as an act of love.

Then his judgement about Mahendranath is far from being convincing. "He's not a puppet, nor anything else you may call him. He has only one defect—he is still the same as every man." (71) In spite of his barbed comment, most readers would agree with Savitri rather than with Juneja ("He's not even half a man!") (69), for Mahendranath as presented in the play is an entirely colourless and spineless character with little to redeem him. So his accusations against Savitri don't carry complete conviction and to this reader at least don't exactly turn the tables on her. Yet they have an unsettling effect on our judgement of her. The certitude with which Juneja launches his attack on Savitri, particularly on her tendency to move from one person to the other in her attempt to escape, tends to cast doubt on her earlier more sympathetic presentation. Who then are we to trust: Juneja or Savitri? According to Juneja, her quest for a perfect mate was futile because her restlessness would have resulted in her disillusionment with any person other than Mahendranath sooner or later. Or are we to trust Savitri who after her disillusionment with Jagmohan and others accuses all her men: "All of you . . everyone of you . . . all alike! Exactly the same. Different masks, but the face . . . ? The same wretched face . . . every single one of you!" (76)

This ambiguity could be traced to the discrepancy between the reactions of Mohan Rakesh's friend on his first reading out his play to them in his Rajinder Nagar *barsati* and his own intention. Recalling his impressions of that first reading, Rajinder Nath says that they mere all stunned and had hardly anything to say. When some of the friends pointed out that "the portrayal of Savitri was not very sympathetic" and that "it seemed as if she were being held responsible for this 'hell'/'no exit' situation. Mohan Rakesh denied it vehemently. Rajinder Nath recalls a similar reaction from the stage and film actress Dina Pathak. He had read to her an earlier version of the play that did not contain Savitri's long speech in her encounter with Juneja. (70-71) She had said that if "she was to play the role she should always have the nagging feeling that she had to say a lot more and the author had not written those lines. It was on her strong suggestion that I reviewed the play and wrote that long speech of Savitri only to redress the balance." (xii-iv) Rajinder Nath then adds that "even after that speech the imbalance remains." (xiv)

Whether one calls it an ambiguity or 'imbalance' the logic of the play as it develops in Act I requires Savitri to be regarded as the central character and her dilemma to be central to the play's meaning. She is a strong character who *acts*—as against Mahendranath who only *reacts*—and she it is who brings in a new element in the form of her enormous appetite for life. And this appetite remains, even after long years of an unhappy marriage. Her experience with different men, Shivjeet, Manoj and Jagmohan, can be interpreted as her attempt to find a perfect mate for herself. That she is disappointed in her quest points to an inadequacy in them all. As Kirti Jain says, "all of them want to evade responsibility and to exploit Savitri."

In spite of the ambiguity in it what we have in the play is essentially male comprehension of a woman's quest for completeness and happiness and this applies to Juneja no less than it does to Mahendranath or his son, Ashok.

Halfway House ends on a sombre note. Disillusioned with all men, Savitri is in a trap, a no-exit situation. The return of the husband completes the circle begun in Act I with all escape routes closed to both of them more firmly than ever. Her plight is much worse because her potential for life must remain forever unrealized.

NOTES

1. Mohan Rakesh, *Aadhe Adhure* (1993; New Delhi: Radhakrishan, 1998), p. 87. This line, curiously omitted in the English translation by Bindu Batra, comes immediately before "That same Mahendra who smiles meekly among friends." *Halfway House*, ed. Dilip Basu (Delhi: Worldview, 1999), p. 69.
2. *Ibid*, p. 69. Again this line has been omitted in Bindu Batra's translation.

3. Kirti Jain, A note on Indian Theatre from the performance point of view, with special reference to Mohan Rakesh's *Aadhe Adhure* (*Halfway House*) and Vijay Tendulkar's *Ghashiram Kotwal*, in *Many Indias, Many Literatures*, ed. Shormishtha Panja (Delhi: Worldview, 1999), p. 78.

Halfway House: Who is Responsible for the Mess?

SATNAM KAUR

Kaur analyses the situation of the family depicted in Halfway House *and finds that Savitri's conduct becomes largely responsible for the disharmony, disorder and disintegration of the family. Savitri's affairs with other men, while remaining married to Mahendranath and while the children are in the process of growing, have an all-round baneful effect on the family.*

Editor

Even though a multi-dimensional writer, Mohan Rakesh established himself as a great literary figure by virtue of his play-writing. During his literary career of nearly twenty-five years, whether in the short stories, novels or plays, this litterateur, like a consummate diagnostician, dissected and analysed the inner turbulence and vicissitudes of the individual human psyche. Alienation of man, not only from his sociological environment but from his own self, becomes the primary concern of Mohan Rakesh in his works. In the author's own words, this loneliness is not the loneliness of the socially isolated individual, but a kind of isolation that comes from existing within a societal framework and it leads not to any kind of cynicism but to the need to exist through it.

During the Sixties and the Seventies, a new awakening had dawned upon the women-folk of India. Women became aware of their independent existence, started moving out of the confines of home and hearth, resulting in greater interaction with men and the evolution of a new relationship between the opposite sexes.

The foundations of marriage as an institution started shaking, germinating a revolt against the traditional idea of keeping a marriage going, at any cost. The female partner started asserting for a room of her own. All these social changes, problems of the female self, man-woman relationship, became the most important thematic concerns for many writers of the age, Mohan Rakesh being no exception. He, too, brooded upon these burning topics with great concern. The incidents of his fictional works revolve around personal problems, frustrations, the various forms and levels of the man-woman relationship, the deep fissures that inevitably result from fractured associations, the collapse of traditional values and their replacement with individualism. Loneliness, suffocation, mutual tension, boredom and many more of such emotional states get depicted through the very titles of Mohan Rakesh's fictional works such as *Doraha, Dhundhlaa Deep, Aparichit, Aadmi aur Deevar, Marusthal, Lakshyaheen, Insaan ke Khandahar*, etc.

Mohan Rakesh wrote a total of 66 stories of which twelve were published during his lifetime. He belonged to an innovative style of story-writing, which was called the 'New Story' (Nayee Kahanee). This type of story writing had more natural expression and simple language of day-to-day life. As a novelist, he published three novels—*Andhere Band Kamre* (1961), *Na Aanewala Kal* (1968) and *Antaraal* (1972). The central focus in these works, exactly like his short stories, is the conflict, disintegration and degeneration of social values and above all the fragmentation of relationship between man and woman. The titles of the novels indicate the darkness and the gloom, which envelop the fictional cosmos of these works. As a playwright, Mohan Rakesh published three full-length plays, *Aashadh Ka Ek Din* (1958), *Lahron Ke Rajhans* (1963) and *Aadhe Adhure* (1969). One play, *Pair Tale Ki Zameen*, was left unfinished and was later completed on the basis of his notings by his close associate, Kamleshwar. The heights attained by Mohan Rakesh as a dramatist were not touched by any other playwright of his times. In 1959, he was awarded the first prize of the Sangeet Natak Akademi for his first play *Aashadh Ka Ek Din* (1958). He has attained a distinctive place in the field of Hindi drama.

Halfway House, published in 1969, deals with the clash between the egos of man and woman, the tension, suffocation, and the disintegration of a relationship. In this play, it is not only the bond between husband and wife, which seems to be breaking, but the whole family is heading towards total disintegration. All the relationships, whether between mother and son, brother and sister or mother and daughter, seem to be going to shambles. An extremely distasteful but a very realistic picture of a modern middle-class family is portrayed through this play. *Halfway House* can be rated as the playwright's masterpiece. It is also regarded as one of the best dramatic works in the world of Hindi Theatre and an important landmark in Indian Theatrical development.

In *Halfway House*, the movement of the story is circular. The play shows disintegration of moral values and the dismantling of a particular family. It is a family of five, where the lady of the house, Savitri, is the sole breadwinner and it is because of her hard struggle and unaided labour that her family has been surviving for twenty-two years. Her husband is a good-for-nothing person, apparently a gargantuan oaf. The elder son, Ashok, is also unable to make anything out of his life. He is also dependent upon the mother and she is trying hard to arrange a job for him. The elder daughter, Binni, has eloped with Manoj, her mother's friend and occasionally returns to her parents's house. Her married life is also disturbed. This time she has come without any bag and baggage, which indicates that perhaps she has left him forever. The younger daughter, Kinni, does not lag behind in creating further chaos in the house. As she is not being properly taken care of and her demands are not being fulfilled, she has become totally uncontrollable and insolent. In the opening scene, when Savitri returns from her workplace, she finds the house in a dishevelled state. This irritates her a lot and she starts castigating the man, who does not extend any kind of help to her. She gives vent to her frustration as nobody in the house shares her workload and loses her temper with her husband, who is an idler. If he cannot go out and work, if he cannot give any financial support to the family, at least he can keep the house in order. He is bullied for his listlessness.

In the meanwhile, the younger daughter has returned and now it is her turn to be scolded, as she is no less irresponsible. She has left her bag and books helter-skelter and gone somewhere. Even as the jibing with Mahendranath is going on, the elder daughter arrives and the problems in her married life are also revealed. The son enters and the arguments intensify. The whole house is in a chaotic state, the man is being blamed for the ruin of the family, as he is projected as a spineless, callous, lethargic parasite. When all this is going on, Mahendra loses his temper and leaves the house in anger. After he leaves, Savitri informs them that she has invited her boss to arrange a job for Ashok, but he does not approve of it and is least interested in the man because of his ostentatious nature. The boss, Singhania, arrives but Ashok refuses to talk to him properly; and after he leaves, an argument flares up between the mother and the son as a result of which Savitri decides not to bother about anyone in the house in future. Nobody in the house ever realises what Savitri has been doing for the family. She gets totally disappointed and in desperation decides to take a new step, which would change her life. She decides to live her own life and for that, she turns to an old flame of hers, Jagmohan. But her plans are dashed to the ground when the man refuses point-blank to oblige Savitri. With a heavy mind she has to return to her eternal hell: her home and her family.

In the beginning, we sympathise with Savitri, as she alone has to bear the burden of the entire family. None among her family members is willing to extend any cooperation or exhibit understanding towards her. But when we analyse the role of the other three men and their relationship with Savitri, our sympathies start shifting. Singhania is Savitri's boss and he has been invited by her to discuss job opportunities for her son. But the son does not want to have a job through such a loathsome person. He does not want to remain in the company of a person who makes him feel even smaller than he actually is. Ashok is unwilling to remain at home when Singhania is expected and the same applies to Mahendra. Hints are provided that whenever Savitri's boss came to visit their place, Mahendra avoided him and this time as well, he does the same. In frustration, he says, "when have I ever been of any use? Only outsiders can be of use here!"[1] He asks Savitri, "why have you always wanted to, . . " (27) By leaving this sentence incomplete, does he mean that she wants to develop relations with other men? Even the son accuses her of inviting such people who are rich, influential, and pseudo-intellectuals. He says, "whenever you've invited anyone, it hasn't been for the person himself but because of his name, his salary, his position." (40) Both the men disapprove of Savitri's relations with other men. Mahendra especially seems to be fighting constantly with this uncomfortable feeling within him. He refers to Singhania with a certain sharpness. This can be one cause of the misunderstanding between husband and wife, which Savitri never tries to clarify. The nature of Savitri's relations with other men also remains hazy. From her own words it appears that she forms these particular relationships to solve her financial problem. Whereas from the words of Juneja, Mahendra and Ashok, it seems that her relations are sexual, illicit from the social point of view and intolerable as far as the family is concerned.

Through Singhania's character, Mohan Rakesh has drawn a satirical portrait of all those employers with base nature, who make show of their knowledge and higher taste by appreciating art and culture, talk errant nonsense and meaningless things and misuse their positions to exploit the women who work under them. He is confused and does not remember anything; his speeches are incomplete and fragmented. He seems to be more interested in Binni rather than in Ashok, thereby revealing his evil intentions regarding the girl.

Jagmohan is an old friend of Savitri. He appears as the Third Man in the play and is worldly and experienced. He comes whenever Savitri calls him but is not too sentimental about his relationship with her and refuses to give her any false assurance. Jagmohan will not do anything that he will have to regret later. He listens to Savitri sympathetically, treats her tenderly but responds only after careful deliberation and with firmness. When Savitri was young and beautiful, he must have made tall promises in order to exploit her and that is why she has so much confidence in him. But when she decides to leave her family and start a new life with him, he turns his back upon her and makes all kinds of lame excuses. Perhaps, Jagmohan has never been sincere; in fact, he has been a mere exploiter. Now his interest seems to be shifting from the mother to the daughter, smacking of the sexual. Savitri had an involvement with Jagmohan before her marriage, had maintained it through all these years and now plans to leave Mahendra and settle with Jagmohan. This makes us suspicious of Savitri's morality and sincerity towards Mahendra. How could such a woman lead a peaceful life with her husband? The clash between Mahendra and Savitri becomes inevitable with the latter's tainted background. The rejection of Savitri by Jagmohan is also indicative of the futility of human relations. He takes the urgency of her decision very lightly and in a very indifferent manner and Savitri's faith is totally shaken. Such an eventuality reflects the result of eroded social and moral values. If Savitri herself is unable to develop a meaningful relationship with her husband, what right does she have to expect sincerity from a mere cad?

Right from the very beginning, the play hints at the fact that Juneja is a money-minded and self-centred man, but at the end, while interacting with Savitri and Binni, he appears to be an honest man, cultured, sensible and a friend of Mahendra's striving for his good. Mahendranath has always turned to him, whenever he wants to escape from home. In the beginning, Savitri too had been close to him and shared her inner feelings with him. The family keeps no secrets from him. Towards the end, Juneja advocates Mahendra's cause, listens to all the complaints and an outburst made by Savitri, but does not hesitate in showing her the mirror where she sees her ugly past. He minces no words and tears her to pieces. Savitri cannot hold Mahendra or the circumstances solely responsible for her ruin; she herself has contributed no less to the dystopian domesticity operating within the family. She is rendered speechless in front of Juneja. His speech reveals that after every few years, Savitri had made a desperate attempt to detach herself from Mahendra and find some way out of her existential predicament. She was attracted to Shivajeet after Juneja because of his university degree and his trips abroad, then to Jagmohan, because of "his excellent contacts, his smart way of life, his generosity." But the feeling remained that each one of them lacked something: "the point is that, if anyone of these men had been a part of your life instead of Mahendra, you would still have felt that you had married the wrong man," Juneja tells her. (73-74) These words amply illustrate the symbolic chasm, the unfathomable vacuum within Savitri's psyche, which any seemingly nice man will find difficult to negotiate.

These harsh revelations shatter the image of Savitri built in the beginning of the play. Had she been a real Sati-Savitri, the woman of strong character, sacrificing and bearing the brunt of time with great patience, the play would have been a great tragedy of the human condition? If Savitri has accused all men for being similar who put on different masks on the same face, she herself has failed to maintain the sanctity of married life. She has also contributed to the erosion of moral values in general and the destruction of the family in particular. One can see the detrimental effect of Savitri's own conduct on the children, all of whom are unhappy and to a certain extent irresponsible. Ashok is a good-for-nothing boy who is not bothered about his future. He, like his father, becomes a failure even though he is young. Binni is inexplicably rebellious in her attitude and actions towards her husband, and leads an unhappy married life. Kinni is a thirteen-year-old spoilt and irresponsible adolescent girl. She is too demanding and least concerned with the problems of the house. She wants her needs to be fulfilled and if they are not met she starts cursing the whole family. She is rude and uses foul language with her elder brother and does not hesitate in being disrespectful towards her mother, too. She is caught by her brother, Ashok, indulging in sex-talk.

It needs to be stressed in conclusion that Savitri's lack of full commitment to the preservation of the family results in its near disintegration. No doubt, she sustains the family economically by taking up a job, after Mahendranath fails in business but her constant open liaisons with other men have a baneful effect on the children and create quarrels with Mahendranath. Everybody in the family becomes bitter, including herself (she is frustrated because of her failure to get away) and such a family cannot escape doom.

NOTE

1. Mohan Rakesh, *Halfway House*, ed. Dilip K. Basu (Delhi: Worldview, 1999), p. 26.

Halfway House: Absurdism of the Indian Middle Class

BHARAT GUPT

Gupt traces the influence of the Euro-American Absurd drama on Rakesh's Halfway House *while simultaneously ranging over diverse issues of family, man-woman relationship, middle-class morality. Though he does not deny that the play contains, in the second Act particularly, a shade of Naturalistic drama, but affirms that the play remains in the tradition of the Absurd by virtue of its clear statement: there are no causes for blind alleys human beings find themselves in and there is no possibility of change as the human endeavour is sure to fail.*

Editor

Mohan Rakesh's *Halfway House* (1968) was written during the decade when the Delhi middle class intellectuals had just acquired a taste for the European philosophies of Absurdism, Existentialism and even Nihilism. There was a reason for these kind of philosophies to appeal to the thoughtful among the educated and literary class, as by the Sixties a certain amount of disillusionment had set in with the ideals of the political leadership of the country and the burdgeoning bureaucracy.

Both in the Sixties and the Seventies, the middle class in India, which was burdened with the proclamation of morality, found that the growing power of bureaucracy and the increasing might of the capitalists knew no norms. Mohan Rakesh's first major play *Aashadh Ka Ek Din* (1958) had already focussed on the artist's plight who wishes to keep alive his creativity under the stifling conditions of official patronage and the whimsical favours of the high and mighty. Through the character of Kalidas he went on to portray that the best creativity was possible in the rural or indigenous conditions of an artist's milieu of his birth and upbringing. The luxurious life of the capital city of the patron was detrimental to fresh thinking and feeling. Taking the paradigm of the ancient story of the legendary Indian poet Kalidas, Mohan Rakesh comments upon the sad story of the writers of the Fifties (and by extension, of artists of all kinds) from small towns and villages who moved to big cities like Delhi and felt that they were oppressed by the system of bureaucratic high-handedness and political apathy. With a vast expansion of educational and research institutions funded by the State including the universities, research, theorising and teaching was also done most often to tow the official line. As the management of cultural institutes, radio, television, and even the press (through the power of handing out advertisements) was in government hands, the paradigm of the stifled Kalidas was very appropriate. In hindsight one can confirm that under state patronage very little creativity has been fostered in the last half a century. Although there may be some different perceptions also by the Indian writers themselves about the newly independent Indian state, Rakesh seems to have made a clear comment that goes against the declared promises of freedom and equality enshrined in the Indian constitution. At the same time Mohan Rakesh does not show any preference for any other political system or philosophy, whether Gandhian, rightist or capitalist. In the absence of any philosophhic moorings or political ideology, the feeling of disgust and disillusionment with the conditions of life prevailing in the Sixties, is best expressed by the Absurdist model that he adopted. That he also adjusted the European experience of the Absurd to the middle class Indian situation, is also shown by me below.

The European Influence

Before we go on to elaborate how *Halfway House* is a cross

between Naturalistic and Absurdist theatre, let us say a few words about both these genres of dramatic compositions. As is well known, the rise of Naturalism occurred in Europe in the nineteenth century, when plays began to follow the model of writing that was being pursued by the novelists for almost a century earlier. The aim of the Realistic and later Naturalistc fiction and drama was to represent not the fantastic, the fabulous, the mythical, the mysterious, the revealed, the ideal or the heroic in life but the actual, the ordinary and the everyday event that is seen all the time by an average observer. They had set aside exalted characters and picked upon mediocre persons and explored their psychological tendencies. This kind of fiction found its best expression in Austen, Balzac and Hardy and in theatre in the plays of Ibsen and Shaw. This artistic vision was a culmination of the rise of the modern natural sciences in Europe and the notions of progress and evolution that were inspired by the optimistic control over natural forces and environment to the comfort and ease of human beings.

A major jolt to scientific optimism came with the two World Wars. That technological excellence can provide sure succour to mankind could no longer be taken for granted. With the crash of faith in what European civilisation had been pursuing for two centuries, a deep despondence began pervading the intellectual milieu and gave birth to the philosophical theories of Existentialism and Absurdism. The first postulated that it was not the social organisation and its betterment that could provide relief to the individual. Most systems of thought since Rousseau had echoed his postulate that "Man is born free but is found everywhere in chains" or in other words that individual unhappiness was caused by social disorders and that if social evils could be cured the individual and the social well-being both would become a palpable reality.

Contrary to this approach, Existentialism sought an answer in the inner being or existence of the individual. Some of these Existential philosophies came up with a positive hope for human salvation reached through inner reconciliations. Others proclaimed that human beings are condemned to loneliness and helplessness in a universe where the cosmic order presides to torture and punish every existence without any reason. Some of the writers like Camus proclaimed that as there was no perceivable purpose or telcology for this Creation, to look for the purpose of one's life was absurd. To symbolise his thought, Camus reinterpreted the ancient Greek myth of Sisyphus. According to the Greek tradition, Sisyphus was the son-in-law of the famous Titan, Atlas, and was known for his cunning which he showed in catching Autolycus, the thief of his sheep. With guile, he also seduced Autolycus's daughter Anticleia, bearing him Odysseus who inherited the shrewdness of his father. He founded Ephyra which was renamed Corinth where he mercilessly robbed travellers. With his cunning, he also avenged himself on many enemies. He knew the secret of Zeus's seducing Aegina, the daughter of Asopus, which he revealed to Asopus after extracting a heavy price. Zeus punished Sisyphus for revealing his divine secrets by sending him to Hades, where the judges ordered him to roll a huge boulder to a hill top and to be pushed across to the other side. "Each time Sisyphus nears the top, the rock rolls back to its place." Whereas the ancients thought of Sisyphus as a deceiver and a crooked king duly punished by Zeus for his many misconducts, Camus has projected him as a victim of the wrath of the Almighty creator damning a human to endless labour. Unboubtedly, the myth does not represent to Camus the justice of gods dispensed to those who are immoral and unscrupulous but the highhandedness and arbitrary dictat of the unchallengeable gods. Creation is seen by Albert Camus as unfair, irrational and, thus, absurd.

A large number of fictionalists and playwrights followed the absurdist notions of Camus, particularly in the Western European states which were under Soviet occupation. Meir Mroshak's *Striptes*, Samuel Beckett's *Waiting for Godot*, Ionesco's *The Bald Prima Dona*, *Rhinoceros* and *Amedee*, Adamov's *Parody* and many more became well-known by the Fifties and early Sixties. The Indian theatre scene, particularly in Delhi where Mohan Rakesh stayed, was touched by this influence in the Sixties when a number of absurd plays were performed by professional and amateur theatre groups. The present writer himself performed *Striptes* which was considered an avant-garde activity at that time. On the larger Indian scene, besides Mohan Rakesh, Badal Sircar, Vijay Tendulkar, many others were impressed by the Existential-Absurdist philosophies and Absurdist theatre techniques as is evident from their earlier works.

Halfway House

In his play *Halfway House*, Mohan Rakesh follows some techniques of the Naturalistic theatre while others of the Absurdist model adjusted to the Indian life. Structurally, the play has a Prologue and two Acts and no scenes as that would have created the illusion of progress and action in the play which the author does not wish to convey. The first Act makes us aware of the personae of the play and their miserably suffocating situation. The second Act demolishes any hope of the action, or even the possibility that dialogue shall lead towards a change in the state of affairs. On the contrary, the dialogue makes it clear that the purpose of this play is to make the audience feel the impossibility of any change. As an absurdist play, there are no episodes in any Act but only the hoping and talking of change in the lives of dramatic characters. The second Act could be called a bit Naturalistic as there is some semblance of action on the heroine's part—she is supposed to have gone out and tried reviving her relationship with an old lover who totally disappoints her.

Prologue

Both the Acts are forwarded with a prologue which is spoken by an actor dressed in black suit and smoking a cigar. This is the beginning of the cross between Naturalistic and Absurd in the play. The speaker declares that the play is going to be an "undefined" one, with "undefined" characters. He makes sure that we do not expect a traditional play, Eastern or Western, with a set plot, episodic development and evolving characters. In fact, he is at pains to tell us that he himself as the prologue speaker is undefined. He says that he is neither just a prologue speaker nor one of the characters of the play that the audience is about to see. But in spite of this statement by the prologue speaker, from the lines that he speaks one gets the impression that he is claiming himself to be the common denominator of all the male characters in the play. He says, "If the woman of the family was replaced by another she would put up with me in a different way . . . or, she would assume my role and I, assuming hers, would have to put up with her. The play would remain equally undefined and it would be just as difficult to decide who or what has the determining role. . . . I, the woman, the circumstances that sorround us or the questions that arise out of our interaction with each other." In other words he is equating himself with the main male character of the play at least to begin with. Also his comment that things would be the same (that is of conflict, hopelessness and alienation) no matter what the character of the woman is, should make it amply clear to the audience that they are going to witness an encounter between a man and a woman that is a symbol of the universal man-woman relationship (a hopelessly absurd one) as presented by Mohan Rakesh. Through this prologue, spoken by a too obviously Westernised nameless persona, Mohan Rakesh introduced his Hindi drama audience to the new current of Absurdist theatre. Unconsciously, there is an admission on the part of the playwright that this is a vision of the hybrid urban dramatic genre which is neither native nor Western. The prologue may seem unnecessary today, as we are by now too familiar with absurdist plays, but in the Sixties it was a useful rite of passage for its audience. For that reason, in my opinion, a director may just wish to dispense with it totally. There is not much spoken by the prologue that the audience cannot infer on their own. In fact, some may even find it pretentious.

The Characters

The play proper in two acts has four men, the husband Mahendra Nath, the boss of Savitri, Singhania, an old lover called Jag, and the husband's close friend, Juneja. All of them are not given any names in the list of *dramatis personae* and according to the playwright are to be played by the same actor. This was one of the common devices that the theatre of the Absurd was using at that time. By this stage device (as postulated by the prologue speaker), the writer wishes to imply that all male characters are facets of the one male person, Mahendra Nath, the husband of Savitri. In the case of women characters, a similar impression is created as the various feminine personalities seem to be parts of the main woman character, Savitri. The elder daughter of Savitri is also alienated from her husband like Savitri is and the younger daughter, too, is likely to be an unbalanced person. The couple's son Ashok is also a good-for-nothing individual like his father. As a result, we have two characters effectually, a man and a woman to make the play.

It is quite clear from the start that by calling his characters "undefined," Mohan Rakesh intends to eschew realistic portraiture. Mahendra Nath is not shown as a man in flesh and blood with some special past, likes and dislikes or personality. He is more of a state of mind. For instance, we do not know why the couple Mahendra and Savitri could never get along and what caused Mahendra to give up work and become such a parasite. The real life events that mould a character are not the concerns of the playwright. We are only told that Mahendra was too dependent on his friends and acted all the time under their influence, but how this came about is not the concern of the dramatist. The causes are not explored in Absurdist theatre, only the resultant state is. No matter what the situation is in life, the consequence is the same, an irrational oddity. This is indicated to us in the Prologue which I have quoted above. One may also add that the same technique of not giving any reasons is followed in the presentation of the characters of the three children of the couple. The eldest daughter has broken off from her husband as her husband feels that she inherits 'something' unnatural from her parents's house. The mother and the daughter are unable to explain their own plight, let alone find any solution. In short, the household is a symbolic universe in which there are no posssibilities of meaningful relationships. Mohan Rakesh is deliberately creating an unexplained situation to reinforce the absurdity of life, so that we may not even try to ask what could have gone wrong. In his last long speech, Juneja, the friend of Mahendra, declares that Savitri is a chronically dissatisfied person. She would have created this hell of unfulfillment no matter who had been her husband.

From the point of view of men, Savitri is to be blamed more than Mahendra Nath. But one should not take the masculine characters's view of Savitri and judge her accordingly. What Juneja says about Savitri is not projected by the playwright as his view. This is certainly not an anti-woman play. Savitri is no blood-sucker who from her dissatisfactions reduces Mahendranath into a pulp. Mahendra is a rotten soul, too. Savitri is shown as caught in the situation of seeking refuge in other men not only because of her bigger dreams but also because her husband is such a good-for-nothing. The disgust is mutual and the failing equally shared by the couple. This is the situation of the total failure of communication which is supposed to reinforce the feeling of Absurdity.

This play is set in the urban middle class family. The ambiguities and the double-standards of the middle class are evident. It is never made clear as to what is the exact relationship of Savitri to other men who frequent the house and make the husband and the children feel so humiliated. Is she prostituting herself or not? The dramatist leaves a doubt. This reaffirms the dubiousness of middle-class values. It also makes another point that sexual morality is not the issue for Mohan Rakesh. The playwright is certainly not making a statement that this family has come to this sorry pass because the housewife bears a loose character. He is not at all anxious to uphold the ideal of family fidelity. Nor is he anxious to state that Savitri is forced to please men other than her husband because she is forced to do so by poverty. This play is not the story of the emotionally passive family bending under economic pressure to forsake its morality. Savitri is seeking more than money in men by going outside her marital bond. She is seeking a dream about which she herself is not clear. The main reason for the breakdown of communication between Mahendra and Savitri is not the jealousy of Mahendra. It is also not a play about a promiscuous wife unacceptable to an upright husband. The dramatist wants to show that no matter what kind of relationship Savitri may have had with men, she will be disappointed. In short, the absurdity of the man-woman relationship lies in the fact that they do not know what they want from each other.

To further reflect the absurdity of the actual conjugal situation, Mohan Rakesh has chosen such names for the protagonists that they parody the ancient meanings and references in Indian literature. In the *Mahabharata* and other puranic accounts, Savitri is the dutiful wife who brings her husband Satyavan back from the world of the dead. She is a paradigm of devotion, sacrifice and clarity of purpose. She had chosen Satyavan because of his elevated righteousness even though she was told that he had a short life. For the sake of fulfilling her aim of living with a righteous husband, she takes a great risk and emerges a winner. The character of this play is the opposite. She does not know what she wants and impatiently runs from one man to another and wishes her husband dead and gone. If Rakesh had called the protagonist as Satyavan, the parallel would have been too obvious. So he chooses a name that serves the purpose in the broader sense. The meaning of the word 'Mahendra' is the king of gods, and the character in the play is just the opposite, a virtual beggar at home. The name signifies a glamorous, powerful and attractive man that the character Savitri wanted for a dream-husband. By using this device of ironical reference to the ancient myth, the dramatist has further heightened the sense of futility of life that the play aims to provide to the audience as a theatrical experience.

The Play in Hindsight

Looking at *Halfway House* at the turn of the century, almost forty years after its first performance, one finds that it does not reflect the accurate condition of the Indian middle-class marital relationships. Mohan Rakesh does not give us a correct picture of the social conditions, even in urban areas, let alone the bigger India, in his depiction of Mahendra and Savitri. Let alone in the Sixties, even today, there is no perceptible feeling that the nuclear family is breaking down. Yes, the divorce rate in India is higher today than it was in the Sixties but there are many reasons for this other than loss of faith in the marital institution. The breakdown of the nuclear family and the impairment of prolonged marital stability has been true of the Euro-American society from the Sixties onwards indeed. There the divorce rate has tremendously shot up and the nuclear family has been partially replaced by "living together" mode. In fact, in actual practice, the affluent societies of the West have almost replaced monogamy by polygamy which has been modified to become "serial monogamy." In other words, you may not have many wives or husbands at a time, but you marry and divorce three or four times in life. This is a Christian modification of polygamy into monogamy. Such a transition of values is an experience of Western societies only. Here in India the perceptible change is a partial breakdown of the joint or the extended family but not at all of the nuclear family so far. One may say that the plays showing absurdity of permanent man-woman relationship in the West are reflective of their cultures. But this cannot be said of any Indian play, and least of all of *Halfway House*.

Sexism and Power Games in *Halfway House*

MANCHI SARAT BABU

Babu traces the marital problems Savitri and Mahendranath face to the inversion of prescribed gender roles. Both are unhappy to be going against the traditional patriarchal roles: Savitri resents having to become the bread-earner and Mahendranath feels frustrated at not being able to succeed in business like other men do. Consequently, they play power games to persecute and rescue each other (and the children) which create an impasse and cause grief for all.

Editor

Mohan Rakesh is a famous Hindi short-story writer, novelist and playwright. He won Sahitya Akademi Award for Literature twice. He belongs to the Modern Hindi Literary Movement of *nai kahani* (new story). He wrote some of his plays, such as *Lehron Ke Rajhans*, first as short stories and then changed them into plays. While pointing out the contribution of Mohan Rakesh, Choudhuri rightly remarks "With Mohan Rakesh (1925-1972) Hindi drama makes a departure from pseudo-modernism and traditional symbolism to the drama of 'non-communication'—the modern man's failure to understand himself or to understand the other person and their mutual failure to understand each other, which is the real tragedy of modern life. The breakdown of communication is handled with a concentration, intensity and subtlety rare in the earlier Hindi drama."[1] Rakesh exploits history and legend in his *Aashadh Ka Ek Din* and *Lehron Ke Rajhans*. He presents the contemporary life in his *Halfway House* and his short plays. He depicts the schizophrenic state of the present day human mind in his experimental play, *Mad Delight.* All his plays deal with the problems of contemporary life, mostly at psychological level. However, among all his plays, *Halfway House* occupies an important place. So, Choudhuri aptly observes: "The crisis of identity and breakdown of communication in human relations and the resultant tragic effect of boredom and despair constitute again the theme of Rakesh's next play *Aadhe Adhure* (The Half and Incomplete, 1969) which is, by far, his best play, devastatingly exposing the fragmented personalities and broken images in a disintegrated society." (513) Rakesh, talking about the emergence of the play, says:

> Yet apparently there is a shift in *Aadhe Adhure*. For this I must refer to two short plays, *Shayad* and *Hunh*, that I wrote before *Aadhe Adhure*. These two plays which I termed *Beej Natak* or Seed Plays, were studies of ordinary middle-class life at middle-age and old age respectively. They were written to discover the drama of being. Another thing that I tried to discover through them was the absurdity of reality itself. These paved the way for the writing of *Aadhe Adhure* where the shift is not because of its 'contemporariness;' but because of its 'ordinariness.'[2]

The play portrays the suffocation of a man and a woman, imprisoned in their roles imposed on them by the sexist culture and the persecution of each by the other in addition to its depiction of the absurdity of their ordinary life.

The incompleteness that torments the characters in the play can be understood by analyzing the fragmented personality of the modern human being. Rakesh himself says: "Everyone of us is living a life in fragments."[3] We are actually born whole human beings, but the division of labour based on gender breaks us into male and female fragments. Each fragment retains only half of the human potential. The retained part overgrows to compensate for the other part that remains underdeveloped. These two polarized, deformed fragments are called men and women. These gender deformities are, thus, caused and gradually canonized by socio-cultural programming of sex roles. They are glorified and children are trained to attain them through socialization since their birth. Hogie Wyckoff, a Transactional Analyst, writes: "As women and men we are socialized to develop certain parts of personalities while suppressing development of other parts. This programming promotes a predetermined, stilted, and repetitive way of acting life."[4]

Every human being has the potential for nurturing, controlling, rationality, intuition, spontaneity and adaptation. To be masculine, men develop the faculties of controlling and rationality while suppressing those of nurturing and intuition. To be feminine, women develop the faculties of nurturing and intuition while suppressing those of controlling and rationality. To be cultured, both men and women develop the faculty of adaptation to culture (but not to Nature), while suppressing that of spontaneity and so neither enjoys life. Nurturing and intuition help women perform their culturally allotted function, child-rearing and house-keeping while controlling and rationality help men perform their culturally allotted function, bread-earning. Adaptation to culture and the lack of spontaneity make both of them obedient to their masters. Thus, men and women become different, except in their obedience. These differences cause alienation and antagonism between men and women. So they find each other mysterious and hostile and fail to communicate with each other. The antagonism and the break-down of communication between Savitri and Mahendranath in *Halfway House* are due to these factors.

Mohan Rakesh depicts the deformity in the personalities of men and women caused by gender distinctions of patriarchal culture in his *Halfway House*. It is about the incomplete life of a middle-class family. At first, Mahendranath is very convivial and his friends like his company. He marries Savitri. He enters into business with his friend, Juneja while she does a job. She urges him to get good furniture and other things for their house. He, therefore, withdraws his share of the capital slowly, and buys all the items one after another and furnishes the house according to the taste of his wife. Consequently, he loses his business and feels very bad about it. His wife goes on nagging him for losing business. This adds to his frustration and he takes it on his wife. As he does not conform to her concept of a masculine man, she considers him impotent. She blames first his parents and later his friends for this. She runs after several men but fails to establish a lasting relationship with any one of them. She feels greatly frustrated and takes it out on her children. All this makes their house a veritable hell.

The play begins with a prologue by a Man in a Black Suit. It conveys that all men behave alike in a given situation. The play proves this through Savitri, the central character. Rakesh points out:

> This woman is the central character and I want the four men to be played by the same actor. What I want to indicate by that is that it's not the individual who's responsible for his situation, for he would have made the same choice no matter what, regardless of the situation. Any choice anyone makes has a certain irony in it, for things turn out the same regardless of the choice.[5]

Savitri, as well as Mahendranath, absorb patriarchal culture and observe it. It makes them think that man is a bread-earner and that woman is a house-keeper. Though patriarchal culture is common to all, individuals differ in their perception and absorption of it. In this context, Savitri is more assertive than her husband. That is, contrary to the patriarchal cultural norms of sexist roles, Savitri has more powerful controlling faculty than her husband. So, Mahendranath meekly yields to the demands of his wife and purchases furniture by withdrawing his share of the capital from the business. Savitri takes up a job and feeds the family while Mahendranath idles away without helping her in her housework. This upsets the cultural norms of patriarchy. Mahendranath wants to be manly and refuses to take up housework. But he does not try honestly to find some employment or other. Savitri resents playing the masculine role of earning the bread for the family and the feminine role of keeping the house, without being appreciated for dual burden. She seems to enjoy more freedom than a traditional wife but she cannot break the patriarchal fetters completely to realize her dreams. Mahendranath can neither play his masculine role successfully nor break himself free from it. Both of them lack the faculty of spontaneity to have other options to come out of the impasse and live happily. The economic realities and patriarchal norms have come into a direct conflict here. This creates a crisis in their family.

Savitri, with her weak rationality, fails to understand the consequence of her demand for furniture in their house. She feels that her husband should, somehow, succeed in business and earn every luxury that she dreams of having. She says to Juneja:

> Why does one get married? In order to fulfil a need . . . an inner . . . void, if you like; to be self-sufficient . . . complete.[6]

She does not toleratc the dependence of her husband on his friend, Juneja and his service to others. Here she sees his friend in the role of a mother-in-law with whom an Indian wife struggles to have more sway over her husband than his mother. She blames others for their misery and refuses to see her part in making her husband what he is now. She expresses her contempt for Mahendra:

> That he's never had any confidence in himself! The test for everything in life has been you. Whatever you think, want, do, he too must think, want and do. Why . . . ? Because you are a man. And he? He's not even half a man! If there's an unsavoury task, Mahendranath will do it . . . a complicated problem, Mahendranath will solve it . . . ! When the press opened it was the same; in the case of the factory, it was the same. To do your dirty work Mahendra was good enough, but what happened when it was done . . . ? 'Mahendranath has already taken his share and spent it.' And what was his share . . . ? (points to furniture in the room) This and this

> and this . . . second, third, fourth-rate things with which he thought he was making a home! (15)

She, thus, accepts the patriarchal concept of a manly man and very much wants her husband to be manly. When Juneja tries to explain to her how she has caused his downfall, she refuses to see reason. As her husband fails to fit her image of a masculine man, she runs after several men but fails to realize her dream. She blames her husband for her failures and frustrations without realizing her part in it. By doing so, she gives away her power, feels powerless and plays power games to overcome her feelings of powerlessness.

On the other hand, Mahendranath, with his feeble intuitive faculty, fails to understand the feelings of his wife. He gives more importance to his friends than his wife. He likes the company of his friends more than that of his wife. He takes the advice of his friends rather than of his wife. He does not understand her need for love and recognition and, moreover, he discounts her sentiments. He blames her for his downfall, without realizing his part in it. By doing so, he gives away his power and feels powerless. Then, he plays power games to overcome his feelings of powerlessness.

Mahendranath and Savitri play power games at familial level. These games involve three roles: the Persecutor, the Rescuer and the Victim and the three roles form a triangle called the Drama Triangle. Usually in a typical patriarchal family, Father plays the Persecutor and Mother the Rescuer while their children play the Victim. When Father hurts children, Mother rescues them. Then, Father becomes her Victim as she persecutes him for hurting the children. Later, she becomes the Victim when the children exploit her kindness. Then, Father rescues her by persecuting them. Similarly, they rescue Mother when Father tries to hurt her. When they grow up, they either rescue or persecute their parents or do both. These roles also change according to the place. Father rescues Mother and children by earning money and arranging things outside the house while they persecute him by being ungrateful for what they are provided and by demanding more things without any consideration for his difficulties. Mother rescues Father and children by doing all the housework and striving to satisfy all their needs while they persecute her by remaining ungrateful for her services and by demanding more service from her without any consideration for her difficulties. Talking about the shifting of roles, Steiner points out: "Every Rescuer-Victim transaction will eventually result in a Persecutor-Victim transaction."[7] The play, *Halfway House*, illustrates the power games at familial level.

Mahendranath rescues his wife by conceding to her status-conscious desire of having good furniture in their house. He withdraws all his capital from the business and purchases furniture. Savitri persecutes him by blaming him for losing his business and for buying the furniture of inferior quality. She says contemptuously:

> And what was his share . . . ? (*points to furniture in the room*) This and this and this . . . second, third, fourth-rate things with which he thought he was making a home! (15)

She rescues Mahendranath by taking up a job to feed the family. He feels frustrated and starts beating his wife inhumanly. He begins blaming his wife for his failure. Thus, he persecutes his wife. She tries to get a job for her son with the help of her boss Singhania. But Ashok refuses to heed her advice.

Savitri resents being victimized by her ungrateful husband and children. She, therefore, decides to persecute them by going away with Jagmohan who she thinks will give her a home. She says to her children:

> Very well, then. From now on I'll only bother about myself. . . . You look after your own lives. (*silence*) I don't have many years to live now. But however few they be, I'll no longer spend them like this. I've done my utmost. It's the end now so far I'm concerned . . . it really is the end. (9)

She has tried to leave the house earlier, too, and live with the man of her choice. But she could not make it and returned home. This time, she firmly decides to leave her house for ever but Jagmohan tells her it is too late for them to live together. So she has to come back again.

Mahendranath also resents being belittled by his wife and children. He, too, wants to persecute them by leaving the house. He says to them:

> I am of no use, of no use at all. I'm only an idler . . . to be kicked and bullied just as you please. Can anyone tell me why I should stay here? (*silence*) You can't, can you?
>
> I'm responsible for ruining my life, your life, all our lives! And I still stick to this house, because I'm a parasite, because I like living off my wife, because . . . (6)

He leaves the house. Actually, he has left the house several times before. But he returns each time. Towards the end of the play, when Juneja is about to leave, he comes back and his son helps him walk in.

This repetition is common in the game and they cannot get out of it as they remain ignorant and as they remain in their favourite roles of the Drama Triangle. All this forms an integral part of our culture, so we take them for granted and do not find it odd. Commenting on their leaving and returning, N.C. Jain remarks: "Both are sick of each other and want and attempt to get away. But being what they are, they do not succeed and are forced to carry on their dreary, unfulfilled life together."[8]

They were not born mentally ill. They have become so because of the psychopathic atmosphere they live in. Their children also inherit their sick personalities. Therefore, the same drama of power games haunt the marital life of their elder daughter. She says to her mother about her problem in her family:

> What reason . . . ? A cup of tea spilt from his hand or a short delay when he returns from work? These little things are not really reasons . . . they become reasons. A strange

> sort of feeling mounts up within me and spreads like poison through my whole being. . . . Everything I touch or see or hear becomes distorted and I stand helpless and fearful under the spell of a destructive fate. . . . But Mama, I don't know why. . . . I just can't see why! It happens unasked, unforeseen. . . . It . . . it . . . tortures me till I think I'm going mad. And in the end he too turns against me and says . . . (4)

She and her brother share their opinions about the predicament of their family. They know something is wrong but they are not sure what it is. None of them knows the real reason behind this. Juneja puts most of the blame on Savitri for their crisis. He says to Savitri:

> Today, Mahendra is bad tempered. But there was a time when he really did laugh. From within. That was when no one made him feel small. When there was no one to tell him what he was not, what he should actually be. (16)

Mahendranath need not have given away his power and could have resisted the attempt of his wife to ruin him but he has not done anything to avert his failure in his business and his life.

Savitri, as a typical middle-class woman, wants to marry a man who can help her go up the ladder of socio-economic hierarchy. Perhaps Mahendranath also wants to scramble up the ladder through his business but he himself aborts his chance of becoming affluent by withdrawing his share of the capital. His frustration is made worse by his nagging wife. He and she begin playing power games instead of solving their problems together and discovering better options in life. Neither his friends nor her lovers help them understand the real situation. Mahendranath and Savitri, thus, have no way of knowing their real problem and so they continue to feel powerful and important through the games that they play. So, it appears to be their fate from which they have no escape and Choudhuri remarks: "But the husband and the wife are found to be destined to live a condemned life in a social prison with no exit. Alienated from each other but at the same time staying together as broken images with unresolved conflicts and tensions these characters hover on the middle-class level of existentialism." (513) The alienation that Choudhuri refers to is due to their deformed personalities caused by our sexist and patriarchal culture as noted above. They are imprisoned not only in the sexist roles but also in the roles the Drama Triangle postulates. There can be individual variations but the games and the roles remain basically the same for all in a similar situation.

NOTES

1. N. Choudhuri, "Hindi Drama," *Contemporary Indian Literature*, ed. K.M. George (Madras: Macmillan India, 1984), pp. 512-13.
2. Rajinder Paul, "Mohan Rakesh Interviewed," *Enact*, May 1971, No. 53.
3. Mohan Maharishi, "Changing Role of Words in Theatre: Mohan Rakesh," *Sangeet Natak*, Oct.-Dec. 1971: 26.
4. Hogie Wyckoff, "Sex Role Scripting in Men and Women," *Scripts People Live*, Claude M. Steiner (New York: Bantam, 1980), p. 196.
5. "Interviews," Mohan Rakesh, *Journal of South Asian Literature*, Vol. IX, Fall and Winter 1973, Nos. 2 & 3, p. 38.
6. Mohan Rakesh, *Halfway House*, Trans. Bindu Batra, *Enact*, May, 1971, p. 15.
7. Claude M. Steiner, *Scripts People Live*, p. 182.
8. N.C. Jain "Rakesh the Playwright," *Enact*, Jan.-Feb. 1973, p. 23.

The Female Husband and the Male Wife in *Halfway House*

SHYAM S. AGARWALLA

The article ranges over several seminal issues in the play: man-woman relationship, influence of western feminist ideas on Indian writers, including Rakesh, life of the middle-class in the metropolis, deconstruction of female-male archetypes. Agarwalla makes copious references to other literary works—both European and Indian—in a bid to put into perspective his arguments on Halfway House.

Editor

Mohan Rakesh's *Halfway House* (*Aadhe Adhure*) is an interesting play, raising more issues than solving them. In this paper, I am going to identify these issues, putting all of them in historical and contemporary periods. First of all, I would like to examine, however briefly, the institution of marriage in the past (not very remote) and the present and examine *Halfway House*. I begin with the assertion of McClintock who says that "Woman's relation to the nation [is] indirect, mediated through her social relation to men, her national identity lying in her unpaid services, through her husband and family, to the volk." This is not thereby to assert women's absence in nationalism's representations of itself. Anuradha Dingwaney Needham writes: "for nationalism is fuelled by a contradictory set of representations with respect to women: at the same time as their material realities and interests are ignored or considered irrelevant, the 'homeland' which is the nation is insistently figured as 'female,' body, violated by colonial occupation, waiting to be avenged, and thus redeemed by (potent) nationalist men."[2]

Hansa Mehta, in her Presidential address to the All India Women's Conference, Hyderabad, Sind, said:

> The more important thing, however, is the woman's position in relation to marriage . . . whether we call it a sacrament or a civil contract, marriage is a union between man and woman legalized by the State. And, therefore, as far as the State is concerned, it is a contract. . . . What is essential are the conditions under which two persons are allowed to unite in a holy wedlock. These conditions, so far as the Hindu Law and Mohammedan Law are concerned, are not very satisfactory and have made the social life of many a woman in this country a hell on earth.[3]

She goes on to define conditions safeguarding the interest of women who desire to marry. I shall quote only three of the five conditions.

1. That neither party must have a husband or wife living at the time of marriage.
2. That the consent of both the parties concerned shall be necessary before their marriage.
3. That either party can dissolve the marriage under certain conditions which will include cruelty, desertion, suffering from incurable disease and impotency. This requires no comment. Even the Hindu Law Reforms Committee has realized the need for this provision and has included it in the draft code.

Mahatma Gandhi was a great champion of the emancipation of the Indian women. On the unspeakable sin of child marriage, he said: "Having once committed the sin of marrying their daughters at very early age, the mothers cannot educate them, or otherwise make their dry life a cheerful one." And he added: "The man who marries a young girl does so not out of any altruistic motives but through sheer lust. Who is to rescue these girls?" Again he wrote in the *Young India* in 1921: "I detest child marriage. I shudder to see child widow and shiver with rage when a husband just widowed with brutal indifference contracts another marriage. I deplore the criminal indifference of parents who keep their daughters utterly ignorant and illiterate and bring them up only for the purpose of marrying them off to some young man of means."

In Mohan Rakesh's *Halfway House*, Savitri is the heroine. When the play opens, Rakesh shows her living in a hell with her husband, Mahendranath, for twenty-two years. The name Savitri automatically, in Hindu minds, connects it with the Savitri of mythology, who fought the Lord of Death to have the life of her husband restored. The marriage of Savitri with Satyavan was held in the old tradition of Vedic rituals. Toru Dutt (1856-77) had written a long poem "Savitri" and I quote only four lines:

> "Ah, whom dear wife, should we select?"
> "Leave it to God," she [her mother] answering cried,
> "Savitri may herself elect
> someday, her future lord and guide."[4]

Dutt's main anxiety is indeed to project Savitri as a *free* woman; "She has a boyish freedom to wander, to choose her friends, and even, under a Calvinistic God's personal guidance, the freedom to choose her own husband. This, the poem insists, was true of all Indian women in an uncorrupted past where there were no *zenanas* (secluded quarters for women). The effort, obviously, is to rebut the negative image the British projected, and redeem, if not the present, at least the past. But more important is the way the poet's imagination, her longings, her straining for freedom, the limits of what she sees as habitable space, and even its forms have been domesticated. In fact, what has been so efficiently controlled are the very terms in which freedom may be *imagined*, not just by the writer but also by the reader."[5]

Toru Dutt *imagined* a free woman in the traditional figure of *Savitri*, Rakesh turns her imagination into reality in *Halfway*

House. Well, Rakesh has the advantage of the passage of a whole century. Rakesh's Savitri is a free woman, before and after her marriage with Mahendranath. To wit:

The Fourth Man: Don't interrupt. . . . But it was obvious even then that you didn't consider Mahendra to be the man with whom you could spend your life.

The Fourth Man: But every other year you've tried to free yourself by looking around for another man! In the beginning I was one of these men. You say you respected me then. . . . After me, you were enamoured of Shivjeet . . . his university degree, his trips abroad, or whatever. In reality he interested you only because . . . he was not Mahendra . . . Then you met Jagmohan. You admired him for his excellent contacts, his smart way of life, his generosity. But the real reason was the same; no matter what he was, he was Jagmohan . . . not Mahendra . . .

The Fourth Man: The point is that if any of these men had been a part of your life instead of Mahendra, you would still have felt that you had married the wrong man. You would still have encountered a Mahendra, a Juneja, a Shivjeet or a Jagmohan and thought and reacted in the same way. Because the meaning of life to you is how many different things you can have and enjoy at the same time. One man alone could never have given them to you, so no matter whom you married, you would always have been as empty and restless as you are today.

Juneja tells Savitri about her flirtatious nature, in the presence of her elder daughter. For her, marriage is not a sacrament nor a contract, but a romantic wandering. Her romantic spree with Juneja, Jagmohan, Shivjeet reminds me of Kamala Das's fictional character Manasi. A married woman, she "rents out" her body to Raje initially in exchange for a pair of diamond earrings but soon determines that "for power I shall rent . . . out [my body] to the most influential tenant I can hope to get."[7] Her affair with Raje is followed by one with the Prime Minister, and it is through these adulterous liaisons that she makes remarkable advances in the political sphere. "While her association with Raje nets her a Padmashri, India's highest literary-cultural award, and enables her to run for electoral office in Bengal, it is her manipulation of the Prime Minister that bags for her the offices of Minister of Information and Broadcasting, then Home Minister, and finally the Prime Ministership itself. Through Manasi, therefore, Das subverts, on various levels, the high nationalist ideology that casts the Indian woman as the guardian of the spiritual (as distinguished from the material) realm, thereby imprisoning her doubly, as traditional and home-bound. "Ablaze with lust, simple, honest, human lust, Manasi is the antithesis of the chaste, Sita-like Brahminic feminine ideal which informed the Indian Independence struggle.[8]

Shirley Lim remarks that "Manasi's only corruption is in the area of the sexual,"[9] while her aggressive sexuality can, in fact, be regarded as dismantling orthodox gender hierarchies and thus as laudable. An one-time Naxalite sympathizer, Manasi discards her idealism utterly, abandons her husband and daughter, turns her mind only to the intricacies of decorating her future "palatial mansion." (147)

The impact of Western education, literature, and movement on Third World countries has been great. The literature of Simone de Beauvoir's *The Second Sex*, Rita's *A Husband of No Importance*, Ella Hepworth Dixon's *The Story of a Modern Woman*, and literature of a host of female writers have a shaping influence not only on male writers but also female writers, in India. R.K. Narayan acknowledges this, when writing his novel *The Dark Room*. Narayan's Savitri is a mild version of Rakesh's Savitri. R.L. Nigam says: "The institution of marriage has worked, so far, almost entirely to the advantage of man. It was, after all, something created by and in a Man's world. Man has had, if not in principle, certainly in practice all the freedoms that woman [wife] is claiming today. . . . There are men eminently successful, eminently prosperous, healthier and handsomer, more cultured, more talented, more magnetic than the man to whom she [Savitri] happens to be tied merely by custom and ceremony, or by signatures affixed to a piece of paper in a fit of romantic idealism. Soon, too soon, the realities of [married] life dawn, and the romantic idealism and mystic trance fade into the light of common day. She begins to rate her man not by *what he is*, but what *he is not*, and by what others are."[10]

Girish Rastogi remarks: "The nature of Savitri's relations with the other men also remains hazy. From her own words it appears that she forms these particular relationships to solve her financial problems, whereas from the words of Juneja, Mahendra and Ashok, it seems that her relations are sexual, illicit from the social point of view, intolerable from the family's. Undoubtedly Rakesh has left this issue in a state of ambiguity which leads to opposing pulls in the play, as also in Savitri's characters. It seems as if two parallel strains are running in Rakesh's mind—a woman's desires, dissatisfied and unfulfilled as she is by the man she has through marriage; and the attempt to solve the economic pattern."[11]

This analysis brings me to raise the issue of the New Woman. The New Woman is neither Sita nor Savitri, of tradition. I had argued by reading the texts of *The Dark Room*, *Gauri*, and *Inside the Haveli*, in my paper titled "Three Modern Versions of the Draupadi Myth: R.K. Narayan, Mulk Raj Anand and Rama Mehta" that "Their creators—Narayan, Anand and Mehta—are neither deep-rooted conservatives, like Saratchandra Chattopadhyaya, as to allow their creations to suffer till death nor are ultra-moderns, like Mukherjee [Bharati] or De [Shoba], as to allow their female creations to perform feats to create disharmony in the family, and then to disintegrate it."[12] Rakesh's heroine, Savitri, is not Draupadi, but, belongs to the category of the fictional characters of Shobha De or Bharati Mukherjee or Nina Sibal or Kamala Das or Namjoshi.

Namjoshi's protagonist, Jyanvi, in *The Mothers of Maya*,

mounts a critique of a heterosexist and progenerative ideology that underwrites the modern nation-state as a masculined domain. Setting up poetry-writing and motherhood as mutually exclusive activities. Jyanvi subverts the very core of the institution of marriage, even in a lesbian relationship as revealed in the poem "Song of a Non-Mother":

> I loved my love with passion.
> She said "Will you marry me?"
> I said "Is this the fashion?"
> She said "It is indeed."
> I cooked and cleaned and scoured.
> I worked myself to the above.
> Her little children devoured
> my labours every one
>
> They were clean and quick and sprightly.
> They scampered in the sun.
> "I must go," I said politely
> and left true love alone. (24)

If 'renting out' one's body to a male is one face of the New Woman in Kamala Das and Mohan Rakesh, then, lesbianism is another face of the New Woman in Namjoshi. In both the faces, it is the family, progenies, that suffer the most.

The disintegration in the family of Savitri and Mahendranath is partly due to the incompetence of the latter and the infidelity of the former. Mahendranath is a piggyback. He is humiliated and abused by Savitri for his failure in business. She has consigned him to the role of the male wife of the female husband. Their son, Ashok, is also modelled on his father by Rakesh. Like father, he "too disappears from home for three days at a time." (11) Mahendranath laments: "I'm responsible for ruining my life, your life, all our lives! And I still stick to this house, because I'm a parasite, because I like living off my wife." (27) Savitri, at the end of Act One, says: "From now on I'll only bother about myself. . . . You look after your own lives. (*Silence*) I don't have many years to live now. But however few they be, I'll no longer spend them like this. I have done my utmost." (43) This last sentence draws Savitri into a circle of the oppressed women, the subalterns, in the words of Gayatri Chakravorty Spivak. But this placing is temporary. Juneja tears off her veil of a victim and exposes her as an oppressor. He says: "You've made him believe that, despite the circumstances, he has no other way of life open to him, no other solution, except to remain with him. And haven't you done everything to ensure that, if nothing else, you should at least be able to hold this wretched pawn in your hand?" (77)

This perpetual indifference of Savitri towards her husband and her son and younger daughter is a story of many 'homes' in cosmopolitan and urban environment. The importation of the concept of the New Woman from the Western civilization to the Indian civilization, dating back to the early years of the twentieth century, finally flooded the literatures of the cosmopolitan centres in India. A rapid survey of this imported product is necessary to understand Savitri.

With the emergence of feminist consciousness in nineteenth-century Europe, the questioning of the very separation of the spheres began. "Ibsen's *Doll's House* (1879)," says Rajeswari Sunder Rajan, "which ends with the female protagonist's exit from the 'doll's house' that represents femininity, the home, the family, the 'private' enclosure, became the most forceful expression of the repudiation of separate spheres. In the colonized countries of Asia, where the women's question was beginning to be articulated in close connection with the issue of liberation and nationalism. . . . Nora's rebellion against male oppression became a symbol of freedom from foreign oppression. . . . The freedom of western women became an inspiration to the colonial bourgeois male intent on fashioning the 'New Woman' for an emergent free nation."[14]

In Charlotte Bronte's *Jane Eyre*, the proper place of the woman is the home. The opening chapter of the novel is a scene of the marginalization and privation of the protagonist: "there was no possibility of taking a walk that day. . . . Out-door exercise was now out of the question. . . . I was glad of it."[15] Gayatri Chakravorty writes:

> let us consider the suggestion, the progress of Jane Eyre can be charted through a sequential arrangement of the family/counter family dyad. In the novel, we encounter first, the Reeds as the legal family and Jane, the late Reed's sister's daughter, as the representative of a near incestuous counter family; second, the Brocklehursts, who run the school to which Jane is sent, as the legal family and Jane, Miss Temple, and Helen Burns as a counter family that falls short because it is only a community of women, third, Rochester and the mad Mrs. Rochester as the legal family and Jane and Rochester as the illicit counter-family . . . It is during this sequence that Jane is moved from the counter-family to the family-in-law. In the next sequence, it is Jane who restores full family status to the as-yet-incomplete community of siblings, the Riverses. The final sequence of the book is a *community of families*, with Jane, Rochester, and their children at the centre.[16]

The sequence in *Halfway House*, from the very beginning, is from integration to disintegration; from harmony to disharmony; from family to units; from love to greed; from the 'legal family' to the adulterous counter-family.

I look for modernist discourse of feminism elsewhere. *Punch* satirizes the New Woman thus: "There is a New Woman, and what do you think? She lives upon nothing but Foolscap and ink!" (April 28, 1894) The New Women were reading Tolstoy, Mona Caird and Ibsen. A popular image of the period was "Donna Quixote." Freud's Dora, in a famous dream after her father's funeral "went calmly to her room and began reading in a big book that lay on her writing-table." Freud interprets the big book as an encyclopaedia of sexual information, and comments: "If her father was dead she could read or love as she pleased." To read and to love as one pleased mingled in the New Woman's programme. Mahendranath, though physically alive, is non-existent as *paterfamilias*. Savitri describes him aptly: "Ever since I've known him, I've always found him leaning on some-one or other . . . when he wanted to marry me, he had to ask you [Juneja]. He can't breathe without asking you!" (68) Provoked further by Juneja, she says more: "Why does one get married? In order to fulfil a need . . . an inner . . . void, if you like; to be self-sufficient . . . complete. But that's not why Mahendra got married! The object of his existence is . . . as if . . . he were there only to fill in the gaps in the lives of others." (62) The older daughter elopes with Manoj and marries him. He was her mother's friend. She occasionally returns to her mother to "try and find out what there is in this house for which I am constantly being humiliated." The younger daughter, Kinni, completely lacking love and care, has become insolent and uncontrollable. Like Freud's Dora, the elder daughter is also the New Woman in this play. Like Savitri, Kinni is the New Woman in the making.

The New Women of the 1890s acknowledged the disappointments and dangers of their vision, but they refused to turn back the clock. As Oliver Schreiner wrote in her parable *Life's Gifts*, her generation had to choose freedom rather than love, but the day would come when women would have both. The generation of Rakesh's fictional women characters chooses freedom, rather than love. Savitri chooses a life of her own, In all of them, there is no love. Only cravings for freedom. The elder daughter explains the nuance of freedom: "That the longer two people live together, breathe the same air, . . . the . . . the more estranged they become from one another." (17) Or, "He speaks with such assurance that . . . that I start . . . I start despising myself. I feel like . . . like smashing everything around me. Like defying him in a way that would." (12)

Feminist radicals and dreamers of the 1890s faced personal conflicts as well. Their theory of the free sexual union—a man and a woman living together in mutual love without legal contract as long as they wished to do so—usually led to tragedy when put into practice. Indeed many *fin-de-siecle* feminist intellectuals came to see themselves as a transitional generation, which had to sacrifice love or motherhood in the interest of women's future freedom.[17] This aspiration for social, economic, and political freedom, for the emancipation of women, demanded sacrifice of love and motherhood. On the other hand, great Indians, like Bankimchandra Chatterjee, Dayanand Saraswati, and Gandhiji demanded no such sacrifice. But, Indian women writers and intellectuals have chosen to cast their lot with the Western radical theorists. Kamala Das, Suniti Namjoshi, Nina Sibal, and Bapsi Sidhwa (Pakistani Parsi), Shobha De, Amrita Pritam, Ismat Chughtai, and Namita Gokhale are some examples. The modernist discourse of feminism still beguiles Mohan Rakesh's imagination, which needs overhauling of decolonization.

Of all the male characters, two are interesting—Juneja and Mahendranath. Mahendranath had partnership with Juneja but Savitri accuses Juneja of depriving him of partnership. In the beginning of the play, Juneja was shown to be a money-minded, self-centred and evil man. In the Second Act, he turns out to be outspoken, straightforward, assertive, kind, genial, accommodative. His concern for his friend Mahendranath has compelled him to come to Savitri. He tells Binni that Mahendranath "never slept a wink last light." (62) But his love for Mahendranath does not deter him from blaming him for marital discord: "Mahendranath himself is responsible." (62) Again he says: "I know . . . that is why I think Mahendranath himself is responsible for what happened to him—were it not so, he wouldn't have been begging me since morning to find some way of talking to her." (64) He plays the role of an impartial mediator.

He confronts Savitri with vehemence, determination, and intelligently, as if he were a one-man-demolition-squad out to demolish her larger-than-martyr-image. He says to Savitri: "And I say that you have him [Mahendranath] in a trap . . . he has become incapable of doing anything for himself." (67) Again, he says to Savitri: "What you have said is not wrong . . . but . . . it's not what you have discovered over the twenty-two years you've been with him. About twenty years ago, I heard these very things from your lips . . . do you remember?" (71) When Savitri asks him, "What do you . . . ," he replies: "What you wanted from me at the time, I'm not quite sure. But it was obvious even then that you didn't consider Mahendranath to be the man with whom you could spend your life." (73) He goes on to tell her about her flirtation with Jagmohan, Shivjeet and himself. At the same time, he admits that Mahendranath is not without his share of faults, and neglect of familial obligations. He is tardy. "He has only one defect . . . he is the same as every man." (71) "Mahendranath was always a bit hasty, I know." (69) He gives Savitri a good talking-to.

Mahendranath is not "a stupendous nincompoop."[18] He is not a puppet, as Juneja rightly assesses him. Savitri says that he cannot stand on his own feet. She accuses Mahendranath of this defect in his person:

> His friends need him to pass their leisure hours. No party is right without Mahendra. No picnic is fun without Mahendra. His main job is to keep his friends happy. . . . The same Mahendra who smiles meekly among his friends, becomes a fiend when he comes home. . . . I want. . . . I want a man, not just a miserable . . . hanger-on! Sometimes I try to wrench my tortured being away from him. There was even a time when I tried to turn him into a man. (71)

Again Savitri accuses him of leaning on his friends:

> Ever since I've known him, I've always found him leaning on someone or other. Particularly on you. He's never been able to do anything, he must ask you. If we went to buy something, he must ask you. When he wanted to marry me, he had to ask you. He can't even breathe without asking you! (68)

Mahendranath, like Panchi of Mulk Raj Anand's *Gauri*, is torn between love and strife. At the severe provocation from Savitri, he leaves his 'home' in a huff. But he cannot live without his wife, his children, for a long time. He sends Juneja to Savitri to strike the right chord in the heart of Savitri. Panchi's utterance finds echo in the heart of Mahendranath. Binni tells

Juneja: "Daddy rages when he tore Mama's clothes to shreds . . . when he gagged her and beat her up behind closed doors . . . dragging her by the hair to the WC." (64) At the end of the play, he comes back to Savitri, haggard, weary, tired, bitten by the love of Savitri. His homesickness arises out of this love for his family, for his wife. Similarly, Panchi burns in desire for Gauri: "I fretted and fretted. . . . I bent my head against a wall one day in despair. . . . Now I can breathe. . . . But first let me hug you . . . Come, come to me, Gauri. . . . I want you."

The loss in business has paralyzed the will-power and guts of Mahendranath. The first half of the First Act nowhere shows him to be a fool. He says to Savitri: "Am I not grateful? Every time a different man starts coming here, I'm always grateful! First there was Jagmohan, then Manoj." (12) Or, "Why do you always try to sweep things under the carpet? Why not ask her a few straight questions?" (13) The discerning mind of Mahendranath knows as to why Binni has come back home. His liberation has not closed his eyes to the hideous infidelity of his wife. Both of them have, in their own ways, made 'home' unlivable. Savitri's burden is undoubtedly great. She has to maintain a family of five. Her irascibility and ironical comments on her husband are understandable. But, her ire against Mahendranath is torrential; Mahendranath's anger against her is a hiccup. One common characteristic of Mahendranath and Savitri is their habit of riding on a piggyback, be it Juneja for Mahendranath or Juneja or Jagmohan for Savitri.

Such incompatible marriages often thwart the ambitions of couples, individually or jointly. Savitri's loneliness is the loneliness of a woman, a wife and a mother—a loneliness conditioned by family and society. Anita Desai's novel, *Where Shall We Go This Summer?* (1975) bears some resemblances to *Halfway House.* Darshan Singh Maini Says: "Whereas the childless Maya's *angst* is existential and metaphysical, Sita's ache is essentially domestic and temporal, though there are moments of pure terror and void even in her life giving her state an existential dimension."[19] Savitri, like Sita of Desai, a desperate woman unable to control her hysteria, plans to panic out of the house in a whirlwind of confused emotions. With another wishy-washy husband, an over-petulant son and a recalcitrant daughter, another married daughter, always coming and going, Savitri accommodated the pent-up misery of her isolation and loneliness, but at the end of the First Act she decides: "From now on I'll only bother about myself. . . . I don't have many years to live now. But however few they be, I'll no longer spend like this. I have done my utmost. It's the end now as far as I'm concerned . . . it really is the end." (43) Is this the end of Savitri's relation with his family? No. Like Cavafy's poem in Desai's novel, she must say "the right No," even though it "crush" her for the rest of her life! Sita concluded her view of life thus: "All was bright . . . Life had no periods, no stretches. It simply swirled around muddling and confusing leading nowhere."[20] The marital discord of Savitri with Mahendranath, after swirling, muddling, confusing, leads nowhere, not to any Utopia.

Halfway House is the story of modern civilization, of metropolis, In the words of Matthew Arnold, this world, "with its sick hurry, its divided aims," is far from days "when wits were fresh and clear, /And life ran gaily as the sparkling Thames." Arnold, like a modern poet, laments:

> Ah, love, let us be true
> to one another! for the world, which seems
> To lie before us like a land of dreams.
> So various, so beautiful, so new,
> Hath really neither joy, nor love, nor light,
> Nor certitude, nor peace, nor help for pain,
> and we are here as on a darkling plain
> Swept with confused alarm of struggle and flight,
> Where ignorant armies clash by night. ("Dover Beach")

T.S. Eliot writes in *The Waste Land* about metropolis civilization:

> What are the roots that clutch, what branches grow
> Out of this stony rubbish? . . .
> I will show you fear in a handful of dust

Mohan Rakesh writes about the lower middle-class society living in a metropolis. Savitri, Mahendranath, Binni, Kinni, and Ashok are the representatives of millions of people living in a metropolis, like Delhi, Calcutta, Mumbai, and Chennai. There is no sparkling Jamuna in Delhi. Wits are jaded and dirty. Life is monotonous, burdensome, fearful, and dull. People have divided aims and sick hurry. Beneath the veneer of civilization, there is rootlessness, void, vacancy, and rubbish. No joy, no love, no light, no certitude, no peace. A metropolis in India is a "darkling plain." Rakesh has portrayed faithfully and skilfully the life of the metropolis—particularly those living in Delhi—the life of a lower middle-class family. The claustrophobic existence of Savitri and Mahendranath in Delhi is the reality, as brutal and convincing as that of Arnold and Eliot. Savitri, Mahendranath and their children are condemned to live under one roof, out of necessity, not out of choice. Here Jagmohan and Shivjeet are parasites, exhibitors of ignorant knowledge and black money. They are selfish, blood-suckers and vulgar. Of course, Juneja is an exception. But, he also takes the soul of Mahendranath as a mortgage, as Singhania and Jagmohan take Savitri's. In a metropolis, for an ambitious person life is like that of a peasant in Premchand's novels, or, that of a bonded labourer, who is always a mortgager of his soul to a mortgagee. The powerful expression of this hapless condition of these people is the highest achievement of Mohan Rakesh.

Halfway House is a play about the subalterns. First of all, the play attempts to set right a perspective that male archetypes have strengthened over time. The asymmetrical man-woman relationship that is so obviously privileged towards men has been deconstructed. The play is a "female space" which represents her desire to be understood, to be harmonized, to be able to withstand the various elements that threaten her existence. It also represents her rebellion against the cramped confines of patriarchal space from which she wants to find her way out. Only the method is wrong in the case of Savitri. Instead of becoming Manasi of Kamala Das, she should have become Draupadi or Gauri of Anand or Sita of Desai. She could have reformed Mahendranath instead of throwing her hands up. Or, she could have walked out of her 'home' and become a social worker like Gauri. For a lower middle-class family the former course is the safest one. Rakesh leaves this option unused at the end of his play, like many unanswered questions. For example, why did Savitri laugh hysterically while confronting Juneja? These unused options and unanswered questions along with several answered ones weave a rich fabric for the play which becomes interesting, absorbing and even unsettling.

NOTES

1. Anne McClintock, "'No Longer in a Future Heaven': Women and Nationalism in South Africa," *Transition*, 51, 1991, p. 107.
2. Anuradha Dingwaney Needham, "Multiple Forms of (National) Belonging: Attia Hosain's *Sunlight on a Broken Column*," *Modern Fiction Studies*, Vol. 39, No. 1, Winter 93, pp. 96-97.
3. Hansa Mehta, *Indian Woman* (Delhi: Butala, 1981), p. 12.
4. Toru Dutt, *Ancient Ballads and Poems of Hindustan* (Allahabad: Kitabistan, 1941), p. 37.
5. Susie Tharu, "Tracing Savitri's Pedigree: Victorian Racism and the Image of Women in Indo-Anglian Literature," in *Recasting Women*: Essays in Colonial History (1989; New Delhi: Kali for Women, 1997), p. 260.
6. Mohan Rakesh, *Halfway House* (*Aadhe Adhure*), trans. Bindu Batra (New Delhi: Worldview, 1999), pp. 73-74.
7. Kamala Das, *Alphabet of Lust* (New Delhi: Orient, 1976), p. 41.
8. Harveen Sachdeva Mann, "'Cracking India': Minority Women Writers and the Contentious Margins of Indian Nationalist Discourse," *The Journal of Commonwealth Literature*, Vol. XXIX, No. 2, 1994, pp. 81-82.
9. Shirley Geokohin Lim, "Semiotics, Experience and Material Self," *Women's Studies*, 18, 1990, p. 155.
10. R.L. Nigam, "*Aadhe Adhure*: A Comment," in Dilip K. Basu, p. 87.
11. Girish Rastogi, "Mohan Rakesh and His Plays," in Dilip K. Basu, p. 112.

12. Shyam S. Agarwalla, "Three Modern Versions of the Draupadi Myth: R.K. Narayan, Mulk Raj Anand and Rama Mehta" in *Feminism and Literature*, ed. Veena Noble Dass (New Delhi: Prestige, 1999), p. 217.
13. Suniti Namjoshi, *The Mothers of Maya Dip* (London: Women's Press, 1989), p. 6.
14. Rajeswari Sunder Rajan, "The Feminist Plot and the Nationalist Allegory: Home and World in Two Indian Women's Novels in English," *Modern Fiction Studies*, Vol. 39, No. 1, Winter 1993, p. 72.
15. Charlotte Bronte, *Jane Eyre* (New York), p. 9.
16. Gayatri Chakravorty Spivak, *A Critique of Postcolonial Reason*, p. 120.
17. Elaine Showalter, "Utopia Comes Alive," *New Statesman*, 13 December 1996, p. 26.
18. R.L. Nigam, "*Aadhe Adhure*: A Comment" in Dilip K. Basu, p. 83.
19. Darshan Singh Maini, "The Achievement of Anita Desai," in *Indo-English Literature*, ed. K.K. Sharma (Ghaziabad: Vimal, 1977), p. 227.
20. Anita Desai, *Where Shall We Go This Summer?* (Delhi: Vikas, 1975), pp. 37-38.

Disintegration of the Family in *Halfway House*

BASAVARAJ NAIKAR

The disjunction between Prologue's claim of interchangeability of roles between himself and the woman and the portrayal of the trapped and even wronged woman is the result of the ambiguity in Rakesh's own thinking: he wished to empathize with Savitri and, therefore, focussed on her positioning and her problems and yet a part of his psyche (conditioned by some of his own personal experiences) castigated woman. We have Juneja's very convincing, lawyer-like, forceful arguments against Savitri.

Editor

Although modern Indian drama is quite rich in various Indian languages, unfortunately very little of it is available in English translation. It is high time for Indian scholars and publishers to turn their attention to the translation of regional drama into English for giving it a pan-Indian and even international recognition which it rightly deserves. Mohan Rakesh, who has been one of the leading figures of the Hindi drama, has tried to hold a mirror to the contemporary society of India in many of his plays. *Halfway House* (1999) offers a microscopic picture of the decadence of a middle-class family in a metropolis and shows the transition of values in the changing society of India. Many critics have rightly pointed out the influence of Shaw and the Absurd dramatists on Mohan Rakesh, though it is neither advisable nor possible to quantify the influence. Yet it should be remembered that Mohan Rakesh was so deeply rooted in the Indian soil that the influence of foreign playwrights could have been only peripheral.

It is true that the changing values of life in the Indian society have created many existential problems for man. But there is a conspicuous difference between the European existentialism and the so-called Indian existentialism. The European existentialist predicament was the result of a metaphysical angst caused by the loss of faith in God. The death of God certified by Frederick Nietzsche had created a metaphysical vacuum in Europe in the first part of the twentieth century. But this kind of metaphysical vacuum is not possible in India which is a land of many religions and philosophies. The existential dilemmas of Indians are mostly social, economic and moral rather than metaphysical. Therefore, the absurdity of the European kind cannot be expected in the Indian life.

Halfway House may be described as an existential play in the Indian context. It offers a picture of the decadence of a bourgeois family in a metropolis of the twentieth century India. It shows the disintegration of the institution of marriage and family and hints at the various factors contributing to the negative process. The extended metaphor of the house is built up all through the play. Generally speaking, a house is a place where the blood relatives live together peacefully, homogeneously and harmoniously.

An ideal home consists of economic security, matrimonial harmony and understanding and the unity among the members of the family—contributing to the general peace and happiness of life.

Right from the beginning to the end of the play, the picture of the house projected by the dramatist is a negative one. As we proceed with the reading or watching of the play, various aspects of reality begin to show up. The entry of the woman into the house after her return from the office sets the negative tone of the play. Obviously, she returns tired after a day's long work in the office and easily feels irritated to find that the house is not kept clean and tidy: "Whenever I come back, the house is in a mess." (7) The initial dialogues of the first scene itself reveal the difference in the nature of the house. Far from being a patriarchal family, it strikes us as a matriarchal family, the chief reason for which is the economic one. Instead of the man or husband being a breadwinner, there is a woman or wife in the present family who is the breadwinner. The man or husband being a non-earning member is reduced to a helpless position and is insulted and taken for granted by all the members of the family. Thus, the traditional roles of the father and the mother are reversed here and, therefore, the 'power' of the house is shifted from the father to the mother, thereby converting the family from the patriarchal to the matriarchal system at least partially. That is the reason why the husband is of no count for the wife. The wife, because of the power of being the breadwinner, asserts herself in the routine matters of domestic life.

She is unhappy with her husband for not having been practical in his business partnership in the past. She complains that he was made to invest some money in a company with his partner Juneja but ultimately put to great loss though Juneja had his usual profit. Mohan Rakesh indirectly shows the evils of modern business partnerships, uncertainties of profit and the risk involved in the whole system. In a way, Mahendra easily brings to our mind Willy Loman of Arthur Miller's *Death of a Salesman*. Like Loman, Mahendra is a failure in life and undergoes an experience of metaphorical death. That is the reason why he complains that nobody cares for him or respects him in the house and that he is used as a 'mere stamp of respectability.' He says sadly as well as angrily, "I am of no use, of no use at all. I'm only an idler . . . to be kicked and bullied just as you please. Can anyone tell me why I should stay here?" (26) Thus being an economic non-entity in the family makes him suffer from a feeling of estrangement. "I am responsible for ruining my life, your life, all our lives! And I still stick to this house, because I'm a parasite, because I like living off my wife." (27) He suffers from a sense of constant humiliation in the family. One may easily notice the irony involved in his name. 'Mahendra' which means the Great Lord Indra, the mythical god known for wealth, luxury and glory provides a sharp contrast to Mahendra who is known for his utter poverty, humiliation and helplessness.

Poverty dogs the family in many details. For example, the younger girl complains that she has no money to spend on her tiffin, "If I am hungry in school, I've no money to buy anything. And at home it takes hours to heat the milk." (20) Likewise she complains that she does not want to be insulted by her teacher for not taking the skeins of thread to the school, "The same thing happened once again in the needle-work class. Miss said . . . If you don't get me the skeins of thread today either, I won't go to school any more. Miss told me in front of the whole class." (21) The younger girl is thus unhappy with her mother for not providing the necessary comforts and amenities of life. The unhappiness of the girl is, obviously because of the overall poverty of the family. The boy quit the college halfway and got a job with Air Freeze Company. But he left his job within six weeks. Now he has been leading a jobless life like his father and is a burden on the family. He buys a tin of cheese mainly because he could buy it on credit and even makes a phone call on credit. Thus, the economic burden of the family is aggravated by the joblessness of two men in the house. That explains why the mother feels the pinch very acutely. "The burden of this house is so great that I need someone to share it with me. I can't manage it alone. Your father lost all our money, and has been idle ever since." (41) It is in order to lighten the economic burden that she invites her boss Singhania to her house and requests him to help her son to get a suitable job. Thus, the entire family is paralyzed by the economic deficiency and consequently converted into a metaphorical 'hell.'

The economic factor has indirectly given rise to other problems in the family. Unlike the traditional housewife who is confined to her home and is obedient to her husband, Savitri is educated as well as employed. The position of a working woman has given her the right to assert herself. Being a new woman and a city-bird, she wants to have sexual freedom not enjoyed by the traditional Hindu wife. Although she invites her boss Singhania to her house under the pretext of requesting him for a job for her son, her behaviour is not approved by her husband or by her son. The boy does not want to get a job through the mother's boss, "I don't want a job. Not through that fellow anyway." (28) He dislikes Singhania for various reasons. Among the mentionable reasons two can be seen. The boy dislikes him because "he doesn't even have the sense to button up his trousers after . . . If he hadn't been your boss, I would have booted him out that day. Lolling on the sofa and scratching himself in the groin! His thoughts stray in one direction, his eyes in another, and I'm supposed to guess that he's addressing me." (29)

Like a modern liberated woman, Savitri does not believe in the sanctity of chastity. Her sexual promiscuity is combined with her ambition. She is deeply interested in material comforts, status, position and wealth. That is the reason why she has had four lovers in the past. She always felt a great temperamental incompatibility with her husband and therefore sought the company of other men like Juneja, Shivjeet, Manoj and finally Jagmohan. Juneja narrates the history of Savitri's extra-marital life very clearly: "it was obvious even then that you didn't consider Mahendra to be the man with whom you could spend your life . . . every year you've tried to free yourself by looking around for another man! In the beginning I was one of these men. . . . After me, you were enamoured of Shivjeet . . . his university degree, his trips abroad, or whatever. In reality he interested you only because . . . he was not Mahendra. . . . Then you met Jagmohan, you admired him for his excellent contacts, his smart way of life, his generosity." (73) But in spite of having these love affairs, Savitri was never happy with anyone of them nor did she stick to any one of them. Savitri was indeed shocked when her own lover Manoj married her daughter Binni. Her affair with different men is strongly resented by Mahendra and her son. So far she has not shown the courage to elope with anyone of her lovers. But now that Jagmohan, her last lover, has come back to Delhi, she wants to go away with him for good. The son who is fed up with her oscillation between marital and extra-marital loyalties, wants it to be decided once for all, "High time the situation changed! . . . I want the whole business to be decided one way or the other." (45-46) But the problem is not to be solved so easily, because of the complex nature of life itself. When Savitri goes out with Jagmohan and desperately requests him to accept her as a life-partner, he refuses to do so. Thus, her route of escape from the matrimonial hell is mercilessly blocked by her fate. She is condemned to continue her life in the matrimonial hell much against her wishes. The frustration is caused by the sense of incomplete contrast to the mythical Savitri who wanted to save her husband from the clutches of death. Unlike the mythical figure, Savitri constantly quarrels with and complains against her husband.

Whereas Savitri has suffered for not taking a drastic step in her extra-marital affairs, her older daughter Binni has been suffering for taking a very drastic step in eloping with Manoj, the lover of her own mother, thereby aggravating the suffering of the mother. In spite of her marrying a man of her choice, she has not been able to live happily with him. Unable to live with him any longer, she has returned to the parental home, thereby adding to the anxiety and liability of the family. Thus, both the mother and the older daughter provide two extremes of sexuality but share in the suffering qualitatively.

Sexual curiosity or obsession seems to be an important ingredient in the make-up of the young people in the family, perhaps because of the wrong role models provided by the mother and the older daughter. This aspect of the family holds a mirror to the slackening of Hindu morality in the changing urban society of India. If the elders indulge in sexuality openly, the younger ones do so secretly or vicariously. For example, Kinni reads the *Memoirs of Casanova* on the sly by stealing it from her elder brother. Likewise, she is interested in discussing with her friends the sex-life of others's parents. Similarly, the son has been courting a girl called Varna, working at the Udyog Centre.

Besides the economic and sexual problems, the temperamental differences among the members of the family also aggravate the unhappiness of the family. Savitri, for example, is a very ambitious woman who wants her husband to be strong in mind and body, successful in his business, earn a lot of money for the family and be a glamorous person. She, therefore, complains that Mahendra has no personality or strength of character or self-confidence. She explains it to Juneja, "Let me tell you about the reality I know. Why does one get married? In order to fulfil a need, . . . an inner . . . void, if you like; to be self-sufficient . . . complete. But that's not why Mahendra got married! The object of his existence is . . . as if . . . he were there only to fill in the gaps in the lives of others." (69) But when she is disappointed with him, she tries to seek those things in her lovers. But even there, she has not been able to have lasting relationship because of the uncertainties and contingencies of middle-class life. She has a bit of Lady Macbeth's ambition in her, but like a Lawrentian heroine, she goes on searching for perfect matrimonial happiness, but gets frustrated at every step. She is not able to solve the problems of her life because of her ambition and desire for pomp and glory and by refusing to accept the contingencies of life with a sense of yogic resignation. Far from accepting her fate and making the best of the reality of her life, she pines for what is not. When she cannot escape from the bondage of matrimony and family, she suffers from a sense of being trapped in it. The Hindu philosophy teaches the great lesson that when the objective world cannot be changed, one has to make one's own life meaningful only through subjective change and sublimation of feelings. Savitri is obviously incapable of such adjustment of life, because of her complaining temperament. The objects of her complaint may change, but the complaints remain. It is the negative approach of Savitri which is pointed out by Juneja, "Whether you were a child or not, you used to speak in the same way you do now. That day you pulled Mahendra to bits . . . you said he was a wimp, had no backbone. . . . But the names of the people who had made him so were different then. You put the blame on his parents." (72) Juneja further analyses her mind very clearly, "The point is that if any of these men had been a part of your life instead of Mahendra, you would still have felt that you had married the wrong man. You would still have encountered a Mahendra, a Juneja, a Shivjeet or a Jagmohan and thought and reacted in the same way. Because the meaning of life to you is how many different things you can have and enjoy at the same time. One man alone could never have given them to you, so no matter whom you married, you would always have felt as empty and as restless as you do today." (74) Savitri's search for completeness or overambitiousness is comic as well as tragic at the same time. She feels angry and helpless at the same time and has no courage either to have sublimated reconciliation with her fate or to snap her relationship with the family. She, therefore, remains an embodiment of frustration.

The same temperamental hauteur can be seen in her older daughter Binni also. But there is a slight difference between their modes of action. Whereas Savitri has a Halketizing tendency, Binni has a Macbethizing tendency. Binni has been bolder than her mother in taking quick and hasty decisions and suffers as a consequence. After having married Manoj, lover of her mother, she has come back to her parents as she could not get on well with her husband due to temperamental incompatibility and Catherine-like defiance. As she herself explains it, "He speaks with such assurance that . . . that I start . . . I start despising myself. I feel like . . . like smashing everything around me. Like defying him in a way that would . . . enrage him. He likes my hair long, so I want it cut. He doesn't like me to work, so I want to have a job. Anything to torment him! But I can't do it. And when I realize this, I feel so crushed that . . . I cut myself off from him for days on end." (19) But in spite of being bolder than her mother, Binni suffers from the feeling of being trapped in the mechanical repetition of the pattern of frustration. "But then, slowly, we start treading the same weary path. Everything happens in the same way . . . until we reach the same abyss once again." (19) Binni, like her mother, is trapped in the emotional hell of the family. The cause of Binni's frustration and estrangement is to be sought in the subjective world rather than in the objective world. "What reason? A cup of tea spilt from his hand or a short delay when he returns from work? These little things are not really reasons; they become reasons. A strange sort of feeling mounts up within me and spreads like poison through my whole being. Everything I touch or see or hear becomes distorted and I stand helpless and fearful under the spell of a destructive fate. But Mama, I don't know why . . . I just can't see why! It happens unasked, unforeseen. It . . . it . . . tortures me till I think I'm going mad. And in the end? In the end he too turns against me and says . . . that . . . it is from the house I have taken something with me which prevents me from being natural." (17-18) Binni, like her mother, puts the blame on the house or on others in the moments of anger. But the cause of their anguish is rooted in themselves, in their temperament although they are not able to understand it.

Like the older girl, the younger girl is also adamant and defiant in nature and, therefore, adds to the irritability of the domestic atmosphere. Kinni is very cheeky and argues with elders disrespectfully. She complains about her loneliness in the house after her return from school when nobody is there to talk with her. When her mother asks her as to why she tore the book, she answers disrespectfully, "It got torn. What can I do? The same thing happened again in the needle-work class." (21) When the mother suggests that they can talk about it later on, she retorts, "You're always telling me to talk later on." (21) When the mother talks disdainfully about her and her Miss, she snaps, "Then why don't you take me out of school? I could also loaf around all day like Shoki." (21) Instead of addressing her elder brother as Ashok, she calls him Shoki. That is the reason why the older girl complains about her, "Mama, you really have turned her into a cheeky little brat!" (21) She refuses to go to school on some pretext or the other and reports the secrets of Ashok to the parents. Also, she has a habit of scandal-mongering and discussing sexual matters with her friends like Surekha, thereby earning the wrath of their parents. She starts crying when people do not oblige her. When somebody calls her a child affectionately, she retorts, "Yes . . . I'm a big girl. Some times I'm told I am a child . . . sometimes a big girl." (61) She calls her older sister and other members of the family "lumps of clay" and exhibits her mannerlessness and hysterical behaviour. She is, therefore, slapped by the mother and locked in a room. But she also bolts the door from inside to rebel against the mother. Kinni is thus a typical representative of adamant and cheeky girls who are uncontrollable and who aggravate the tension in the family and make the domestic hell more intolerable than it normally is.

Mahendranath also suffers partially due to his peculiar temperament. Though once upon a time he was a successful business partner, now he has fallen on bad days due to the cut-throat competition in the commercial world. The present state of poverty has reduced him to the level of a non-entity and affected his mind and heart adversely. He feels hurt to notice that he commands no respect from anybody in the family, especially from his wife who questions his very manhood. "For how many years have I been bearing the burden of life? And for how many years have I been looking after this family? And despite that, what have I come to . . . that everyone answers me back, is rude, disrespectful, impertinent . . . what is my status in this house? Silent acceptance, perpetual snubs, constant insults, is that all I deserve after so many years?" (25-26) He is unhappy to know that he is regarded "only as a stamp of respectability, to be used when the need arises." (26) It is true that poverty has reduced him to a non-entity, but he has no strength of character to face the situation boldly. He suffers from inferiority-complex, self-pity and self-accusation, "I am of no use, of no use at all. I'm only an idler . . . to be kicked and bullied just as you please. Can anyone tell me why I should stay here? . . . I'm responsible for ruining my life, your life, all our lives! And I still stick to this house, because I'm a parasite, because I like living off my wife, because . . . I know I'm like dry rot in this house, eating away at its very foundations." (26-27)

Mahendranath is a failure as a husband not only because he is not the breadwinner now, but also because of his psychological dependence on others. He is incapable of taking independent decisions about life and seeks help and guidance from others. Savitri complains, "Ever since I've known, I've always found him leaning on someone or other. Particularly on you. He's ever been able to do anything without asking you. If we want to buy something, he must ask you. If we want to go somewhere, he must ask you. When he wanted to marry me, he had to ask you. He can't even breathe without asking you. . . . And what has been the result? That he's never had any confidence in himself. The test for everything in life has been you. Whatever you think, want, do, he too must think, want and do. Why? Because you are a man. And he? He's not even half a man!" (68-69) Mahendranath seems to have neglected his own family in his eagerness to make his friends happy. This is indeed a very grave deficiency in any householder. Savitri is right when she complains about it to Juneja, "His friends need him to pass their leisure hours. No party is fun without Mahendra. His main job is to keep his friends happy. And not only is it *his* main job, but it should also be the only concern of his family." (70)

Although Mahendranath is a meek husband now, he had been dominating and cruel to his wife in the past. Savitri sees a contradiction in his public amiable behaviour and his private cruel behaviour. She complains, "That same Mahendra who smiles meekly among his friends, becomes a fiend when he comes home. One never knows when he may scratch one's eyes out or drink one's life-blood! One day he makes a bonfire of his clothes in anger. Another day he sits on my chest and bangs my head against the floor." (71) It is on account of his extremes and contradictions that he is disdained by his wife.

Another feature of his personality is his helplessness in dealing with the wife's extra-marital affairs. Although like any self-respecting husband, he dislikes his wife's lovers, he does not have the courage to oppose them openly or the generosity to ignore them. On the contrary, he talks only ironically about them and indulges in self-pity. He has neither the patience to stay with the family nor the courage to go away from there. When he goes away from the house in a fit of anger and stays with Juneja, he comes back again to his house because he says he loves his wife in spite of the temperamental clashes. Because of his eccentricities, he creates a psychological hell for himself as well as for others.

Mahendra's son is an extension of his personality. The son, like his father, has been a failure in his education and job. He is not serious about anything in life. He has no clearly defined goal or desire for any achievement. As his mother complains against him, he is "only interested in three things . . . in sleeping all day, in cutting out those pictures and . . . taking out things from home." (30) Otherwise he will loaf around in the city or chase a girl or read pornographic books. Although his mother seriously tries to help him by getting him a job through the influence of her boss, he does not understand her motherly concern for him. On the contrary, he puts embarrassing questions to his mother about the boss. He does not want to get a job through the influence of Singhania. Further, he draws a cartoon of Singhania and makes fun of him after the latter's departure from their home. Like his father, he is useless. He does not understand the sacrifices made by his mother for the family. Although he himself is a useless boy he questions everybody in the house about their past and present actions. Through his cheekiness and satirical approach, he aggravates the atmosphere of the multi-dimensional hell called their family.

Thus, all the five members of the family suffer from economic, sexual and temperamental problems and undergo the experience of hell caused by incompleteness, fragmentation and the resultant frustration. The tension between the desire to escape and the inevitable bondage to harsh reality continues in a repetitive circle. All the members of the family are disoriented from one another for various reasons, but seem to be trapped in the prison of the house. *Halfway House*, thus, presents the predicament of the modern man in the Indian context and offers a picture of a family on the brink of disintegration. Although existentialistic dilemma and the human predicament form the theme of the play, the theme itself cannot be described as Absurdist. On the contrary, it is the technique of the play which has certain elements of the Absurd drama. Even the dialogues are quite logical and sensible in their style. There is nothing mysterious or inexplicable about the problematic of the play. That there is no harmony or alignment of interests and goals among the members of the family or that they have no freedom of choice is clear enough.

The Absurdist technique of *Halfway House* can be seen in its static nature. The principle of indirection seems to be the dominant technical feature of the play. For example, there is very little direct physical action in the play whereas the indirect action is comparatively more. The characters constantly refer to the past to understand the cause of their frustration in the present. In other words, the present seems to be haunted by the ghost of the past. There is more talking than doing in the present. The principle of indirection may be seen in the revelation of characters's hidden motives also. This is an epistemological problem in the play. Almost all characters in the play do not reveal their nature through their actions, but are revealed or interpreted by others. Mahendra is interpreted or explained by Savitri. Binni is explained by Savitri and by the boy. Kinni is explained by the boy and vice versa. Mahendra and Savitri are explained by Juneja. Many times these explanations or interpretations are exaggerated or negativized on account of their own subjective prejudices and eccentricities. Everyone explains the other from his/ her own point of view and never has the willingness or imagination to interpret the other from the other's point of view. Thus, they come out with half-truths and are incapable of arriving at the whole truth.

NOTE

1. Mohan Rakesh, *Halfway House*, trans. Bindu Batra, ed. Dilip K. Basu (Delhi: Worldview, 1999).

Uncertain Circumstances, Undefined Individuals: A Study of *Halfway House*

S.G. BHANEGAONKAR

Bhanegaonkar focusses on the institution of family by discussing the particular Savitri-Mahendranath family and points out how this hoary institution comes under stress because of the lack of mature emotional responses from the husband and the wife who refuse to make adjustments. However, there is hope for the family at the end of the play, because it does not finally break up fully and irrevocably.

Editor

Reading translated works of art is not just a literary exercise, but an indication of the readers's willingness to participate in the process of global literary, socio-cultural interaction. It is the readers's open-minded approach to share the social, religious, cultural, and literary heritage of both the languages—source language and target language. The readers of translations exhibit a natural liking for the source language, its social and cultural processes; while the translator indeed does a noble job by bringing two distinct literary cultures into a wedlock. Translation is a sort of recognition of the immense creative potentiality of the source language; it is also an acknowledgment of the target language's readiness to embrace the source language in toto. Moreover, in times of literary unproductivity, the art of translation has even a greater role to perform—it keeps literatures and languages alive by way of socio-cultural inter-communication. The very fact that Mohan Rakesh's *Aadhe Adhure* has been translated into English as *Half-*

way House suggests the tremendous creative capacity of Hindi literature.

Mohan Rakesh (1925-1972) was a versatile genius—short story writer, novelist, and playwright, all combined in one. The publication of *Aadhe Adhure* in 1968 marked a surprising shift in the thematic concerns of Hindi literature, particularly the conventional themes of the Hindi theatre. Mohan Rakesh deserves to be complimented, as for the first time in the history of Hindi literature, some one ventured to talk about the hollowness and deteriorating values and status of the institutions of family and marriage. In the Sixties, a serious discussion started among men of letters who predicted a total collapse of marriage as an institution. It was also feared that the working women would hold their families to ransom and the concept of family, which is peculiarly Indian in spirit, would disappear. Mohan Rakesh's *Halfway House* is a play which concentrates largely on the fear and anxieties of his time, but it finally conveys an optimistic message that the institution of marriage would survive despite several glaring problems involved in marital relationships.

The Prologue describes Mohan Rakesh's chief concerns in *Halfway House*—depiction of thoroughly undefined individuals and the devastating circumstances into which they are plunged. According to the Prologue, the circumstances are beyond control, the characters have no identity, and the play itself is undefined. The play is about "a particular family and its particular circumstances!" (5) The theme of marriage is sociologically so important that any comment made in relation to any particular family is liable to be taken as a generalization and thus, achieve wider dimensions of controversy. *Halfway House*, therefore, portrays Mohan Rakesh's conviction of the failure of marriage in the 1960s—a theme which attracted more attention than any other social issue. The Prologue puts forward an important question—Who is the culprit? Savitri? Mahendranath? Or the circumstances? In modern times, human life has become on ocean of uncertain circumstances and individuals are victims of a general purposelessness, and these are, precisely, the factors responsible for disintegration of family. Life, and especially marital life, is a game of frightful uncertainties and the people involved have no concrete roles to play. Mohan Rakesh's *Halfway House* represents the controversy about the collapse of the marriage as an institution. Representing contemporary social issues in literature is the hallmark of a great creative writer, and that is what Mohan Rakesh does in his play.

Mahendranath's is a small, middle-class family, but it is struggling hard to cope with the contradictions within itself. Love, care, affection, and faith are actually the ingredients of a happy home, but these are exactly the values this 'particular family' is devoid of—there is no proper co-ordination between the members. Savitri, Mahendranath's wife, is hardworking and committed to the economic progress of the family, but she lacks integrity of character which is the essence of marital life. The children—Binni, Ashok and Kinni—are quarrelsome and Mahendranath himself is an idler, incapable of doing anything, for himself or for others. Savitri indeed works very hard for the betterment of her family, but she is treated by her husband and children as 'a machine'; they are always asking her for tea, books, and money. Mahendranath is himself frustrated, bangs his head against the drawing-room walls, bullies his children, tears Savitri's clothes to pieces, gags her and beats her up behind closed doors, dragging her by the hair. Ashok, Kinni and Binni are brought up in an atmosphere of domestic violence, and when they grow up they do not mature but retain their original childhood characteristics—stubbornness, disrepectfulnesss, quarrelsomeness, eccentricity, and mental stagnation. There is no bond of love or care that could connect them together and Kinni, the youngest daughter, feels "like a stranger in this house." (46) and calls her parents, brother, and sister as "lump of clay! All of you . . . lumps of clay!" (66) Mahendranath fears that his wife and children are conspiring against him because they are always answering him back, are rude, disrespectful, and impertinent, and regard him "only as a stamp of respectability to be used only when the need arises." (26) Binni, the elder daughter, makes an apt comment when she desperately cries—"My home . . . yes. And I come here to look for the cause of my trouble!" (19) Mahendranath's house is virtually a battlefield where serious threats are issued, abusive language is used, enemies are warned of serious consequences, curses are showered and violence is brought in as a proof of physical strength. Mahendranath, Savitri and their children treat one another like a disease forgetting that each one of them has the germs of infection within himself/herself. Who, then, is actually responsible for this utter chaos? Binni, the elder daughter, probably knows the secret—"it's . . . it's just the air we breathe" (17) and "that the longer two people live together, breathe the same air . . . the . . . the more estranged they become from one another." (17) Binni's argument sounds logical because when the individuals are undefined, it is the mysteriousness of circumstances that takes over.

It is only Savitri who is always trying to bring some order to these violent chaotic conditions. She wants to arrange a job for her son, Ashok and, therefore, invites her boss to her house. Ashok is sent to college but he quits halfway, a job is arranged for him with Air Freeze but he leaves it in six weeks and now he spends time in quarrelling with his mother and sister, Kinni. He is a young boy but does nothing except idling away his precious youth in cutting pictures from magazines, sleeping, and quarrelling. Savitri indeed does a nice job for her family but her efforts are never recognized either by her idle, parasitic husband or irresponsible children. She is a dutiful, caring and committed mother, but, like other members of her family, she is not free from weakness of character. She is easily carried away by the status and position of her male officers, and wants her husband and children to accept silently the presence of her male friends when she brings them home. The husband goes away everytime his dominating careerist wife brings home a different man. Savitri was previously in love with Juneja. Then with Shivjeet . . . whose university degree fascinated her and his foreign trips charmed her. Then she was drawn to Jagmohan for his excellent contacts and his smart, impressive life-style and his handsome salary. But her charming ways of attracting these handsome, professional men receive a terrible setback when Manoj ditches her and elopes with her daughter, Binni. Thus, professional worries and familial frustrations are the reasons for Savitri's psychic anxieties. The play is indeed a high quality drama replete with accusations and counter-accusations. Savitri is accused of infidelity, but she in turn, accuses Mahendranath of inaction and expects him to be a man, and have strength of character. Savitri invites her boss to arrange a job for Ashok, but Ashok feels ashamed of facing "respectable people who make [him] feel even smaller than we actually are." (40) Ashok is conscious of his mean, small inferior existence. The typical problem with this family is that its members go on accusing each other indiscriminately and disrespectfully. The series of accusations is completed by Mahendranath's friend, Juneja, when he takes Savitri to task for this utter chaos and points to a serious flaw in her own personality: "the meaning of life to you is how many different things you can have and enjoy at the same time." (74) The individuals in the play have no confidence in themselves or trust in others and the whole family moves without a sense of direction. The parents have no time for their children, nor do the children have any respect for their parents. What the members of Mahendranath's family are devoid of is the affectionate attitude towards others. Mahendranath's family is already in a state of economic uncertainty and the heavy loss in business adds to the woes and miseries of the family. The members of the family so seriously lack in love and care that at one point, reconciliation appears to be a distant possibility. The woman clearly points this out in her final outcry:

> Haven't I said that's enough! All of you . . . every one of you . . . all alike. Exactly the same. Different masks, but the face . . . ? The same wretched face . . . every single one of you! (76)

All the individuals in *Halfway House* are escapists and, therefore, their behaviour appears to be abnormal. Savitri spends most of her time out of her house to escape from her quarrelsome children and furious husband; the husband does not come home for days together in order to avoid his wife's unpleasant male friends; and the children run away from their brutal parents. According to the old principles of psychology, running away from home is considered as an escapist's shirking of responsibilities and his inability to work in the atmosphere of stress and psychic tensions. It was viewed as a symptom of a weak mind and personality. Contrary to this view, modern psychologists believe that escapism is not a weakness but the sensitive individual's desire for some higher values which he does not find in the conditions he is placed in. He, therefore, tries to escape from such futile conditions of life that offer him no hope. The escapist's quest may include 'anything' like love, money, protection, peace of mind, and even human relationships. Mahendranath mostly stays with his friend, Juneja, for in his friend he finds the possibility of a new relationship. It also offers him mental relaxation which he does not experience in his home. Binni runs away with Manoj, not that the heat and passion of love compel her, but out of her desire for protection and peace of mind. Kinni and Ashok live in their own worlds to escape from the fearful existence of their wrangling parents, and Savitri escapes into the embrace of her male friends who offer her some relief, if not love. All the members of the family know that a friendly congenial atmosphere needs to be created, but nobody is mature enough to take the initiative. And instead, they create their own isolated worlds and sacrifice the integrity and happiness of the family at the altar of their personal frustrations and anxieties.

Individuals fail, not the institutions. The institution of marriage was established to promote a stronger, healthier, and humane society which would become the pride and glory of mankind. The institutions of family and marriage are as old as mankind itself; their existence is very necessary for the process of human civilization and social balance. The pains, efforts, and devotion of millions of people have gone into their making. The domain of family is important not only for the individual's personal health, but it is vital for the greater benefits of the whole society; and a disintegrated family can only damage such interests. Mahendranath's is a disintegrated family, for every individual is a divided self. The Mahendranath-Savitri relationship is a failure, and Binni's marriage is also on the verge of collapse. Manoj thinks that Binni has brought something from her parents that prevents her from being natural. What is it that Binni has inherited from her parents? It is probably the art of failure. The pyramid of successful institutions is built only when wise and emotionally mature people are associated with the construction work; but immature, undefined, and directionless individuals can only help to destroy this historical structure slowly. Mohan Rakesh's *Halfway House*, thus, attempts to perceive how the undefined individuals like Savitri and Mahendranath spoil the prospects of a happy and successful marital relationship. Towards the end, the play seems to suggest that repairs can be made and reconciliation can take place, for, while there is life, there is hope.

NOTE

Mohan Rakesh, *Halfway House*, trans. Bindu Batra (Delhi: Worldview, 1999).

There is Something in this House that . . . Makes it a Halfway House

N.S. DHARAN

Dharan is of the view that Halfway House *dramatizes the existential predicament of the urban middle-class whose lives are guided not by love and concern for each other but by materialistic considerations. Since the members of the family are estranged from each other, and their relations with each other are ruptured, their 'home' inevitably becomes a 'halfway house' which cannot give them succour or support.*

Editor

The 1960s and 1970s which witnessed a resurgence of Indian drama were marked by fervent theatrical activity in the regional languages, especially Bengali, Hindi, Kannada and Marathi. Badal Sircar in Bengali, Mohan Rakesh in Hindi, Girish Karnad in Kannada, and Vijay Tendulkar in Marathi burst on the Indian theatre firmament with explosive plays, unconventional in content and innovative in form. The reader-audience were jolted out of their complacent, middle-class smugness, and for the first time, they were forced to take a good look at themselves and their milieu. Urban-born, urban-based, urban-educated, urban-oriented and middle-class, these playwrights address the issues unique to the urban milieu. Needless to say, the modern middle-class urbanites are their *dramatis personae.* All the problems that beset the urbanites are delineated in their plays. Each play of theirs is a subjective response to a potentially dramatic situation. Their plays are subjective in the sense that they have their origin in their experiences. Therefore, one may say that Badal Sircar, Mohan Rakesh, Girish Karnad and Vijay Tendulkar focus on a common theme, as both their texts and contexts have the urban middle-class milieu as their matrix.

A versatile writer, Mohan Rakesh contributed in no small measure to the growth of Hindi literature during the early post-Independence era, with his short stories, novels, plays, essays and translations. Sixty-six short stories, three novels and three full-length plays constitute his creative ouvre. In all of them he delves into the society he lived in and the experiences he went through. However, it is as a playwright that he continues to appeal to us most. His first play *Aashadh Ka Ek Din* (1958) deals with the delightful man-woman relationship between Mallika and Kalidas. In *Lehron Ke Rajhans* (1963), his second play, he deals with the tense man-woman relationship between the husband and the wife Nand and Sundari. In *Halfway House* (1969) we see Mahendranath and Savitri, the husband and the wife, who lead a hellish married life which disorients their three children. Curiously enough, there is a deterioration in the man-woman relationship, from the delightful bond in *Aashadh Ka Ek Din* to the bitter, acrimonious, disintegrating conjugal conjunction in *Halfway House*.

Halfway House is a significant play in the sense that it has earned Mohan Rakesh both the praise and the ire of theatre critics. While many acclaim it as a work of great literary merit and a well-wrought theatrical piece, some, nonetheless, do dismiss it as a wilful gimmick. The fact, however, is, to quote Rajinder Nath: "It still continues to be staged not only by well-known theatre groups in the major cities but also in smaller towns where plays are staged even just once a year." (ix)[1] It is evident, hence that the play enjoys an abiding popularity, and its continuing success may be attributed to the contemporaneity of its theme which, to quote Rajinder Nath once again, is:

> Here is a class (urban middle-class and educated) where all human bonds of love and concern for one another have been replaced by very mundane and materialistic compulsions. Whenever bonds of love are replaced by materialistic

> compulsion, the 'hell' is inevitable. And that is what *Aadhe Adhure* is about. (x-xi)

The play revolves around an urban middle-class family which consists of a jobless idler husband, an employed self-willed wife, their educated drifter son, runaway, married daughter and an adolescent daughter. Each one is alone, despite being a member of the family. The refrain "No one's ever at home" occurs again and again in the play. This expression of despair is indicative of the existential dilemma that the members of the family experience. The play is rooted in Mohan Rakesh's credo as a fictionist, which to quote him is:

> Most of my stories are about people living through the torture of relationships in their loneliness, where I have tried to depict through the individual his environment. This loneliness is not the loneliness of the socially isolated individual but the loneliness that comes from living within society and it leads not to any kind of cynicism but to the need to live through it. (95)

The play, when analyzed in the light of these words, assumes all the characteristics of an existentialist drama. Each individual in the family feels lonely, but none dares to leave the coop. And, if at all anyone leaves, it is only to come back. The play, in effect, portrays loneliness in the midst of relationships, and also the impossibility of escaping into the world outside. One goes out only to come back and live as one used to in the past. The wheel goes round and round, but the spokes are precariously hinged, likely to fall off any moment. But nothing happens, the stasis is frightening.

Mahendranath has been rendered an idler by his failure in business which he started as a joint venture with Juneja. While the business flourished they never felt any want, and eventually "What ever [he] had invested, [they] took and spent." (10) Now he has nothing to turn back to or look forward to, for he realizes "What have I come to . . . that everyone answers me back, is rude, disrespectful, impertinent and . . . " (26) Savitri insults him saying that he lives on her salary and he is of no use to them. He stoically accepts his plight, for he knows, "Only outsiders [like Singhania and Jagmohan] can be of use here." (26) Savitri's taunts torture him and he pities himself. He tells her: "I'm responsible for ruining my life, your life, all our lives! And I still stick to this house, because I'm a parasite because I like living off my wife." (27) Eventually he resolves to leave, saying: "I know I'm like dry-rot in this house, eating away at its very foundations. But I'm no longer hungry. I'll never be hungry again." (27)

Savitri, on her part, decides to persuade Jagmohan to accept her, her patience already having been worn by the irresponsibility of Ashok who refuses to humour Singhania for a job, by the stubbornness of Kinni, her youngest daughter, and also by the indecisiveness of Binni. Jagmohan takes her out, but politely tells her that he will not be able to offer her what she expects from him. Disillusioned and enraged, Savitri returns only to find Juneja waiting for her.

The conversation between Juneja and Savitri is the most poignant and revealing part of the play, and occurring as it does towards the end, assumes all the intensity of a *denouement*. The past stands revealed, and Savitri, who so far has impressed us as a wronged wife, emerges as a woman who runs after men in her search for comforts in life. Juneja's ruthless exposure of Savitri's past startles us. She strikes us as a woman who prefers societal labels of power, money and position to her husband's steadfast, unalloyed affection. Here is a woman who wrecks the family with her single-minded pursuit of societal recognition through material trappings. In this context Rajinder Nath's statement on the theme cited earlier assumes significance.

Halfway House has been referred to by many as a woman-centred play which is anti-woman. Consequently, much critical attention has been given to the man-woman relationship in the play. Not surprisingly, the role that the modern urban middle-class society plays in the creation of the materialistic craze that governs its members, which is a vital element in the play, seems to have been ignored. As a matter of fact, it is the society that largely determines an individual's attitude, his way of life, in short, his personality. The family, as we know, consists of individuals who have been brought into a conjunction, a bond that need not always be harmonious, with the individuals working not for the common good, but for their selfish purposes. Needless to say, such a family is bound to disintegrate. And, it is precisely this process of disintegration that we witness in *Halfway House*.

Woman-centred plays are a unique phenomenon of the post-Independence Indian literature. For instance, Vijay Tendulkar has contributed such gynocentric plays as *Silence! The Court is in Session* and *Kamala*, and Girish Karnad's *Hayavadana* and *Naga Mandala* which have in them women playing prominent roles. All the three plays of Mohan Rakesh are also woman-centred. Man-woman relationship is, no doubt, his forte. However, in *Halfway House*, the woman, Savitri, far from being the traditional Indian woman, is the modern, educated, independent lady to whom societal trappings like money, position and education matter most. This lady cannot, by any stretch of imagination, be expected to hold a family together. On the contrary, she hastens the disintegration of the family.

The play gains intensity and poignancy from the conflict in the relationship between Mahendranath and Savitri on the one hand, and from Savitri's relationship with the other men, namely, Manoj, Singhania, Jagmohan and Juneja, on the other. Manoj, as we are told, used to visit the house as Savitri's paramour. Singhania is her boss whom she seems to oblige to secure a job for her son, Ashok. She is enamoured of Jagmohan for he is a person who, she knows, posseses all that her husband lacks. Juneja, whom she derides in her husband's presence, was once considered her saviour in distress. All in all, Savitri, despite her apparent care for her family, especially for her children, fails to win our sympathy. Juneja reveals towards the end that Savitri has been selfishly pursuing purely personal goals meant to further her status in the society through acquiring money, position, and power.

Mohan Rakesh's insistence that the same actor should play

all the five roles, namely the Man in Black Suit, Mahendranath, Singhania, Jagmohan and Juneja shows his meticulous care for dramatic techniques. The same man playing five roles is a unique dramatic innovation. However, it should not be regarded as a mere dramatic contrivance, designed for the sake of novelty. This device is of immense dramatic significance, for in real life too we have instances of the same man acting out different roles, often making it difficult for us to distinguish between the real face and the mask. In the absence of genuine lasting relationships, man considers it a risk to reveal himself. In other words, he remains an actor, always careful to put up a facade, and to hide the real self, according to the demands of the situations he finds himself in.

Family is a group of individuals and its healthy continuance depends on the healthy interaction between its members, and this interaction proceeds from mutual understanding, affection and regard. In *Halfway House*, the family does not hold together, for Mahendranath and Savitri do not understand each other. They do not meet, but always confront. Accusing her husband of turning their son Ashok into an idler, Savitri tells Mahendranath, "just as you've ruined your life, he too is . . ." (11) Reacting sharply, Mahendranath retorts: "And your daughter? From whom did she learn to ruin her life? I had never thought of running away from home!" (11)

Instances of such acrimonious exchanges between the care-worn husband and aggressive wife occur aplenty in Act I. Binni, their elder daughter, says in connection with her present estrangement with Manoj, "the longer two people live together, breathe the same air, . . . the more estranged they become from one another." (17) This remark holds true of the married life of her parents too. Familiarity has, indeed, bred contempt. Binni, the Older Girl, observes reflectively:

> My home . . . yes. And I come here to look for the cause of my trouble! Can you tell me, Mama, what it is and where it is? It is in the doors and windows of this house? In the walls, the ceiling, the floors? Why can't I see it?

> Can you see it Mama? Can Daddy? Can Kinni? Can Ashok? (19)

This half-reflective, half-accusative query imposes silence. Kinni barges in, and sensing the tenseness of the atmosphere, sums up the situation tellingly, "One never knows what's going on here!" (20)

Realizing that he has no status in the house, "that silent acceptance, perpetual snubs, constant insults," (26) are his only lot, and that he has never been of any use, for "Only outsiders can be of use here," (26) Mahendranath, decides to leave the house for ever. Unperturbed, Savitri tells an anxious Binni: "He'll be back before nightfall. This keeps happening every other day." (27)

She busies herself with arranging for the imminent visit of Singhania. On Singhania's departure, Ashok taunts his mother, saying, "Whenever you've invited anyone, it hadn't been for the person himself, but . . . because of his name, his salary, his position." (40) Implicit in the young man's observation is his knowledge of Savitri's craze for societal labels.

That Savitri visits Singhania, a widower with a daughter, Baby, who seems to have in the house many an aunty as a visitor is evident in Singhania's words, "She loves her Aunties!" (35) When Ashok, her son, wonders, "I don't know why you invite them, but you do invite only such people," and asks her, "Tell me, why . . . ? Why?" (41), Savitri tells him, "Because I hope, somehow, something might come of it. If I try and keep up contacts with certain people, it's not for my sake but for all of you!" (41) Ashok's indifference irks her and she declares, "If no one else is bothered, why should I alone go on? Why shouldn't I enjoy life?" (41) She resolves:

> From now on I'll only bother about myself. You look after your own lives. . . . I don't have many years to live now. But however few they be I'll no longer spend them like this. . . . It's the end now as far as I am concerned . . . it really is the end. (43)

But this is not the 'end,' as we discover soon. Her hopes of finding her much longed-for life with Jagmohan are shattered. Jagmohan's response is cold. Dejected, she returns home in a huff and then there ensues a conversation between Juneja and Savitri which reveals to the reader/audience that Savitri does not consider Mahendranath man enough for her. Juneja mercilessly tears apart her past and the play ends with Mahendranath returning home, a literally heart-broken man.

Halfway House is a play that compels attention and admiration, for its apt title, struggling and suffering characters (their innocuous anonymity suggestive of the commonality of such relations in urban middle-class milieu), terse dialogues (often reminiscent of Beckett's plays,) and the sombre tense atmosphere. Acknowledged as subjective, Mohan Rakesh's plays dwell on man-woman relationship as lived and experienced from an authorial perspective. People like Mahendranath, Savitri, Ashok, Binni and Kinni are not unknown in the present day urban middle-class milieu. The tensions in their relations and the resultant ruptures are poignantly portrayed in the play. There are no homes for these hapless urbanites, their habitats are only *halfway houses*, where the inmates are not bound by any lasting relationships, but are just strangers to each other.

NOTE

Dilip Kumar Basu, ed., Mohan Rakesh, *Halfway House* (Delhi: Worldview, 1999).

Halfway House: A House but not a Home

GEETA KUMAR

The writer significantly picks on the "theme" in the title, Halfway House, *to point out how this house disintegrates because of unresolved (perhaps unresolvable) tensions that characterize the relationships in the family. This house has no chance of turning into a home.*

Editor

Eminent drama critic R.L. Nigam commenting on Mohan Rakesh's *Halfway House* makes a valid point when he says that the play in addition to being a highly significant creative work about breakdown of marital relations in a modern nuclear family also incisively highlights the plight of children caught in the quagmire of such a crisis in the family. The squabbling parents make the home a veritable hell for the children, rather than a sanctuary as it should be. Nigam says: "In the environment so created, 'each for himself or herself' will be the ruling ethics. In the recurring crises resulting from this situation, man can be the greater sufferer even as the woman has been the exclusive sufferer in the past, exceptions notwithstanding. It is the sins of his forbears being visited on him, and as surely the sins of the present ones will be visited on their children. We can see this already happening in the case of the three children of the Savitri-Mahendranath family in *Halfway House*. What makes for the tragedy is that it is always the innocents who suffer." (87)

As the play opens, we find that the play is set in "a disorderly living room—with several pieces of broken furniture." This setting in the prologue is repeated in Act I as "the same living room," but with the additional information that "a high-school satchel lies open on a teapoy with half the books spilt out." (7) One would conjecture that there is a school-going child in this house who is careless and irresponsible. Savitri, the heroine and the mother, on entering immediately notices this and blurts out in exasperation, "This child is impossible. Another torn book!" Irritated as she is, she finds fault with her older child, the twenty-year-old Ashok, who wastes his time in cutting pictures of film actresses, which she sees lying around. She says: "Elizabeth Taylor—Audrey Hepburn—Shirley Maclaine—That's right, just live for these pictures." (7) Everything seems to be in disarray and her question to her husband as to whether Kinni, the younger daughter was given her glass of milk seems to be unnecessary as one is sure that this ritual would definitely not have been performed. Neither the father nor the mother is at home to look after the basic needs of an adolescent child. A little later, one finds the husband and the wife blaming each other for ruining the life of the children. The wife says: "Just as you have ruined your life, he too is—" (11) This is a reference to Ashok, who is idling away his life according to Savitri. And the husband Mahendranath quickly retorts: "And your daughter? From whom did she learn to ruin her life? I had never thought of running away from home." (11) The mutual recriminations may or may not be true, but certainly two points are established right at the beginning of the play. The marriage is on the verge of a breakdown, and secondly the tension between the parents has had tremendous impact on the three children's lives and irreparable damage has been done to their psyches.

As the parents argue, the older girl Binni arrives, and it is clear that she has quit her husband's house. Savitri turns pale as the older girl comes home in a "crumpled sari" and with a "look of distraction on her face," with only a rupee and "not even having fare for the scooter-rickshaw." The older girl is evasive and gets nettled on being asked how she is and blurts out, "How do I look? As though I've got consumption? As though

I'm about to die?" (16) The older girl thinks that everything is wrong in her married life. Even though her husband is not bad-tempered, unfaithful, poor, or ill, "it's the air we breathe" that causes problems. She asks her mother, "Why is it that the longer two people live together, breathe the same air . . the . . . the more estranged they become from one another." (17) When the mother insists there must be a reason, Binni says, "What reason? A cup of tea spilt from his hand or a short delay when he returns home from work? These little things are not reasons; they become reasons. A strange sort of feeling mounts up within me and spreads like poison through my whole being. Everything I touch or see or hear becomes distorted and I stand helpless and fearful under the spell of a destructive fate." (17-18) The older girl wants to do things to her husband, just to "enrage him." Interestingly, she comes home to "look for the cause of my trouble" as her husband says that "it's from this house that I have taken something with me which prevents me from being natural." (18) Binni is "afraid" of her husband who does not want her to work. The implication is that she can neither have economic independence, nor a short respite from the suffocating atmosphere in her house if she had been working. Binni is a replica of her mother. Both are at crossroads in their lives as their marriages are going through tumultuous phases and it is quite possible that Binni, like her mother, in the future may take outside support to fill up the cracks in the edifice of her marriage. And surely this outside support in the form of incomplete liaisons will only lead to another "halfway house."

From a psychological point of view, Kinni, the younger girl, is the most sharply etched character. She is a thirteen-year-old girl whose present and future are terribly uncertain as a result of parental conflicts at home. She comes back from school only to find nobody at home. She has got into the habit of throwing her school-bag on the teapôy and running out to waste her time in the streets. She has no money when she goes to school, no milk on time at home, and usually no one at home to look after her needs. When she goes to school without the skeins of thread for the needlework class, the mother, instead of buying her some, only says: "You and your miss! It's almost like a disease." (21) Upon Kinni's suggestion that she should be taken out of school so that she could also loaf around all day like her brother "Shoki," she is scolded for being mannerless. The older sister calls her "cheeky little brat." Kinni has to wear torn socks to school, gets no skeins of thread, has no hair clips, and gets no new uniform for the Founder's Day in her school. The mother only asks her to put away her satchel. She is caught reading "Memoirs of Casanova" by her brother, who consequently pulls her hair hard. Ashok is of the opinion that "A girl of thirteen is thirteen, and she should be thirteen, while this one—" (25) Constant neglect and lack of affection have made her free with her tongue. Probably she will also leave this house in the future, as there is no bonding here with the other family members. Possibly she may elope like her sister Binni and have a discordant and disharmonious married life. The atmosphere at home has already driven her to adopt clandestine ways, and deviant behaviour is the consequence. She discusses with her friend, Surekha, about "how her father and her mother [Surekha's parents]—but not together." (49) The implication is clear. Kinni, more mature than her thirteen years of age, knows a lot about the man-woman relationship. Ashok, perchance, listens to the conversation and beats her up. In retaliation, she teases him about Varna at the Udyog Center, whom he apparently keeps chasing. Later, for indulging in loose talk, she is insulted by her friend's mother and is beaten by her mother at home and locked up in a room for calling all in the family "lumps of clay."

The tension of twenty-two years of married life of Savitri and Mahendranath, during which period three children were born, encapsulated in this play of about twenty-six hours [Savitri returns from her office in the evening, calls Jagmohan in the morning, and comes back dejected in the evening] has taken its toll on the personalities of all the three children, but the worst sufferer has undoubtedly been Kinni. Kinni mimics her elder sister and even says, "Beat me as much as you like." (60) She is locked up in a room, which is not opened, despite her repeated desperate cries of "Open the door—open the door!" She finally bolts the door from the inside and does not open it till the end of the play. As Savitri takes a decision to leave the house, it is the older girl Binni, sympathetic to the mother, who takes charge of the house. She makes tea and cheese sandwiches, decides to tidy the room before Uncle Juneja comes, and advises her mother to reconsider her decision of quitting the house: "Think it over, Mama." She wants her parents to reconcile but is definitely more supportive of the mother. The mother asks Binni to stay and listen to what she says about Mahendranath. But Binni is horrified to learn during their conversation that her mother's last "futile attempt" was to attract Manoj. Juneja further says to Savitri, "But you suffered a terrible blow when he took your daughter." (75) The shock is too much for Binni but she can only blink away her tears.

Everyone in this "Halfway House" seems to be on his or her own ego trips. The father says that his fate in the house is nothing but "silent acceptance, perpetual snubs, constant insults." (26) The mother has run out of patience and would like to quit the house and terminate her relationship with her husband. Neither the father nor the mother seems to be bothered about what would happen to the children and where or with whom they would stay.

Ashok, the twenty-year-old son of the family, is as emotional, impulsive, argumentative and impractical as his father. He cannot concentrate on anything. He can't make compromises even where his own interests are involved. He has neither been able to finish his studies, nor work at one place with regularity. His mother through flattery tries to get a job for him through her boss, Singhania, but just like his father (who gets irritated with Singhania and disappears before his arrival), Ashok too can't stand him. When his mother forces him to stay at home, instead of listening to Singhania's nonsensical talk, he keeps on drawing cartoons and makes fun of him by making sarcastic remarks and is not at all desirous of getting a job through him. According to him, Singhania is a man who is not a man, but a man with a name-plate of five thousand rupees a month. Not at all worried about his future, he makes no effort to look for a job. It is extremely probable that he would grow into a Mahendranath in course of time, whose wife too would find him to be a half-man.

Ashok frustrates all his mother's efforts to get him a job and sometimes even insults her. He is contemptuous of the "pompous ass" Singhania. Savitrí castigates her son, saying categorically: "You are interested in only three things—in sleeping all day, in cutting out these pictures, and—in taking things from the house and—" (30) She implies that he has been selling things. Ashok makes fun of Singhania who has said that many people resemble each other, and that he has an uncle who looks just like Morarji Desai "from the back." Ashok immediately retorts: "We have an aunt. If you cut off her head, she looks just like Gina Lollobrigida." (32) When Singhania refers to a speech by a Maharishi whose name he can't remember, Ashok playfully suggests that it could be "Maharishi Nirodh." Singhania readily agrees. Singhania with a salary of five thousand a month (a substantial sum in 1969 when the play was written) only inspires Ashok to draw his cartoon with his ears on top of his head. He asks his mother in exasperation, "Why do you have to invite people who make us feel even smaller than we are?" (40) Ultimately it is because Ashok tells her to take a decision one way or the other that Savitri decides to quit the house. She emphatically says at the end of Act I, "It really is the end." Ashok tells her that all her efforts have been useless, as if whatever she did for the family, has come to nothing. The older girl ran away, Kinni gets more spoilt by the day, their father has been reduced to 'nothing,' and he himself has been the most useless of all.

In Act II, one finds Ashok playing the card game "Patience," usually played by lonely old people. In this house, children discuss their parents's problems instead of the other way round. The older girl is sympathetic but Ashok is realistic. He tells Binni, "There is something in this house—Better not admit it. But even if one manages to deceive others, how can one deceive oneself?" (46-47)

Finally at the end of the play, it is Ashok who takes charge and brings back his father, who enters "ashen-faced" and asks the older girl to get the walking-stick as Mahendranath has to get off the auto-rickshaw and is not well.

The disintegration of the family is complete. No doubt the mother has come back dispirited and dejected, and the father is also back, but what kind of a haven it is going to be, especially for the children, is debatable. Children, considered to be an insurance against family disintegration, are here denied affection, and so interpersonal relationships suffer. Everyone seems to be selfishly pursuing his or her own happiness. The malaise in the parents's marriage and Savitri's efforts at social and vertical mobility lead to her decision to desert the family. For the children, it has meant a kind of emotional starvation and psychological malnutrition. Lack of desired compatibility between the spouses in the family has led to maladjustment and frustration all around. One sees cruelty not just towards the wife by the husband (the older girl talks of "Daddy's rages when he gagged her [his wife] and beat her up dragging her by the hair to the W.C."), but also others. Mahendranath bullies the children, Savitri beats the younger girl and sneers at her son Ashok by lisping sarcastically, and Ashok pulls at Kinni's hair and the older girl scolds Kinni. Poor Kinni can only grit her teeth and stomp off to the inner room. Ashok's rudeness, Binni's emotional dissatisfaction and Kinni's defiant, quarrelsome and aggressive nature are due to the tense atmosphere in the house.

Mohan Rakesh, who lost his father at the young age of sixteen, had to spend a night with the dead body of his father in a terrible state of mind, as the landlord's son declared that unless the house-rent was paid, the cremation of the dead body would not be allowed. The sensitive teenager spent the whole night resting his head against the cold window bars in the winter night. He had to take charge of the family—his mother, a seventeen-year-old sister, and a younger brother. But first the funeral rites had to be performed. The mother's bangles were sold in the morning and the dead body cremated. But that night was a kind of bridge between two worlds of carefree adolescence and responsible adulthood. For Rakesh, for many years the nightmarish night was still not over. Some of the bitter experiences of the teenager Rakesh, especially concerning economic hardship made him place his plays in just such a context. He himself was a rebel, an extremist and unstable as a teenager. These personality traits are reflected in the portrayal of Ashok in *Halfway House*. Ashok doesn't shave for days on end, and when questioned says he is thinking of growing a goatee. He quits college halfway through, leaves the Air-Freeze job within six weeks. Singhania is shocked at his "violent attitude" as Ashok squashes an insect crawling in his trousers.

The images of an unopened cheese tin, the scissors that cut noisily, the inside room where Kinni is bolted in, the insect crawling inside Ashok's trousers and later squashed by him are powerful dramatic devices to reinforce the main theme—the alienation and breakdown of relations in a modern marriage. Savitri quits the house towards the end of the play, bag in hand, like Ibsen's Nora in *A Doll's House*, in a festive sari, probably full of stars in her eyes. However, unlike Nora who stood for women's liberation in 1879 (when the play was written), Savitri comes back dejected and dispirited in 1969, as Jagmohan fails her, symbolizing the unfortunate women in modern times who are condemned to live in hells of the halfway houses. As far as the children are concerned, they simply have no choice. They did not choose their parents or their halfway house and must continue to rot in the hell. Lack of choices for all in the family and a disharmonious atmosphere in the house would lead to precarious situations again and again in the future. Parents's frustrations would continue to be taken out on the children. However, as children are not puppets but independent living entities with minds of their own, the future looks bleak for all concerned.

NOTE

Mohan Rakesh, *Aadhe Adhure*, translated by Bindu Batra into English as *Halfway House* (New Delhi: Worldview, 1999).

Halfway House: A Play of Incomplete Utterances

VEENA NOBLE DAS

The theme of the play, thinks Das, is woman's search for a complete man while trying to keep her family from disintegrating. She goes on to approvingly quote a critic's comment. Savitri's quest could more appropriately be called "a Doomed Woman in Search of Hell." The theme is reinforced by the playwright by the use of incomplete utterances.

Editor

With his desire for more words and new situations, Rakesh embarked on his third play *Aadhe Adhure* (*Halfway House*).[1] To those who are never tired of crying themselves hoarse about the absence of modern Indian plays, despite some notable examples to the contrary, came a powerful answer from Mohan Rakesh with his play *Halfway House*.

In this play, Rakesh has brought to light the way of living of a middle-middle-class all but on its way out, with their personal and social problems. It is a family torn between the middle-class morals and respectability on one hand and the hindrances that stop them from achieving them. All the five members of this family are linked together through unresolved conflicts and tensions.

Rakesh has chosen the theme of the middle-class family, because the crisis of the Indian society of today is in large measure a crisis of the dead illusions of many years of the rising middle-class. This he expressed in an interview:

> Many of the writers today not only come from the middle-class, but more specifically from the urban middle-class; those from the rural middle-class have also been urbanised, for the most part. The country today at all levels—lower, middle and upper classes, urban and rural—is becoming middle-class. The playwright identifies the consciousness or mentality of the middle-class as that uppishness, that status hunting, that struggle for attainment of material possessions, the going to any lengths to attain all of this. This is the morality of the average man, almost anywhere, belonging to any class.[2]

The play begins with a Prologue in a disorderly living room of once a well-to-do middle class family. A man in a black suit is sitting on the sofa, smoking a cigar. The man introduces himself as one who cannot be identified with any name or character. He has no role in the play and the play is as undefined as he is.

A Prologue as a brief introductory note is conventionally accepted in the drama of both the East and the West. In ancient Sanskrit drama and the Restoration plays it appeared as a regular feature. According to Frank Thakurdas, "a prologue which seeks to serve more than as a prefatory note, to establish a highly dubious theory of dramatic literature, is something questionable." In the Prologue to this play, Rakesh declares a thesis—a statement of the situation of which the play is a demonstration, that is, the hero, Mahendranath and his friends, or more precisely his wife's casual acquaintances, could be any one in the audience. Therefore, what matters is not the individual and all the subtle attributes that define his personality but the situation that is sovereign compelling him to a particular mode of behaviour. Stated in such bold terms it appears to be the most tyrannous type of determinism in which human volition is reduced to nullity and all the psychological factors motivating conduct are declared irrelevant to the understanding of a human being in a particular human situation.

Frank Thakurdas's contention relates to the thesis of the 'Prologue' that far from demonstrating it, the play actually repudiates it and, therefore, in a sense the prologue is a trifle redundant. However, he feels that it does not interfere with the enjoyment of this beautifully structured play; a triumph of craftsmanship in which the balance is so evenly held as to be deceptive. According to the Prologue, Rakesh would have us believe that Mahendranath, a feckless individual, is either a hero with a thousand faces or a faceless self, into whose shoes any one of the equally faceless persons can step in and behave identically; or into the shoes of his three alter egos, or as his wife imagined him, behaving in an identical manner as the situation commands. We know "that functional characters are analogous to some basic types. It is she and not her weak husband who has generated the morally suffocating atmosphere at home. She is the cause of the malaise in the domestic scene driving her sensitive children to a rebellious mood and conduct.

There is a subtly drawn parallel between the disillusionment of the eldest daughter who married in haste to escape the clogging atmosphere at home, and her mother's disillusionment which is the constant refrain of the play. Here is a sharply drawn character of a woman, wishing to live a class above her own, a domineering type who never really loved her husband, who thrived on his weak moral nature, tortured and deserted him. The husband, in desperation, beat and bullied her to win her love which he realized he never had. Her highly intelligent and sensitive children see through her deceptions, and pretensions, the unsuccessful camouflage with which she wishes to cover the moral defiance. In the final idiosyncrasies of her restless self in the last scene which is a brilliant 'tour de force' of economy in dialogue, she accuses Juneja for her husband's failure and very nearly convinces the audience till he turns the searchlight on her grand illusions and her fruitless attempt to realize them.

This exposure has a shattering effect on her, as he holds up the mirror to her and ruthlessly tears the veil of her self-deception and holds her as the force for the painful domestic scene:

Fourth Man: You've made him believe that despite the circumstances, he has no other way of life open to

> him, no other solution except to remain with you and haven't you done everything to ensure that if nothing else, you should at least be able to hold this wretched pawn in your hand? (17)

Savitri's desperate attitude when she is exposed is seen in what she says:

> There is no need for him to come and live in this house. And I too have absolutely no need for this pawn as you say, this man who neither moves ahead himself nor permits any one else to do so. (17)

But this attitude of the critic can be contradicted in the sense that the searchlight falls on the wife and the story is wound round her and becomes important, only because Mahendranath is in background throughout. Savitri's role in the play would not have been so important had she not reacted in different ways to everything Mahendranath upheld. Thus, one need not agree with Thakurdas that the thesis of the Prologue is repudiated in the play.

The woman's search for a complete man while trying to keep her family from disintegrating, forms the theme of the play. For Rakesh, the central character is incidental, 'situations' converging round any character are bound to place that person in the limelight. The play is the story of how much of a lost soul a woman could come to be who, while having a passion for possessing any soul that crossed her way, had also the knack of either scaring it away or suffocating it in her effort to possess it. Developed thus, the play turns out to be a pointed impeachment of a rare human type than a rounded indictment of a universal social phenomenon. That a play such as this has a right to social attention cannot be denied, but that it also possesses a social purpose is open to question. Portraying a woman as a curse rather than as a problem to herself and to all around her, the play, one is inclined to feel, could be more appropriately called "A Doomed Woman in Search of Hell."[4]

The play portrays the woman who is the sole economic source of the family as a working woman let loose. For twenty years she has been trying to hold on to any man, who she thought had masculine perfection. But it resulted only in torture and humiliation and she dehumanized her self and her small domestic set-up driving the members of her family to mental and moral decomposition. Her unsuccessful husband, Mahendranath, has been turned into a writhing worm and her son, Ashok, into a hissing reptile. The elder daughter elopes with Manoj, who was one of Savitri's ex-suitors and the younger daughter Kinni exhibits signs of promiscuous precocity.

Savitri, however chooses to go ahead with her exploration of the possibilities of masculine perfection, which brings on the scene her boss Singhania and her old friend Jagmohan, both of whom indicate their readiness to reciprocate her advances and to accept her favours if the cost of what they get is well within reason.

The device of five divergent roles for one single person seemed evidently to have been meant by Rakesh, as both a philosophical symbolism and a theatrical novelty designed to bring added depth and distinctiveness to the play. But the flimsy theory advanced frivolously by Savitri of their being split personalities in masculine form around her was exploded in no uncertain terms by Juneja, who having been given the last say in this matter by the writer, fittingly retorted that all those who had happened to come into her life were full-fledged persons having their own diverse peculiarities and what made her see them as fractioned entities was but a figment of her own diseased imagination, The philosophical symbolism having been smashed by the author himself, what remained of it was more or less a gimmick. Whether five divergent persons in these five roles would not inject greater vitality into the play is a matter that only an actual experiment can decide. According to K.K. Verma, "this play is capable of providing immense sadistic thrill to those who crave for it. Savitri stripped of all her matriarchal sentiments and thrown to universal contempt reminds one of the disgraced criminal whose naked public execution to vast jeering used to be a sportive occasion."[5] The play, thus, portrays the family of Savitri-Mahendranath as one in which individuals are not considered important at all. Savitri is considered important as long as she provides the means for the family to survive. All her other relationships were not accepted in the Indian society and, like Nora in *A Doll's House*,[6] who is in search of some sanctuary, in *Halfway House* whether it is Mahendranath turning to Juneja or it is Savitri turning to one of her admirers, it is the self-same phenomenon—the soul's search for a sanctuary. These sources whoever or whatever they may be, are bound to be dearer to the individual concerned than anything or anybody in the family. The situation can only add to the existing tensions which will make the need for a sanctuary all the more imperious. The vicious circle runs on. At certain levels, the level particularly to which this play belongs, the situation of crisis originates from and is made more vicious by the breakdown of marriage. This is explicable not only in the case of Savitri-Mahendranath affair but even in the marriage of Binni and Manoj, which, according to Binni, is almost on the verge of breakdown.

Older Girl:	That the longer two people live together the more estranged they become from one another.
Woman:	Is that how you both feel?
Older Girl:	Well at least I do.
Woman:	Then there must be a reason.
Older Girl:	What reason . . . a cup of tea spilt from his hand or a short delay when he returns from work? These little things are not really reasons; they become reasons. A strong sort of feeling mounts up within me and spreads like poison through my whole being. . . . Everything I touch or see or hear becomes distorted and I stand helpless and fearful under the spell of a destructive fate. But Mama. I don't know why. . . . I just can't see why? It happens unasked, unforeseen. It tortures me till I think I'm going mad. (3-4)

This breakdown is significantly related to the emancipation of woman. In this play Savitri is the principal figure in the breakdown in a way. She appears to be the principal accused. The point, the dramatist is trying to make is that it is not the individual who is responsible for the situation, for the individual would have made the same choice, regardless of the situation. Any choice anyone makes has a certain irony in it, for things turn out the same regardless of the choice and this is how Savitri gets herself entangled in this kind of situation.

What makes for the tragedy in the play is that it is always the innocent that suffer the most. Like Binni who is frustrated, the other children also suffer in different ways. The boy for whom the mother is trying to fix a job is frustrated at her actions. When the mother invites her boss, Singhania, home, he says,

Boy: Why do you have to call people who make us feel even smaller than we actually are.

Woman: What do you mean?

Boy: For the glamour of it all. An intellectual, A man with a salary of five thousand. A Chief Commissioner. Whenever you've invited anyone, it hasn't been for the person himself but . . . because of his name, his salary his position. (9)

It is an outrageous burst of an adolescent who is not able to reconcile to the fact that a woman belonging to a middle-class family with the sole responsibility of her family on her shoulder tries to keep contacts with men in higher positions, so that one day they would be of some use to her. She tells him the reason as to why she does so:

> If I try and keep up contacts with certain people, it's not for my sake, but for all of you. The burden of the house is so great that I need someone to share it with me. I can't manage it alone. Your father lost all the money and has been an idler ever since. You, far from doing something on

> your own, even consider my efforts to help you, an insult. If no one else is bothered, why should I alone go on? Why should not I enjoy life? If I did that you wouldn't feel small would you? (9)

The younger girl suffers in a very different way. In this strange household she feels very insecure, no one to care for her, to stand by her in times of need. Her disgust about this house can be summed up in these lines when she says: "Lumps of clay! All of you are lumps of clay!" (14)

That Savitri represents the predicament of the new woman becomes clear in her encounter with Juneja towards the end of the play where the character of Savitri, her relationships, her problems, her attitude, her frustrations in the *Halfway House* are unveiled. A half way in which she tries to find wholeness, a completeness in an incomplete thing.

Juneja begins by saying that Mahendranath is not a free man. He is in a trap.

Fourth Man: And I say that you have him in a trap . . . he's become incapable of doing anything for himself.
Woman: When was he ever capable of doing anything? (14)

The character of Mahendranath is revealed through a discussion about him between Savitri and Juneja. She feels that Mahendranath is devoid of any strength of character and she does not like the idea of her husband being a parasite on Juneja. Her attempt to change him and make him a man was always thwarted by his friend. She accuses Juneja of making him a puppet. Juneja retorts: "He's not a puppet nor anything else you might call him. He has only one defect . . . he is the same as everyman." (15) Juneja feels that Savitri would not have been happy even if she had married any other man, because the meaning of life to her is how many different things she can have and enjoy at the same time, because one man could not have given her complete satisfaction, whether it was Mahendra, Shivjeet, Jagmohan, Juneja or even Manoj who married Binni. Savitri screams in a frustrated tone:

> Haven't I said that's enough! All of you . . . everyone of you all alike . . . exactly the same. Different masks. Different masks, but the face? The same wretched face . . . every single one of you. (15)

The play ends with Mahendranath coming back home and the problem of the family remains unsolved. Savitri and Mahendranath living in the same hell again reveals a great truth of contemporary life. The experience of contemporary life within the universe of the present discourse is the experience of well-caught in a cleft anchor, which is an experience of agony and helplessness. Some like Mahendranath are so much in love with the idea of the anchor that they would rather suffer the eternal agony than let the cleft anchor split all along the length and be free. Others like Savitri only seek to shift from one to another cleft anchor though they may not realize the significance of their moves till the operation is complete. The tragedy all the time is not that the anchor is cleft, but that somewhere at some point it is still joined; that is the tragedy in *Halfway House*.

The playwright has seized from life a general and larger truth which is expressed in the play. Certainly the concern of the playwright as an artist is not with propagation of truth, sociological or moral. His concern is with the form which he must give to the truth he has seized from life. He tries to transform the experience of truth into an experience of beauty which is a joy in itself both to the one who creates and the one who contemplates. But the experience of beauty is, in the last analysis, the experience of the contemplation of form. Hence the supreme concern of the artist with the form. Rakesh, too, has been concerned with the form in no small way. His idea of a single person appearing in four different roles, the use of Prologue and certain other features are significant to the total form which he gives to the experience that is expressed through the play.

The structure of the play can be experienced in parts only; it has all the basic ingredients of modern drama. It is part existentialist, in the sense that there is no exit as all the claustrophobic conflicts remain unresolved. It is also Brechtian, in the sense that people though apolitical prey upon each other and highlight their inadequacies—an inevitable link in the process of alienation. According to J.D. Sethi, the play is doubly Ibsenian in that people cannot survive without illusions and that the apparently insane babbling of perfectly sane persons is the human condition of hidden fears and fantasies. A lone shadow of O Neill's despair falls on the whole setting—the room-walls, furniture, books etc. all suffocatingly distanced from their masters. There is also an all pervading Miller's sense of decay without disillusion and revolt. Of course, all these aspects are found only in parts and patches, linked through Indian family's age-old conflicts between bondage and freedom, between small hopes and gigantic pretensions, between self-doting and the masquerade of sacrifice.[7]

The language of the play can be viewed from different aspects. First, it is simple and yet so telling that it could come only from a master craftsman. The play is an uninhibited expression of fierce realism and, again, unlike the plays that are built on powerful dialogue, it suffers from no riot of words or colours. There are no faded cliches, no determination, no ugly introspection through an interior monologue, no psychic oddities and fallacies etc., which have crowded out drama from modern plays. The argumentative ratiocination, the exposure technique, which were present in *One Day in Aashadh* and *The Great Swans of the Waves* are also present here but reduced admittedly to work-a-day language. The admired "stripping" of Savitri by Juneja is a speech which speaks too much. Rakesh, the sincere artist that he was, admitted that the denouement should have been felt in the body of the play. The play through its language can be seen as a protest against anonymity imposed on human beings after the Industrial Revolution. An incident can be quoted from Tolstoy's *War and Peace*. Prince Andre tells Pierre: "Pierre you must be something." "Yes I know but what?"[8] which shows that there is depreciation and irony about the value of being something itself.

Such depreciation and irony are impossible for Savitri and millions like her who are being dumped in astronomical numbers on the historical scene, they all want to be "something." To use a hoary vein from sociology, they have become other-directed from being "inner-directed." Traditional and parent-inspired controls are gone. All of them hunt for paradigm recognition and approval by the "models" which is the chief source of direction.

It is not merely money or security that Savitri desires. It is a certain style of life, a certain ineffable distinction which will lift her above the grey mass, She hopes to attain this by merging the world of culture (Manoj) and of style (Jagmohan). It is Rakesh's insistence on this craving, this distinctive anxiety as a psychological lever, that lifts this play from the ordinary and makes it stand up as "modern drama." Savitri is not searching for a complete man. Her search is for a touchstone which will confer identity on her.

The play is a hunt for a paradigm in another sense. It marks a stage in Rakesh's frantic search for a language of 'being' rather than "knowing"—a language which will create "is-ness," rather than a language which will rationally describe or justify. His dramatic idiom in this play has shed a lot of its earlier ornamental quality and literary artificiality, and has become more direct, incisive and economical.

The other aspect is that of incomplete utterances found in the dialogues between the woman and the four male characters. The incomplete utterances and the ways in which they are uttered throw light on the inter-action process, reject and reinforce the nature of social relationships among the male and female characters and function as a means of expressing subtle nuances of meaning, attitudes and feelings. Rakesh has exploited the potential of the process of incomplete utterance to his great advantage in literary communication and depiction of character.[9]

Rakesh has by dramatic exploitation of this technique and also by giving one person four roles has been able to handle the major counterparts of the theme. True to life, the characters are seldom all of a piece. they are the broken images of a decomposing society.

Thus, *Halfway House* will be cited for years to come as the play which not only marked a dramatic break with the past, but also ushered in a neo-classical phase in Indian drama, if one agrees with Edmund Wilson's definition of classicism: "In the domain of politics and morals a preoccupation with society as a whole and in art an ideal of objectivity."[10]

NOTES

1. Mohan Rakesh, *Halfway House*, trans. Bindu Batra, *Enact*, No. 53, (May 1971).
2. "*Journal of South Asian Literature Interviews: Mohan Rakesh*," *JSAL* 9, No. 243, Fall and Winter (1973), pp. 19-20.
3. Frank Thakurdas, "*Aadhe Adhure*—A Comment," *Enact*, No. 28 (April 1969).
4. K.K. Verma, "*Aadhe Adhure*," *Enact*, No. 42, June 1969.
5, *Ibid*.
6. Henrik Ibsen, *A Doll's House*, in *The Collected Works of Henrik Ibsen* (London: William Heinemann, 1919).
7. J.D. Sethi, "Rakesh's *Aadhe Adhure*—A Breakthrough," *Enact*, No. 27 (March 1996).
8. Leo Tolstoy, *War and Peace*, trans. Rosemary Edwards (Middlessex, England: Penguin, 1957), p. 18.
9. Hans Raj Dua, "The Function of Incomplete Utterances in Character Depiction and Literary Communication in Mohan Rakesh's *Aadhe Adhure*," *JSAL*, 17, Winter-Summer (1982), p. 238.
10. Edmund Wilson, *Axel's Castle* (New York: Charles Scribner's, 1959), p. 2.

The Incomplete Incompleteness in *Halfway House*

P. DHANAVEL

The article contends that the central theme of the play is inherent incompleteness of human beings but Rakesh fails to convincingly establish the point. Instead of depicting the incompleteness of all men (as also of women), the play ends up only denouncing Savitri, through the forceful tirade against her delivered by Juneja. To this extent, Dhanavel regards Halfway House *as artistic failure.*

Editor

The major theme of Mohan Rakesh's *Aadhe Adhure*, translated into English as *Halfway House* by Bindu Batra, is incompleteness. It has been brought out mainly through the central character of the play, the woman, whose name is finally revealed as Savitri. However, the incompleteness of Savitri seems to remain incomplete as presented by Rakesh. This is one of the reasons for the critical problem the play poses with regard to the hiatus between the technical device of one actor playing four different characters and the thematic thrust of incompleteness. Hence, the need for a close examination of this technique and the major theme.

An intratextual analysis of the play is inadequate, as it is seen in the writings of some critics. While some have defended the dramatist, others have attacked him on the same score. Even Rajinder Nath's moderate approach seems to miss the point when he observes: "The point the playwright makes through the device is to show how conveniently and according to one's own convenience the same man can put on different masks according to the situation in which he is placed." (xi) If Nath's observation is valid, the play must have clearly emerged as a feminist drama. But it does not. On the contrary, it is a misogynistic play, though it is woman-centred. Surprisingly, Savitri's daughters have been used against her, not for her and her defeat is not even honourable.

It is, therefore, believed that an intertextual analysis of *Halfway House* in relation to Jean Anouilh's *Ring Round the Moon*, Girish Karnad's *Naga-Mandala* and Abdulla Al Mamoon's *Kokilara* will be very useful to throw light on the technical aspect. Besides, a similar analysis of the play with reference to Girish Karnad's *Hayavadana* will be fruitful to illuminate the thematic angle. These two analyses will be helpful to identify Mohan Rakesh's conceptual problem in *Halfway House*.

Jean Anouilh's *Ring Round the Moon*, as its sub-title indicates, is about a charade with music. A poor but beautiful ballet dancer, Isabelle, is invited for a ball by Hugo. She is under the impression that he is interested in her for a possible marriage. Soon she realizes that she has to leave him after the ball is over. Hugo arranges the ball, only to have a dig at Diana, who is engaged to Frederic but is secretly in love with him. The funniest and most important factor is that Frederic and Hugo are twins and their characters are played by the same actor. Understandably, the theme of mistaken identity gains significance. Hugo is mistaken for Frederic and vice versa by various characters at various times. However, both Frederic and Hugo do not meet with each other on the stage. When both have to be present, Hugo is hidden behind a sofa. Only his words are heard by Isabelle. This Hugo-behind-the-sofa is played by a double. Later, when a reply is required from Hugo, it is sent through a letter. Though all these may appear to be theatrical gimmicks, Aniouilh's drama succeeds very well. The device of one actor for two characters with a double does not create any problem at all.

Closer home, there is Girish Karnad's play *Naga-Mandala*, which goes a step further in using the device of one actor for two characters. This play deals with a newly married young woman and her problems in adjusting to the new situation. Rani is the young woman married to Appanna. She is left alone in her house for most part of the day and night, as her husband continues to live with his concubine. To charm Appanna to herself, Rani prepares a paste and puts it in a glass of milk, meant for her husband. On seeing the red mixture in the glass and afraid, she pours the milk into a nearby anthill. From there comes a Naga, which takes the shape of a human being, exactly like Appanna, and meets Rani, usually during the night. The husband during the day and the lover during the night are played by the same actor. They enter and leave the stage separately. There is no meeting between them.

What is interesting about *Naga-Mandala* is that the Naga changes into Appanna suddenly at one point. In a stage direction, Karnad records: "She turns away. Naga takes a step to go. They both freeze. The light changes sharply from night to mid-day. In a flash, Naga becomes Appanna: Pushes her to the floor and kicks her." (52) This sudden change of Naga into Appanna is not a theatrical gimmick. It serves the dramatic purpose of showing the whimsical, unpredictable, and conflicting behaviour of a husband as perceived by a wife. The split roles effectively bring out the bewilderment and suffering of a young woman after her marriage. Karnad's technique coheres with his theme excellently.

Similar is the case with *Kokilara*, a Bengali play by a Bangladeshi playwright and director Abdulla Al Mamoon. I had a chance to witness a performance of *Kokilara* on 19 January 2000 at the Town Hall, Agartala. The play was presented by the Theatre Group of Bangladesh to a well-attended audience. The three different characters of the play with the same name were played by the famous actress Firdozi Majumdar. Despite the fact that the whole performance was done by only one actress and also that the audience were irritated by the long delay due to the inaugural function of the six-day long Drama festival, the play was a great success.

The theme of the play is gender injustice. It aims at creating feminist awareness of female suffering in a patriarchal society. Its aim is achieved effectively through the plight of three women in three different situations. The first, Kokila is a very ordinary village girl. While working in a house as a maidservant, she falls in love with a man and becomes pregnant. She is called a thief and sent to jail. Later, she commits suicide by falling on the railway track. The second Kokila is an ordinary housewife. Living according to the patriarchal tradition, she is devoted to her husband and has two grown-up daughters. Yet the husband chooses to marry his lady personal assistant and throws Kokila out by divorce. These cases of injustice against women come to the third Kokila, who is an extraordinary lawyer. She argues her cases exceedingly well and pleads for justice forcefully. Yet she fails in her endeavour because the judge who listens to her arguments is a man and so he dismisses the cases for want of proper evidence and support. Thus, the play shows how all women suffer at the hands of men. These three Kokilas are representatives of their class as a whole. By giving the same name to three different characters, the playwright adds a symbolic significance to Kokila.

As mentioned, all these three characters were played by the same actress. This technique of one actress for three characters plus the same name for them contributes remarkably to the feminist theme of the play. It also suggests that women are denied their individual identity and existence in a male-dominated society.

Jean Anouilh's *Ring Round the Moon*, Girish Karnad's *Naga-Mandala* and Abdulla Al Mamoon's *Kokilara* pose no critical problem to the readers and audience in any way, even though they employ the technique of one actor for more than one character. The theme of each play is well integrated with its technique. Each dramatist is unambiguous in his theme as well as technique. All these plays are women-centred and feminist. When Mohan Rakesh's *Halfway House* is compared with them, it becomes clear that Rakesh is successful in his use of the technique theatrically but unsuccessful thematically. It is necessary, then, to examine Rakesh's play closely.

In the Dramatis Personae page of the play, Rakesh directs that the roles of the Man in a Black Suit, The First Man, The Second Man, The Third Man, and The Fourth Man should be played by the same actor. While the Man in a Black Suit speaks the Prologue and does not have any other function, the four men are intimately connected with the play as a whole. The First Man is the Woman's husband, the Second Man is her employer. The Third Man is her lover, whereas the Fourth Man is her husband's friend. Except the Man in a Black Suit, all these four men have individual names, viz. Mahendranath, Singhania, Jagmohan, and Juneja, respectively. These men, however, do not have a separate identity of their own. Each of them is defined mainly in relation to The Woman, whose name is Savitri. All these four men plus Manoj and Shivjeet are objects of the Woman's love as well as hatred—of love when they please her and of hatred when they do not. Every one's relation with her begins in love and ends in hatred, leading her to condemn all men. Ironically, however, the play ends in a worser condemnation of the Woman. The problem is that this irony is not built in as part of the play from the beginning. It is rather imposed upon through the words of the Fourth Man, whose meeting with Savitri and his exposure of her militate against the general tenor of the play.

The function of the Man in a Black Suit, like Sutradhar, is to introduce the play, its subject matter and its characters. Interestingly, he performs his job in the living room of the First Man's house and thereby he participates in the location of the play. He sits on the sofa, smokes a cigar, and strolls up and down in the living room. He begins, as if, telling the story but defines himself paradoxically in indefinition: "amorphous" and "undefined." (4) He imposes his own indefinition on the play, its characters, and the audience. Clearly the major issue that he raises for himself and for the play is identity crisis, the incompleteness of human beings, which is synecdochically foretold in the title of the play as *Halfway House*. The Man asks himself "who am I?" but does not answer the question. In fact, he says he has abandoned the question altogether. However, he offers a working definition of himself as "the man you bump into by chance in the street." (5) Beyond this, he does not want to complicate matters. All he asserts is that "there is something of me in each one of you and that is why, whether on or off the stage,

I have no separate identity." (5) Through his words, he suggests himself to be everyman and simultaneously a no-man.

Likewise the Man in a Black Suit characterises the play as undefined and he takes the responsibility for its evolution or dissolution. He reveals the subject matter of the play as "a particular family and its particular circumstances." In his elaboration of the same, he relates himself to the woman of the play but does not define his role. Evidently, he is going to play the roles of four men with whom the woman is associated in different ways. Further, he indicates that the characters and circumstances are complex which do not lend themselves to unambiguous understanding. He also hints that the play is amenable to improvisation. In this regard, his last words disarm the audience by his seeming trust in them. The trap is laid for them when the Fourth Man enters in Act Two and starts exposing the Woman. But most of the audience cannot react immediately because the Fourth Man's revelations are so powerful as to silence them, before one begins to think critically, the First Man appears drawing the audience's sympathy. The whole drama plays with the emotions of the audience and benumbs them at the end.

The amorphous and undefined nature of the Man in a Black Suit can be seen in all the four men and other characters in the play. The First Man is the husband of Savitri, the father of three children—Binni, Ashok and Kinni—and the friend of a businessman, Juneja. Yet he is seriously plagued by the question of identity "Who am I?" Once he was a business partner with Juneja and had a source of income. When he failed in his business, he lost not only his income but also his status as the head of a family. As he could not succeed in any other way, his wife took up a job and started shouldering the family responsibility. Disappointed in business and also in family, he has turned out to be an escapist. Consequently, he does not have any sense of belonging to any place or person. Most often he prefers to be silent but is provoked by his wife to react. Often he makes efforts to be patient but is forced to fight. Naturally, he is increasingly alienated from his family.

As husband, Mahendranath expects his wife to stay at home.

He eagerly looks forward to strikes in her office. He does not want other men to visit his wife in his house. As father, he is interested in the welfare of his children but he can do nothing. He takes pains to persuade his wife to enquire about the problems of Binni, the Older Girl. When he intervenes to know more about what his son-in-law had to say about his house, his wife cuts him short saying, "If you really considered this your house." (18) Neglected and abused in his house, he spends his time in the market, in reading newspapers, or going to his friend's place, almost regularly. Whenever he loses his temper, he leaves the house. On one such occasion, he gives a picture of his status in the house. Though he has looked after the house for many years, he feels that "everyone answers me back, is rude, disrespectful, impertinent." (26) His rewards have been "silent acceptance, perpetual snubs, constant insults." He feels, he is a stamp of respectability to be used when the need arises." (26) In his fit of impotent rage, he takes the responsibility for ruining the entire family. He describes himself as a useless parasite, living off his wife; his last words are striking for the image of the dry rot and for his assertion: "I know I'm like dry rot in this house, eating away its very foundations. But I'm no longer hungry. I'll never be hungry again." (27) He leaves the house not to return but finally comes back. The reason given by Juneja for the First Man's return is that Savitri has bound him as a slave to her.

Who is the First Man then? He is Mahendranath, which means Maha + Indra + Nath. Ironically, however, he is neither Nath (Shiva, the destroyer), nor Indra, the God of heaven. The addition of Maha, great, to Indra and Nath accentuates the irony. He is criticized for drinking a lot of tea. He is asked an explanation as to how he spent his money. He is directed to heat milk for his Younger Girl. He accepts all these situations without a murmur. When it comes to receiving his wife's employer, however, he rebels. He cannot understand how a man could visit his house to arrange a job for his son just for the asking. He suffers from lack of self-worth and doubts whether others too have any self-respect. Undoubtedly, his problem is his own identity crisis.

The Second Man is the second incarnation of The Man in a

Black Suit. He is the employer of Savitri. A leading personality of the town, he seems to be acquainted with several women. As an upper middle class man, he is a reader of *Reader's Digest* and a visitor to many foreign countries. He talks glowingly about America, Japan, Italy, and other countries and countrymen. True to his class, he denigrates India and all that is Indian: "In our country there's just trash; one never sees a good magazine." (31) He advertises himself as a Past President of the Literary Forum at the university and bloats up his importance by saying that he was a member of some interview boards.

Such a big man is naturally invited by many people to get favours from him. He mentions Mrs. Mathur and Mrs. Malhotra. Savitri belongs to the same category. He is keenly interested in them and their daughters. But he cannot distinctly remember them and what they spoke. Savitri invites him to her house to talk about a job for her son, Ashok. But he is delighted to converse with her daughter Binni about her job. He pretends to show interest in Ashok's future and asks him to come near him but gives a lecture on Italy. When Ashok squashes an insect, he describes it as a "violent attitude" and then talks about "national values". According to him these values are best propagated by Maharshi Nirodh, whose name he cannot remember immediately.

This man is often forgetful and confused. He is a chatterbox who jumps from one topic to another. He confuses between people and cannot remember them distinctly. One thing he does not forget is to ask Savitri to come to his house for some office work. He also reminds her that his daughter likes the aunts who visit him. Obviously, he is an unscrupulous man out to exploit the women who come his way. Not surprisingly he remembers Maharishi Nirodh half-heartedly. But Savitri gives him a lot of respect and entertains him happily. The simple reason is that he is a man with a salary of five thousand and a car, though it needs pushing for a start.

His empty, aimless and manipulative talk reveals another facet of identity crisis in the play. If Mahendranath's crisis arises from his unstable family, Singhania's crisis originates from his unstable social and work environment. The latter is a manager of a whole office but he cannot manage himself properly; it appears that he is a wifeless man, looking for a wife in every woman he comes across. There is a certain amount of wantonness in him, which he does not understand. As long as gullible and vulnerable women like Savitri are there, he will continue to flourish, not as a complete and self-realized man but as an incomplete and incoherent man.

If the First Man is amorphous and undefined as the head of a family and the Second Man as the head of an office, the Third Man is formless and indefinite as the lover of a woman. Not accidentally, his name is Jagmohan = Jag (world) + Mohan (the eternal lover Krishna). That is, he is a lover of the world, especially of women. He is able to draw Savitri's complete devotion to him by making her feel that she is more important than himself. He loved her and admired her but did not marry her. His transfer from Delhi to another place came as a blessing to him to be away from Savitri for some time. Now that he has been transferred back to Delhi, he establishes contact with her without any problem. He appears to be sympathetic, understanding and tolerant. However, he is not willing to be lost in and swayed by Savitri's emotional outbursts.

Like the Krishna of the *Mahabharata*, the Third Man has a philosophy of life, which is recalled and articulated by Savitri. The first statement is "If thinking led anywhere, it would be worth thinking" and the second is "There's a difference between yesterday and today." (56) Perhaps there may be many other interesting ideas of his but these two are remembered by Savitri. With such consoling words, he is able to create self-confidence in Savitri. Hence, she looks at him as her saviour in distress. However, his powers are very limited. He can come to her, when called in. He can listen to her with sympathy and understanding. He can take her out for tea, lunch or dinner to any hotel. He can give her some money. More than these, he cannot do anything. Particularly, he cannot provide her emotional support and security that she desperately longs for. Perhaps he realizes that no man could fulfill Savitri's expectations because her imaginary world of freedom and enjoyment does not exist in real life. Even Krishna could not prevent the atrocities on Draupadi. How could Jagmohan do anything more than what a friend in need could?

Obviously Jagmohan's needs and compulsions are different from those of Savitri. His problem is that he is looking for romance without responsibility. He is not willing to sacrifice himself, his job, and social standing for the sake of Savitri. He is caught in a tangle but is careful enough to disentangle himself. His imperfections, then, are intimately connected with his socio-economic context.

Like the Fourth-Tempter in Eliot's *Murder in the Cathedral*, the Fourth Man in *Halfway House* is more difficult to deal with than the rest of them. He is a former business partner and a good friend of Mahendranath. Emotionally, economically, and perhaps socially, he is superior to the other three men. He did not try to exploit Savitri's emotional dependence on him. He did not discard Mahendranath, after the latter lost his partnership. As a good friend, he has remained a source of support to him for several years. His virtue is that he understands himself and others. Even then his personality is ridden with problems. For he takes peculiar delight in destroying Savitri's very selfhood.

Like Stanley Kowalski who rapes Blanche Dubois, albeit not a virgin, and sends her mad to an asylum in *A Streetcar Named Desire*, Juneja strips Savitri of her illusions and wakes her up to the harsh reality of her helpless dependence on Mahendranath, who, she thinks, depends on her. He tries to play fair with her by listening to her exposure of Mahendranath as a useless man. In the end, however, he critically analyses her relationship with different men to show how she has deceived herself in searching for a complete and perfect man with money, status, contacts and all that a materialistic society promises to offer to an ambitious person. He explains her condition: "the meaning of life to you is how many different things you can have and enjoy at the same time. One man alone could never have given them to you, so no matter whom you married, you would always have felt as empty and as restless as you do today." (74) This is not all; he shatters her further by exposing the maniac fear in her and her futile attempt to attract Manoj, who chooses to marry her daughter.

One of his important functions is to reveal the names of both Mahendranath and Savitri. Even this seemingly harmless act gains a persecuting force of its own and attempts to strangle Savitri right in front of the audience. The mythical pair of Satyavan and Savitri inevitably comes to the audience's minds. This subconscious juxtaposition points to the stark difference between the ideal husband and wife, and the actual husband and wife. The fact that the difference is enormous pushes both Mahendranath and Savitri to the abyss of hell, for which Juneja holds her responsible to a large extent.

Believing that nothing could be done to restabilize the family of Mahendranath and Savitri, Juneja strives to liberate his friend and so asks her, "Can't you free that poor man somehow?"(67) He argues that Mahendranath has become incapable of doing anything for himself because of her. As he explains a little later, "Because today he thinks he's helpless. You've made him believe that, despite the circumstances, he has no other way of life open to him, no solution, except to remain with you. And haven't you done everything to ensure that, if nothing else, you should at least be able to hold this wretched pawn in your hand?" (77)

Thus, the Fourth Man wants to release the First Man from the Woman but the latter returns to her, as if he were a prey bewitched by its predator. However, it is clearly seen that both Mahendranath and Savitri are tied to each other to torture themselves. As the Fourth Man is also a witness and participant in their torments, he is not free from their imperfection and incompleteness. He shares their amorphous and undefined nature more so in a very complex way.

When the First Man returns to Savitri at the end, the Man in a Black Suit's identity crisis turns its full circle. In the process, the psychological and sociological problems of Binni, the Older Girl, Ashok, the Boy, and Kinni, the Younger Girl, as well as those of the Woman are brought into sharp focus. Each character faces the question "Who am I?" in his or her individual way. Their suffering is very painful. Kinni's disorientation draws the attention of the audience for its unusual pathos. And the cycle of suffering continues for the incomplete human beings.

In the final analysis, the technique of one actor for four different characters is not in itself defective nor is it just a theatrical gimmick. It does reveal the various dimensions of the ideal man as perceived and pursued by the Woman. It does underscore the amorphous and undefined nature not only of these four men but also of the Woman. It does add power to Savitri's accusation against all men "All of you . . . every one of you . . . all alike. Exactly the same. Different masks, but the face . . . ? The same wretched face . . . every single one of you." (76) Nevertheless the whole endeavour of the Fourth Man to liberate his friend by exposing Savitri undermines the thematic thrust of her search for completeness. In this connection, a comparison of Savitri with Padmini in Girish Karnad's *Hayavadana* is instructive.

Karnad's *Hayavadana*, written, published and performed around the same time as that of Rakesh's *Halfway House* also deals with "the mad dance of incompleteness." (126) Aesthetically and emotionally, however, Karnad's play is much more satisfying than Rakesh's. It is not just the folk form, nor the *Vetalapanchavimsati* story via Thomas Mann, nor Karnad's invented story of *Hayavadana* that is superior to that of Rakesh. It is the complete and holistic presentation of imperfection and incompleteness by Karnad that deserves due appreciation.

Both *Hayavadana* and *Halfway House* are woman-centred plays. While the former is unmistakably feminist, the latter is ambiguously anti-feminist. If Karnad shows Padmini's search for completeness through the episode of the transposed heads with the objective correlative of both *Hayavadana*, the horse-headed man and Ganesha, the elephant-headed God, Rakesh uses the technique of one actor for four characters who manifest different aspects of Savitri's ideal man. Karnad's Padmini dies with the happy realization that she cannot have her complete man of head and body in one man. Whereas Rakesh's Savitri has no such realization, one does not feel deceived by Karnad's techniques or themes but Rakesh gives scope for questioning his very theme and his technique as they work at cross-purposes. It is not a process of deconstruction that is seen in the play but a single-minded destruction of one individual character, that is, Savitri.

If the dramatic purpose of Rakesh is to suggest that today's woman cannot be yesterday's Savitri, it is well and good. He has the artistic freedom to paint her in the worst possible colours, though feminists may have their objections. As a responsible artist, however, he cannot afford to sacrifice his artistic integrity. Shakespeare gave that famous definition of woman in *Hamlet*, "Frailty, thy name is woman" but he is not taken to be an anti-woman. His play explains adequately the reason for such a devastating generalization within the framework of the play. Despite his denial that he had any anti-feminist intention, Rakesh's play exhibits certain disturbing misogynistic tendencies. He may have tried to depict the battle of the sexes as August Strindberg did in play after play. Unfortunately, however, Rakesh's dramatic conception is not as clear as that of Strindberg.

Mohan Rakesh's problem, then, is his inability to achieve clarity of purpose in *Halfway House*. Henrik Ibsen's Nora could walk out of her house in *A Doll's House*. Strindberg's Julie could maintain her dignity even in demeaning circumstances. Pirandello's six characters could come together to enact the drama *Six Characters in Search of an Author*. But Rakesh's Savitri loses all her elements of humaneness. Christopher Marlowe's Faustus could exclaim about Helen "Was this the face that launched a thousand ships/ And destroyed the topless towers of Ilium?" Shakespeare's Enobarbus could affirm about Cleopatra, "Age cannot wither her, nor custom stale/ her infinite variety." But Rakesh's Savitri has to lose even what she possesses in her search for completeness. Why? This question is left clouded in prejudices.

Arthur Miller's *Death of a Salesman*, a family drama par excellence, is a modern American classic. As the playwright explains its greatness:

> If . . . the struggle in *Death of a Salesman* were simply between father and son for recognition and forgiveness, it would diminish in importance. But when it extends itself

> out of the family circle and into society, it broaches those questions of social status, social honor and recognition, which expand its vision and then lift it out of the merely particular towards the fate of generality of men. (223)

Though Rakesh's *Halfway House* is a family drama, it does not "expand its vision and lift it out of the merely particular toward the fate of generality of men." Rightly it has not been included in K.M. George's *Masterpieces of Indian Literature.* It is Rakesh's first play *Aashadh Ka Ek Din* that is considered a masterpiece by Satyendranath Taneja. The same play is given full coverage in *The Encyclopedia of Indian Literature* by Mrinal Pandey. Perhaps some critics like I.N. Choudhuri are doing injustice to Rakesh by projecting his weakest play as "his best play." (513)

Halfway House succeeds at best in creating, increasing, and maintaining the Woman's feeling of disgust for her husband and finally for all men. But then disgust alone does not make a great work of art. Take, for instance, Shakespeare's *Hamlet.* The play deals with Hamlet's frustration, expressed in his first soliloquy:

> O, that this too too solid flesh would melt
> Thaw, and resolve itself into a dew.
> Or that the Everlasting had not fixed
> His canon against self-slaughter!
> O God! O God! how weary, stale, flat, and unprofitable,
> Seem to me all the uses of this world.
> Fie on't! Ah fie! 'tis an unweeded garden,
> That grows to seed; things rank and gross in nature
> Possess it merely. That it should come to this.

The perspective of Hamlet is that of a son whose father has recently been killed by his mother's lover. A similar family drama is found in *Halfway House.* Though alive, Mahendranath is effectively dead. Ashok's anger against his mother is very much visible. Yet the play fails to achieve the artistic integrity found in *Hamlet.* The reason is not to be sought in the change in perspective but in the distortion of perspective. Shakespeare does not make the audience hate Hamlet for all his indecision, but enables them to see Hamlet's condition feelingly. On the contrary, Rakesh uses Savitri's hatred against herself and persuades the audience forcefully through the Fourth Man to condemn her to hell. Such an authorial manipulation cannot be justified by any dramatic theory and practice.

In conclusion, Mohan Rakesh's *Halfway House* is incomplete in its presentation of the theme of incompleteness as seen in the protagonist Savitri. While Jean Anouilh's *Ring Round the Moon*, Girish Karnad's *Naga-Mandala* and Abdulla Al Mamoon's *Kokilara* are successful in integrating their technique of one actor for more than one character with their theme, Rakesh's play poses critical problems. There is no doubt about his effective handling of the technique of one actor for four different characters. However, to what effect does Rakesh use this technique is certainly doubtful. The course of the play is in the feminist direction but it reaches the anti-climax of anti-feminism. The tragic irony of the independent woman depending on her husband is not convincing at all. Karnad's *Hayavadana* also deals with the theme of incompleteness. In comparison, *Halfway House* falls flat. Despite the fact that *Hayavadana* is a folk drama with certain in-built alienation effects, the audience feels moved by the tragedy of Padmini. But *Halfway House*, though a partly realistic play, fails to evoke from the audience any sense of sympathy for Savitri. On the contrary, they are moved to hate her. Such a resolution is not befitting for a great play, though it may please a large number of critics. Therefore, Mohan Rakesh's *Halfway House* is only half way to greatness.

NOTES

1. Jean Anouilh, *Ring Round the Moon*: A Charade with Music, adapted by Christopher Fry (1950; London: Methuen, 1968).

2. I.N. Choudhuri, "Hindi (Drama)," *Comparative Indian Literature*, ed. K.M. George (Madras, Macmillan and Trichur: Kerala Sahitya Akademi, 1984), Vol. 1, pp. 506-15.
3. Girish Karnad, *Three Plays: Naga-Mandala, Hayavadana, Tughlaq* (1994; New Delhi: Oxford Univ. Press, 1995).
4. Arthur Miller, "The Family in Modern Drama," *Modern Drama: Essays in Criticism*, ed. Travis Bogard and William Oliver (1965; New York: Oxford Univ. Press, 1971), pp. 219-33.
5. Mohan Rakesh, *Halfway House*, trans. Bindu Batra, ed. Dilip K. Basu (Delhi: Worldview, 1999).

Halfway House: The Problem of Incompleteness

P.S. KASTURE

Kasture pinpoints incompleteness as the essential condition of human beings. Tragedy results from the characters' attempts at finding completeness which, they do not realize, is an impossibility.

Editor

The central aesthetic problem of the modern writer is the problem of rendering "complete human personality . . . in an age of lost values, lost men, and lost gods."[1] The twentieth century has been rightly called "the Age of Alienation."[2] The modern man is doomed to suffer the corrosive impact of alienation, which manifests itself variously in the form of generation gap, the credibility loss, the compartmentalization of life, the stunting of personal development and the conspicuous absence of a sense of meaningfulness of life. As Edmund Fuller suggests, in our age "man suffers not only from war, persecution, famine and ruin, but from inner problems . . . a conviction of isolation, randomness, and meaninglessness in his way of existence."[3] The malaise of the contemporary man has been considerably aggravated by what Spengler calls "the crisis of the present." The present century has seen the dissolution of old certainties and, as Paul Brunton points out, "never before have many people plunged in so much uncertainty, so much perplexity and unsettlement."[4]

Modern literature is derived from a shared sense of cultural crisis, the collapse of all systematic explanations of the world and the consequent questioning of all the established ways of forming experience. These artists admit the chaotic nature of the universe and at the same time they affirm the power of art not to make order, but to discover it.

In this process, the artist has a special function. He is expected not to evade darkness, but to search for light that emerges through darkness. "If the world were clear," says Camus, "art would not exist." So a work of art attempts to clarify our universe, defining mystery where it can, and bringing that mystery into sharper focus where it cannot penetrate it altogether. To enter such realms is necessarily to confront darkness and dilemma at every level, but the serious artist is willing to grapple with whatever drives him forward in his search for meaning, aids in his exploration of human problems. By shaping experience as only it can, a work of art itself becomes one of our essential experiences, because it provides the insight, intelligence and coherence which life alone never offers.

Mohan Rakesh's *Halfway House* is one of the significant modern dramas that powerfully echoes this modern malady, transcends time and space and symbolizes eternal human predicament. The pervasive sense of alienation has corroded human life from various quarters. Modern man has shrunk in spirit languishing in confusion, frustration, disillusionment and alienation. His very notion of reality has profoundly changed on account of Bergson's theory of *duree*, Freud's postulates about the subconscious, Einstein's concept of relativity and Heisenberg's uncertainty principle. Consequently, he suffers from an acute sense of rootlessness, which manifests itself as "the alienation from oneself, from one's fellow men and from nature, the awareness that life runs out of one's hand like sand."[5] The hiatus between what the individual aspires for and the harsh reality of what he achieves, what he professes and what he practises, what he really is and what he would like to be taken for, has crumpled his life, leaving an insidious effect on his inner being. The injuries inflicted and the scars left on his psyche make him realize his helplessness. He finds life 'infinitely vast' without any proper 'linkage' to hold it together from falling apart.[6] Painfully aware of his precarious position, man feels tragically self-alienated.

These men often suffer from a gnawing sense of disintegration within and disjunction from the world around. The man-woman relationship is used by Mohan Rakesh to bring out the essentially alienated condition of human beings. His protagonists are alienated from the world, from society, from their families and even from themselves as in *Aashadh Ka Ek Din* and *Lehron Ke Rajhans*. The psychic breakdown is quickened by the marital discord as in *Halfway House*. Rakesh is quite aware, as seen by his dramatic experiments, that there is no easy or final solution to these problems. Still his characters go on living intensely and he goes on fathoming their minds deeply. It is a creative act of living with the tragic sense of life.

II

Mohan Rakesh's *Halfway House* has evoked a strikingly diverse range of critical opinions, from highly laudatory to severely hostile. "Within the tradition of Hindi drama, this play has enjoyed a canonical status," says Sanjay Kumar.[7] Recipient of a number of awards, the play is regarded as the best work of Rakesh, the most complete drama in Hindi and an important landmark in Indian theatre. (98) Some critics have compared it with the plays of Brecht, Ibsen, Strindberg, O'Neill and Arthur Miller. On the other hand, others denounce the play as being sentimental and commercial, superficial and hollow. (106)

Most of the critics regard the play as a scathing critique of the tragic disintegration of the decadent modern middle-class family. The situation of each of the characters points to the bitter fact of contemporary life. This specially lifts the play high above other Hindi dramas.[8] From a director's point of view, it is the first Hindi drama, says Om Shivpuri, that truly represents the contemporary life.[9] According to Ramesh Kumar Jadhav, this social drama truly represents modern middle-class head and heart with all the implicit contradictions.[10] To delineate contemporary man's misery, Rakesh took help of historical figures in *Aashadh Ka Ek Din* and *Lehron Ke Rajhans*, but all the characters in

Halfway House live in the present. His *Halfway House* expresses modern man's miserable lot and the crisis of his existence.[11] Though most of the critics regard *Halfway House* as a truthful reflection of contemporary life, Sunderalal Kathuria disagrees with this claim. He feels that Rakesh as usual deals with some specific references, exceptional situations and not with the general scene.[12]

Critics also differ widely regarding the vision of life presented by the play. To R.L. Nigam, "*Aadhe Adhure* is a highly significant play sociologically." (83) Dilip Kumar Basu thinks that the play "hesitates structurally between the naturalistic and the absurdist." (126) He argues that the four variations of 'Man' presented in the play do not combine to give a powerful impression of 'Everyman' systematically revealed, though the Prologue together with the naming of the characters as The First Man, The Second Man etc., all to be played by the same actor, do encourage such a search. The 'Everyman factor' (128) is distributed in different locations in such an arrangement that the well-known absurdist methods of presenting the essential predicament of man by locating them either in one solitary character or in paired couples is not observed here. The contradictions arising out of these two pulls—naturalist and absurdist—make its meaning ambiguous. In spite of its leaning towards the Absurdist tradition, it is devoid of the Absurdist theatrical images. Devaluation of language, a marked characteristic of the Theatre of Absurd is also absent here. The play also does not take "the ultimate absurdist position of dismissing historical time as a dimension of Reality." (131) Sanjay Kumar, too, feels,

> *Halfway House* shows the obvious influence of modern western theatrical and philosophical traditions. The strongest influence is of the Theatre of the Absurd (discernible in the debt both to Camus-like notions of the Absurd and to the theatrical ideas of dramatists like Beckett, Ionesco and Pinter). The influence of the Theatre of Ideas, particularly works of Sartre and Shaw, is also strongly there (obvious in the too long discursive section at the end). The themes

> and tropes of the play place it in the universalistic idiom. (133-34)

These diverse claims at lineage do not point to any inherent confusion, but to the multiplicity of meaning implicit in a great work of art. A successful work of art is a complex whole woven out of diverse elements. If we want to understand its true nature and meaning, we have to examine it from many angles. A new possibility of interpretation always remains open. Ernest Hemingway, in an interview, talking about his Nobel Prize winning novel *The Old Man and the Sea*, remarked: "I tried to make a real man, a real fish, and a real shark. But if I made them good and true enough, they would mean many things."[13]

III

In spite of the diversity of interpretations, critics agree that the essence of *Halfway House* is constituted in the alienated individuals groping in the pervasive meaninglessness. Each of the characters experiences a sense of isolation, loneliness, alienation, absence of communication, loss of identity and the loss of values. They are frustrated, dissatisfied, skeptical and vexed at their familial relationships. They feel trapped in the contemporary social pattern. The sense of incompleteness also serves as a trap for them.

Man always runs after a mirage. He does not value what he has but tries to run after the unattainable. He is quite aware of his mortality, and still, perhaps because of it only, pines for immortality. Man has envisaged the ideal state of completeness in the Godhead. Being a man, it is not possible for him to attain it in this life. This is his human limitation. Still he pines for completeness. This search for the unattainable continues throughout his life. The nature and form of the search taken differs from person to person depending upon his innate character.

In his epoch-making drama *Halfway House*, Mohan Rakesh deals with this problem of incompleteness through the discord in the man-woman relationship. Mahendranath and Savitri are happily married, but the colour of marital concord soon fades away. Ironically each becomes intensely aware and intolerant of other's incompleteness, forgetting his/her own. They never realize the possibility of being each other's complement. Though this pining for completeness is present in every individual, this search becomes much more intense in Savitri.

With the rise of the curtain, Savitri is seen constantly nagging, insulting, denouncing Mahendranath, and deliberately making him feel small. Mahendranath feels that he is slighted by all:

> What is my status in this house? Silent acceptance, perpetual snubs, constant insults, is that all I deserve after so many years? (26)

He feels that they use him only as a convenient stamp of respectability. Savitri puts him down with a satirical question, "Aren't you exaggerating your importance, slightly?" and snubs him with a direct blow: "When has he ever been any use? On what grounds does he say." (26) She tries to justify her behaviour as a natural response to the present oppressive burden of her family she alone has to bear:

> (sits down on cane pouf, removes tablecloth from her face, tearfully) I can't manage any longer, Binni. I just can't. (23)

Savitri is not ready to accept Mahendranath as he is. She fails to understand the meaning of conjugal life and love. One who only talks and walks like a man is not a man. "To be a man involves something more. . . . Personality. . . . Strength of character." (68) To her, Mahendranath is not even half a man. Her pining for perfection makes her so bold as to openly say, "I want a man, not just a miserable . . . hanger on!" (71) Even twenty-two years back, when they were newly married, Savitri felt the same way about him. "That day too you pulled Mahendra to bits. . . . You said he was a wimp, had no backbone," (72) says Juneja. It was obvious even then that Savitri did not consider Mahendranath to be the man with whom she could spend her life.

Juneja unveils the reality by discovering the root of all the trouble in Savitri's concept of life. He agrees that today Mahendranath, at times, becomes bad-tempered, but there was a time when he was happy by nature—he laughed from within. It is Savitri who always makes him feel low. Juneja feels that she has trapped Mahendra, to use him as a 'wretched pawn' (77) at the moment of crisis. He claims that it is her attitude that is responsible for this state of affairs.

Savitri aspires for a life, which Mahendranath cannot give her, which no man can possibly give her. These twenty-two years have not been spent in "any interpersonal adjustments as she would have us believe, but in search of escape routes and a sanctuary." (88) Juneja's words are relevant: "The point is that if any of these men had been a part of your life instead of Mahendra, you would still have felt that you had married the wrong man. You would still have encountered a Mahendra, a Juneja, a Shivjeet, or a Jagmohan and thought and reacted in the same way. Because the meaning of life to you is how many different things you can have and enjoy at the same time. One man alone could never have given them to you, so no matter whom you married, you would always have felt as empty and as restless as you do today." (74)

Savitri's search for completeness ends disastrously. Even as she is trying to attract Manoj, he takes away her elder daughter, Binni. In a desperate frenzy, she makes hysterical attempts to find a way out. Just then she hears that Jagmohan is back. Seeing all doors closed before her, she tries "to step into the past." (75) When she goes out with Jagmohan the whole new life is before her, but Jagmohan does not fulfil her heart's desire. Choking with frustration, she has to come back to the 'clammy' halfway house. Savitri feels disillusioned and frustrated that all men are alike, no one is able to help her:

> All of you . . . every one of you . . . all alike! Exactly the same. Different masks, but the face? . . . The same wretched faces . . . every single one of you! (76)

Juneja emphasizes the futility of all her attempts with a sardonic question:

> And yet you felt you had a choice? . . . was there really any choice? Tell me, was there? (76)

This is the inevitable end of Savitri's mad search for completeness. Though Girish Rastogi feels, "The contradiction and struggle between incompleteness and search for wholeness could not be elevated for viewing at a very high creative plane," (112) the play goes much beyond Savitri, the individual—'ambitious' or 'psychic.' (14) She blames all the men as being alike, but fails to apprehend the truth—all human beings are alike in being incomplete. A sense of wholeness can be experienced only when two complementary fragments are put together. Being complementary to each other may perhaps be the answer to the problem of incompleteness. The moment of awareness slips from her hands. In her futile efforts to achieve more, Savitri loses whatever she has. She is the real loser.

Mahendranath's return at the end serves as a foil to that of Savitri. Surely, both of them are destined to come back, but in a different sense. Mahendranath also wants to get away from the hell. He wonders why he continues to stay there. He, too, feels desperate and declares that he won't come back to eat up the foundations of the house: "But I'm no longer hungry. I'll never be hungry again!"(27) In spite of himself, because of his love for Savitri, he comes back at the end in a miserable condition. This is the human predicament. There is no total meaninglessness, no unmitigated gloom, but no grand tragedy either in *Halfway House*. Rakesh is quite conscious of the futility of any positive solution. The moment of fruition is never realised in this incomplete world, but the possibility always remains halfway open because there is no total loss of positive values in the world of *Halfway House*. Everything in this world is incomplete—halfway, since man himself is incomplete.

No wonder that Rakesh does not take the extreme Absurdist position. This is a bleak picture of a disintegrated family, but no total breakdown is intended. They cannot live together happily, but cannot leave each other either. This is not Rakesh's failure in characterization, as some critics feel, but a mature understanding of the nature of human existence. This is no 'rationalization,'[15] as Meena Pimpalapure claims, but an intuitive apprehension. Rakesh is not trying to solve the riddle of human existence. No wonder, the question remains unanswered. There is no action, the play goes nowhere. This is not Rakesh's failure. This is the implicit meaning of that experience.

This incompleteness is not a curse. It is a condition of existence. It is but natural that the drama *Halfway House* cannot be pigeonholed in any one slot—the Absurdist/ Naturalist/ Universalistic. Rakesh's vision of life transcends all the established categories. It is not the story but the vision that forms the crux of the play. So it does not matter whether the original story be of Rakesh or be based on Anita Aulak's short story "Din se Din."[16] The essence of a Shakespearean play lies not in the common well-known story, but in Shakespeare's vision of life. This is the difference between Thomas Kyd's *The Spanish Tragedy* and William Shakespeare's *Hamlet*. Mohan Rakesh's *Halfway House* symbolises not only a halfway modern house, but stands for the whole human world, which is incomplete.

NOTES

1. Harry J. Moony Jr. and Thomas P. Stanley, ed., *Shapeless Gods* (Pittsburgh, 1968), p. 3.
2. B. Murchland, *The Age of Alienation* (New York, 1971).
3. Edmund Fuller, *Man in Modern Fiction* (New York, 1958), p. 3.
4. Paul Brunton, *The Spiritual Crisis of Man* (London, 1952), p. 7.
5. Erich Fromm, *Zen Buddhism and Psychoanalysis* (New York, 1970), p. 86.
6. Carl Jaspers, *Man in the Modern Age* (New York, 1956), pp. 202, 210.
7. Sanjay Kumar, "*Halfway House*: A Critical Commentary," in

Halfway House, A Translation of *Aadhe Adhure*, Mohan Rakesh, Eng. trans. Bindu Batra (Delhi: Worldview, 1999), p. 133.

8. Mahesh Anand, "Samakalin Jindagi aur Rangamulyon ki Talash" in *Natakkar Mohan Rakesh*, ed. Sundarlal Kathuria (New Delhi: Kumar Prakashan 1974), p. 92.
9. *Ibid.*, p. 85.
10. Ramesh Kumar Jadhav, *Mohan Rakesh: Vyaktitva Evam Krititva* (Lucknow: Nitin, 1986), p. 109.
11. Ramesh Gautam, *Hindi ke Pratik Natak* (New Delhi: Nachiketa, 1980), pp. 288-89.
12. Sundarlal Kathuria, *Natakkar Mohan Rakesh*, p. 197.
13. Ernest Hemingway, quoted by U.S. Mathur, *Ernest Hemingway: The Old Man and the Sea*, p. 188.
14. Mahesh Anand, *Natakkar Mohan Rakesh*, pp. 90-91.
15. Meena Pimpalapure, *Mohan Rakesh Ka Nari-Sansar* (New Delhi: Prakashan Sansthan, 1989), p. 95.
16. Quoted by Ramesh Gautam, p. 294.

Contributors

SHYAM S. AGARWALLA	Dr. R.M.L. College Ranchi
MANCHI SARAT BABU	Government Degree College Srisailam Project
S.G. BHANEGAONKAR	People's College Nanded
NILIMA CHANDRA	Kalindi College University of Delhi
SUBHASH CHANDRA	S.B.S. College University of Delhi
VEENA NOBLE DASS	S.P.M. University Tirupati
P. DHANAVEL	Anna University Chennai
N.S. DHARAN	S.T. Hindu College Nagercoil
BHARAT GUPT	College of Vocational Studies University of Delhi
NARESH K. JAIN	School of Correspondence Courses University of Delhi
SATNAM KAUR	University of Jammu Jammu
DEEPSHIKHA KOTWAL	University of Jammu Jammu

GEETA KUMAR	S.P.M. College University of Delhi
P.S. KASTURE	R.D.G. Women's College Akola
ARTI MATHUR	P.G.D.A.V. College University of Delhi
BASAVARAJ NAIKAR	Karnatak University Dharwad
O.P. SHARMA 'PRAKASH'	Ram Lal Anand College University of Delhi